ENTER THE ACTRESS

The First Women in the Theatre

ISABELLA ANDREINI
From a painting said to be of the Gelosi at the
Carnavalet Museum, Paris

ENTER THE ACTRESS

The First Women in the Theatre

BY

ROSAMOND GILDER

WITH ILLUSTRATIONS

Theatre Arts Books

1960 FIRST PUBLISHED BY
THEATRE ARTS BOOKS
333 SIXTH AVENUE
NEW YORK 14
PRINTED IN THE U.S.A.

CONTENTS

ILLUSTRATIONS

ILLUSTRATIONS

ILLUSTRATIONS

INTRODUCING THE LADIES

OF all the arts that mankind has invented to clothe its concept of reality and to ornament its leisure moments, none is more suited to the genius of the female of the species than that of the theatre. Women have risen to greater heights of achievement as actresses than in any other art. There are no more glowing names in the theatrical firmament than those of Siddons, Bernhardt, or Duse. The theatre, in all its branches, is a rich field of enterprise for any woman with a ray of natural endowment in its many lively arts. We find them in every one of its branches, stage manager as well as actress, director as well as playwright, business agent, stage designer, electrician, choreographer — anything and everything. The stage door is wide open, and the surly doorkeeper must needs let all the world pass in and out. The invasion is so complete we have almost forgotten that once the theatre was an Eveless paradise — that once, like so many other professions, avocations, and guilds, it was a closed shop, reserved for men only; that once no distracting and competitive female was allowed within its sacred precincts. The recorded history of the European theatre covers some twenty-five hundred years, but only during the last three hundred and eighty have women been allowed any official part in its development. The processes by which they have won their place in the artificial sun of candle flare and footlight, against more than two centuries of rooted custom and prejudice, has seemed worth recording in the following pages.

This book does not attempt to be a history of great actresses — their number is legion, and their stories, always lively and diverting, have often been told. The Adrienne Lecouvreurs, the Clairons, Woffingtons, Rachels, and Ristoris will not figure here. It is their little-known predecessors, the true innovators who dared to face a hostile tradition and earn their living or try out their ideas in a new profession, whose adventures are here recorded. Wherever possible one of these pioneer players has been chosen as an example of her type, while the theatrical conditions that immediately preceded and surrounded her have been sketched in as a necessary corollary to her first steps. A fleeting glimpse of her companions in adventure has been given, for these first actresses did not arrive singly, but in groups and coveys, fluttering bands of pretty girls, tricked out in their best clothes and flushed with the double excitement of youth and untried adventure. Where one actress appeared on the stage, whether in Italy, Spain, France, England, or Germany, others promptly followed; but there is no difficulty in selecting one in each group who, by her unusual merits or by the accident of her connection with some important theatrical figure of the day, has left a sufficient record in history to distinguish her from her fellows.

There were actresses before Isabella Andreini, but none as talented; there were older, and in their day more famous, comediennes than Molière's wife and mistress, but none whose history has been so minutely studied, so endlessly discussed. In England, where women came to the stage later than on the Continent, the field was so rich in candidates that it seemed ungracious not to take several of these dazzling ladies into consideration, as well as the pioneer among them, that quiet, competent, and patient Mrs. Betterton who is sometimes forgotten among the naughty ladies of King Charles's royal theatres. Less choice was possible among pioneer playwrights, for they are too few in number to allow of much variety. Blue-stockings from the days of Queen Elizabeth and Margaret of Navarre have diverted themselves and their admirers by the elaboration of poetic effusions entitled comedies and tragedies, but having little other relation to the stage. Very few women, however, until our own day, have produced anything solid in the way of dramatic fare. England boasts the greatest number of women playwrights, with Aphra Behn and the crowd of lesser 'Female Wits' in the van, but the playwrights, unlike the actresses, cannot hold their own against their masculine competitors.

It is even more difficult to discover, in the incomplete records of the theatre, who were the first women managers and directors. These functions were less definitely specialised in the past than they are to-day, and there were comparatively few managers, men or women, who were not first of all actors. Several actresses of the *commedia dell'arte* were directors of their own companies: La Béjart, Molière's mistress, organised and directed the troupe in which the future playwright served his apprenticeship; Carolina Neuber was primarily a directress; but it was not till we come to La Montansier in eighteenth-century France that a woman appears who merely managed theatres and theatrical enterprises and did not act at all. She can hardly be held up as a model of personal or business integrity, but her career proves, once again, that the ladies differ very little from the gentlemen in putting business before the abstract virtues.

For a long time women's contribution toward the scenic investiture of the stage was confined to their own charming presence. They graced it with their personal beauty, their gorgeous and fashionable clothes, their glowing presence. At first they had little interest in the scene as a whole, but as time went on their natural taste prevailed. Mademoiselle Clairon brought about the first important reforms in costume on the French stage, and Madame Vestris, in England, was one of the most enterprising and ingenious directors of her day.

The pioneers whose adventures in these various fields of theatric art are here recorded opened the way to a host of followers. The road is by now trodden broad and clear. But the actress of to-day still owes a gesture of gratitude to the Isabellas, the Madeleines and Armandes who led the way; our present writers of comedy should not forget the valiant Aphra Behn, who fought for a hearing less than three hundred years ago. Vestris invented and executed prodigies of scene-mounting when stage design was not part of the college curriculum. Even the somewhat shady Montansier was not without her courage and imagination, leading the way for the many stage managers and business women who are now running theatres all over the world. To all these Amazons of Thespis we owe a debt of admiration and gratitude. They gave much joy and delight in their day, forgetting, when they appeared before their public, the struggles and difficulties that surrounded their pioneer enterprise and the devious ways by which they had mounted to the stage. Now, once again, evoked from dusty books and seen for a moment, shadowy figures on a distant stage, they have brought to at least one observer a renewed sense of their vitality and charm.

ENTER THE ACTRESS

ENTER THE ACTRESS

· ·

CHAPTER I

FROM PRIESTESS TO PROSTITUTE

THE GREEK AND ROMAN STAGE

THE history of women in the theatre begins, surprisingly enough in view of their classic exclusion from the stage, at the very source and centre of its being; begins in that dim primeval grove where our first forbear, priestess of life, protectress of fertility, propitiated the unknown in mystic dances of magical intent. If we can believe the learned archæologists who have spent their lives deciphering the hieroglyphics of the past, religion and the theatre were born together, there where the eternal mystery of the continuation of life was first realised, feared, and longed for. While primitive man hunted and fought, destroying in order to live, the women of the tribe made the first attempts at agriculture, tilled the soil, planted seed, protected the useful creatures, bore and reared the children — were, indeed, the vehicles of a tangible immortality. And when any of these processes went wrong, it was the woman who must call upon and obtain the aid of those hidden forces with which she was so mysteriously allied. Clothed in the symbols of desired increase, the head woman of the tribe took upon herself the attributes of godhead. By costume and mimicry she became the very power she invoked, forcing it to do her bidding by the magic of her gestures. Around her, her companions enacted the dance-drama of their needs, the crudest of all dances before the Lord — the first tragic chorus.

We know these things but vaguely through a haze of

tradition and a smoke screen of contending theories, but
certain popular festivals, such as the selection of the Queen
of the May in England, have survived even to our own
day to bear witness to an immemorial custom, and in the
mythologies of both Europe and Asia, the Earth Mother
and her priestesses carry about them the flavour of an
antiquity greater even than recorded history. In Phrygia
she was called Cybele, Great Mother of the Gods; in
Babylonia and Phœnicia, Ishtar and Ashtoreth; in Egypt
they hailed her as Isis, Queen of Heaven; but wherever
she appeared, she was the prototype of that first actress-
priest of the primitive grove, and her attributes remained
the same — the symbols of fertility — the child who dies
to be reborn and the band of attendant women dancing
the drama of birth and death and resurrection.

Little by little the function of the mother took on form
and substance. The cyclic year became itself a god, until
finally the cult of the son overshadowed that of the mother
from which it sprang. But the Incarnate Year was still attended by the followers of the older faith. The Mænads,
the skin-clad Bacchæ, clothed in the fragments of the
sacrifice, the nymphs and woodland creatures recalling a
vanished order, all these survivals of a primitive cult can
be seen depicted on the vases and fragments of ancient
reliefs attending the young god as they had once followed
the Earth Mother. Nor were the nymphs and Mænads of
the Greek vases merely mythical figures. They had on
earth their very human prototypes in the priestesses and
worshippers who sacrificed and danced in honour of Bacchus. This ritual of birth and death and reincarnation has
been sung and danced and mimed in every land and under
a thousand aspects, but we know it best in Greece, where
the Dithyramb of Dionysos took on more and more distinct outlines as a form of singing and dancing from which
the tragic chorus and tragedy itself at last took form.

It is at this point, where the dithyramb merges into the
tragic chorus, that women are supposed to disappear

MÆNADS
From a fifth-century Greek vase (cylix) in the
Metropolitan Museum of Art

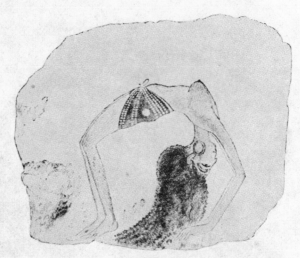

AN EGYPTIAN DANCER OF THREE THOUSAND
YEARS AGO
From a potsherd in the Museum of Turin

A GREEK DANCING-GIRL
From a Greek vase in the British Museum

completely from the scene. But it seems unlikely that
this exclusion was as sudden or as complete as is usually
thought. The transition from dithyramb to tragic chorus
was necessarily gradual, and no one knows exactly when
or where it took place. We do know, however, that women sang and danced in the dithyrambic and cyclic
choruses that preceded the tragic chorus. Homer himself
danced in the midst of a choir of Delian maidens, just as
Apollo danced with the Muses and Bacchus or his human
representative danced and sang surrounded by the Mænads, in each case, as Gilbert Murray points out, 'a con-
ductor surrounded by a chorus, usually female.' This
same chorus of Delian maidens seems to have been at the
disposal of all the various competing poets and could sing
in all the different dialects that were required. Women
took part in the dramatic mysteries of Eleusis and led the
secret Bacchic orgies in the hills of Bœotia and Thrace.
Plutarch describes the women of Elis who summoned
Dionysos in their hymns of spring — the bull-driving
dithyramb of Dionysos. The five days' festival in Athens
known as the Thesmophoria, held in honour of Demeter,
the Earth Mother, was celebrated entirely by women,
while certain phases of the mysteries of Bacchus were
confided to a group of fourteen women chosen by the
archon and presided over by his wife in the guise of a
temporary queen. Sparta, too, was famous for the dances
of her young girls, the Emmeleia and Partheneia described
by Pindar. Mimetic dances of all sorts were known
throughout Greece: monodies in which a woman alone
sang and danced to the accompaniment of cymbals; songs
for two voices wherein song and action formed a miniature
drama; and the larger choruses of girls and boys dancing together in honour of the gods and in celebration of
the higher virtues. All these forms of dramatic expression enriched the stream which finally developed into the
classic theatre of Greece, and in them all women as well as
men took active part.

It seems, therefore, not too fantastic to believe that the women of Greece were present at the birth of tragedy, even though they were eventually excluded from its noblest flights. There are, indeed, scholars bold enough to suggest that women may possibly have formed part of the tragic choruses in the Golden Age of the Greek drama, that they may have moved to the noble rhythms of the Æschylean line, and that the fifty daughters of Danaus, the ocean nymphs, the mourning women, the furies and the maidens of the classic choruses, were actually women and not men in disguise. This shattering suggestion, so at variance with the accepted tradition of a classic stage where no women were allowed to appear, cannot be proved to-day but it serves as a reminder of the incompleteness of our historic information. There is no incontrovertible evidence one way or the other, but if women danced one day in the hieron of Dionysos in a dithyrambic or cyclic chorus, why should they not dance the next in a tragic chorus? Why should women, who had long been intimately associated with the worship of Dionysos, suddenly cease their ministrations because a form of monody was introduced into the midst of the dithyramb? And finally, why should the tragic poets have thrown away so admirable an instrument as the fully developed chorus of mixed voices, when they began to develop the Greek drama as we know it to-day?

The poet Thespis is supposed to have made the great innovation by which the diversion introduced between parts of a choral song was given a new impulse and importance and became part of the chorus itself instead of a mere accidental interpolation. No one, however, has ever known — or ever will know — whether the chorus into which this first dramatic discourse was introduced was a chorus of men, of women, or of men and women together. Phrynicus followed Thespis with a further development of the dramatic recitative. He is reputed to have introduced the first woman character to the newly created

stage, but we have no knowledge whatsoever of the constitution of his chorus. Following Phrynicus and with a
dazzling rapidity, Greek tragedy leaped to its supreme
heights. The genius of Æschylus burst upon the world,
Sophocles and Euripides followed almost immediately —
the Western theatre was created, perfected, polished, in
the small space of a hundred years from 525 to 406 B.C.

In considering the details of the production of Greek
drama, we must remember that we have the words, more
or less incomplete, of the great poets, but we know aston-
ishingly little of the functioning of their theatre, and this
in spite of the volumes of comment and reconstruction
that later scholarship has produced. It is more than probable, however, that by the time Æschylus had introduced
the second actor and the Greek drama was fully established, women had disappeared entirely from the tragic
chorus. Whatever faint possibility there may be that
women once appeared in the early choruses, there is no
doubt at all that the actor, invented by Thespis and
doubled and trebled by Æschylus and Sophocles, was always a man. Here, indeed, we are on firmer ground, for
the names of actors have survived on tablets of stone, and
no woman's name is among them. We see on vases and
bas-reliefs actors masking for their rôles — men dressed as
women ready to interpret the noblest feminine rôles ever
written. For, curiously enough, though the theatre had
become and was to remain for almost two thousand years
a man's world, it was not a world of men. The greatest
creations in the greatest period in the history of the
theatre, the Golden Age of Greek drama at Athens, are
women characters. Electra, Clytemnestra, Antigone,
Iphigenia — they stand to-day silhouetted against the Attic sky, incomparably noble, passionate, and alive. If the
theatre that saw their birth knew no women actors, it was
obviously not because its poets were incapable of portray-
ing women characters, or indifferent to the complexities of
human psychology in all its manifestations.

From the technical point of view the fact that women were not allowed to act on the Athenian stage would present little difficulty to the poet or choregus superintending the production of a play. All the actors wore masks and flowing robes which entirely covered them, giving them a majesty and force in harmony with the words they spoke or chanted. The voice alone could betray the fact that Antigone, Electra, or Clytemnestra was being portrayed by a man, and this particular difficulty was overcome by the great care given to the training of the actors, for in the Greek theatre the flexibility, power, and beauty of a voice was the actors' greatest glory. It was not merely the size of the open-air Greek theatres that made this development of voice desirable, for as a matter of fact the acoustic properties of the theatres were so remarkable, as we can judge to-day, that the slightest word could be heard at an immense distance, but more particularly because the theatre was still closely associated with its origin, was still somewhat musical in form, so that even the dialogue was probably chanted or at least recited in a musical and stylised manner.

The choruses were evidently both chanted and danced, and it is unfortunate that we have no trace of Greek music by which we might be able to judge whether women's voices were needed in the choral melodies. The plays themselves, the comparatively few texts that survive of Æschylus, Sophocles, Euripides, and Aristophanes, give no irrefutable information on this point, though now and then in the latter we have a brief and tantalising glimpse of theatrical customs. In the *Thesmophoria-zusæ*, for instance, the poet Agathon rehearses his chorus on the stage. He addresses the choristers — who are near him on the raised platform stage, not in the orchestra, where the chorus of the play itself was stationed — as 'young girls' — which might possibly mean that they were in reality women, and not men. The indications, however, are so slight that little weight can be given them, and we must in the end bow to the tradition that kept women entirely off the classic Greek stage.

If our information concerning the actual make-up of the Greek chorus is uncertain, we are almost equally in the dark as to the audiences. In spite of the volumes that have been written on the subject of the Greek stage, to ask so simple a question as whether the women of Athens attended the dramatic contests sends a flurry through the ranks of scholarship. Interpretations of passing allusions in plays or the deciphering of broken fragments of inscription can vary so violently that contending theorists reach diametrically opposite conclusions from the same premises. It is hard to believe, however, that the Athenian women, who took such an active share in religious ceremonies, would tolerate exclusion from the theatre. The semi-Oriental isolation in which Athenian women were kept was forgotten when the great festivals were celebrated. Young maids and matrons of the noblest families walked through the streets unveiled, gorgeously dressed and attended, and forming an accepted part of the great processions in honour of the gods at the City Dionysia.

They took part also, as we have seen, in the Eleusinian mysteries, returning from the temple barefooted, carrying symbolic offerings and honouring Demeter and Persephone by their dances, songs, and ceremonies. It seems unlikely that they, who were so intimately connected with the worship of Dionysos, would not have shared the greatest of all celebrations in his honour, the dramatic contests held in the theatre of Athens. A. E. Haigh in his *Attic Theatre* marshals the evidence in favour of their presence on the great days of the tragic contests, and quite rightly supposes that if they attended the tragedies they remained in the theatre for the satiric plays. It hardly needs Mr. Haigh's apologetic explanation, that after all even Aristophanic ribaldry came under the protection of the broadminded Dionysos, to believe that the women of Athens were not too squeamish on the score of humour. Aristophanes wrote his comedies some twenty-two hundred years before nineteenth-century prudery had been invented, and the lusty heroines of the Old Comedy were exaggerations but probably not pure inventions of his genius.

It is difficult to believe that the women who could inspire the noblest creations of poetry as well as stimulate the robustious comedies of the day would have submitted tamely to an arbitrary exclusion from the theatres. Plato's remark that 'tragedy is a kind of rhetoric addressed to boys, women and men, slaves, and free citizens without distinction' is strong evidence in favour of their presence in the theatres, as is also his statement that, if an audience were called upon to say what they were most pleased with, the little children would vote for the conjuror, the boys for the comic poet, the young men and the more refined sort of women for the tragic poet. Probability and evidence would, therefore, lead us to believe that the good-wife of Athens, as well as her noble sisters of the Eupatridæ and the brilliant and highly cultivated courtesans who were the intellectual leaders among the women of the period, took their places with their peers in the theatre on the great days of the City Dionysia and watched the tragedies and comedies of that Golden Age of the world unfold in a glory of poetry, music, dance, colour, song, and splendour which have never since been reached or rivalled.

While the official Greek theatre, forgetful of its sources in the cyclic dance and the dithyramb in which women had taken part, closed its doors to feminine participants in its elevated mysteries, that other theatre, forever effervescent at the heart of humanity, the theatre of pure diversion, continued its unfettered course. Ever since Eve invented costume, and, coached by the Serpent, enacted that little comedy by which she persuaded Adam that the bitter apple of knowledge was sweet and comforting, there has been something satanic in the very nature of the theatre. Born of ritual and of revelry, it is at once child of

God and offspring of the Devil. We see it simultaneously reflecting the noblest aspects of the mind of man, stemming from his aspiration toward beauty and goodness and blossoming in the highest forms of art, and at the same time we find it creeping up from the gutter, befouling the image of its creator and reducing him to something a little lower than the beasts. In this double aspect it very fairly mirrors the larger human scene, and not least of all in its attitude toward woman. When, as in Greece, the nobler aspects of the theatre were closed to her, she came in, as was to be expected, by the Devil's way.

If women did not dance in the tragic and comic choruses in the theatre of Dionysos, they danced everywhere else. Aside from the serious and religious dances we have already mentioned, which were the direct forerunners of the tragic chorus, we find a whole class of dances performed in the streets, along the highways, and in the private houses of ancient Greece. Women dancers, tumblers, jugglers, and contortionists, usually slave girls and foreigners, were always at hand to enliven the idle hours of the tired business man of Athens. As the customs of the country became more luxurious, as 'the good old days' were forgotten and banquets became less a feast of reason than a festival of the senses, professional entertainers grew in numbers, skill, and importance. Already, in the Golden Age, Aristophanes gives us a glimpse of these dancers and flute-players of the street-corner, bringing them on the stage in the *Thesmophoriazusæ*, and speaking of them repeatedly in other plays.

It is impossible to draw a line between dancer, singer, mime, and actress. One form of entertainment merged into another. The dances were mimetic and descriptive, the singer enacted the drama she recited; music and movement reënforced the fable. These miniature dramas were an inevitable accompaniment of every feast, wedding, or funeral, and became more and more elaborate and gorgeous as time went on. Xenophon in his *Symposium* describes such a dance given at the close of a banquet in honor of Callias, in which the loves of Bacchus and Ariadne were performed with great skill and dramatic effect. Other mimetic dances were concerned with the exploits of Ajax, the adventures of Apollo, the rape of Ganymede, and the interminable loves of the gods, of Zeus and Danaë, of Venus and Adonis, and the rest. Under Alexander the Great and his successors, aristocratic entertainments grew to vast proportions; dancers, singers, and musicians swarmed in the houses of the rich. Pageants and semi-theatrical displays of all sorts were part of the pomp and circumstance of a decadent civilisation, and in all these shows women were in demand as dancers, actresses, musicians, and general entertainers.

Nor were the common people without their lighter forms of amusement. Aristophanes' little flute girl picked up on the street-corner is typical of the entertainers who have flourished in all ages and civilisations. A whole school of unofficial theatrical entertainment flourished side by side with the nobler forms of drama housed in the theatres and supported by the state. These impromptu actors who entertained the citizen in the market-place or the villager at the crossroads, with improvised scenes and unlicensed witticisms, were later known as mimes, and were very much like their Roman successors or the vaudeville and cabaret performers of our own day.

At first improvised, the mimes were later written, usually in verse, and given with the accompaniment of music. Their subject-matter, as far as can be discovered, ranged from parodies of the heroes of mythology to direct satire of the notables of the day or of prominent people in the assembled company. They were played largely, if not exclusively, in the phallic mode, and were as completely untrammelled as such merry-making has always been and always will be. Reënforced by the women, whose presence added nothing of decency or order to the performance, these mimes even invaded the orchestra of the great theatres of Greece. Literally barefaced and flat-footed, wearing neither mask nor cothurnus, brazen in every sense of the word, these ribald comedians were not permitted to mount the stage still sacred to the memory of the great tragic poets. Even their occasional presence in the orchestras of the theatres was looked upon by the conservative-minded as an outrage. It was considered shameful that their antics should find a welcome from a people who had once known better things, but the truth was that the great days of the official Greek theatre were over, and that the strength it lacked was finding expression in the improvised and unlicensed theatricality dormant in the heart of the people.

II

Transported to Rome, the classic Greek theatre received no renewal of vitality. Imitative in all its aspects, it was also imitative in its exclusion of women from the serious stage. Roman poets rewrote the great tragedies and made attempts in the grand manner for themselves. They confided these works to Greek slaves to be performed, who reproduced as nearly as possible the traditional Greek theatre where men acted women's parts. By the time of Seneca in the first century of the Christian era, even these remnants of a great tradition were disappearing. Tragedies were written to be read, and the Greek heritage survived only in imitations of the New Comedy of Menander successfully reincarnated in the works of Plautus and Terence. These, too, stemming from the Greek school, were performed by men only, and kept alive a tradition which by this time had become an accepted law. Even the purely indigenous Atellanæ were probably acted entirely by men. In these little plays, Maccus, Bucco, Pappus, and the rest wore masks, and such women's parts as existed were played by men or boys.

The more serious forms of the drama which existed for

a time in Italy were, however, doomed to extinction under the heavy hand of the Roman populace. The theatre is a product of its public as well as of its creators and performers, and in Rome a new element was present in the audiences that filled its theatres and circuses — an audience, it must be noted, composed of women as well as men, for if there is some question as to whether women were allowed to attend the performances in the theatres of Greece, there is no doubt that the Roman matron had this privilege. Her presence, however, did nothing to soften the attitude of this new public.

The Roman was a realist and demanded the most complete realism in his dramatic entertainments. He preferred the sight of captive kings led forth in chains to make a holiday to the consideration of the purely imaginary peripeteia of mythical heroes. He preferred real blood on the sands of the arena to red paint spilled on the floor of a stage. If a fable called for the death of the hero at its climax, the Roman demanded that he should die in actual fact in as public and spectacular a manner as possible. Captives and criminals were always at hand for this type of pastime, and realism can go no further than it went in the Roman amphitheatre, where, says Tertullian: 'We have seen the castration of Atys and a man burnt alive to represent Hercules' living pyre on Mount Œta.'

Martial describes a scene representing Orpheus charming birds and beasts with his music, but in the end 'the poet died, torn asunder by an ungrateful bear, and the death of the actor was as real as everything that is told of Orpheus is legendary.' All this has nothing to do with art, except, perhaps, as a horrid example of where realism can lead the unwary, but it is an indication of the strong fare on which the Roman public was fed. The fascinations of this sort of performance, of gladiatorial combats, of animal baitings, and wholesale slaughterings of men and beasts must be remembered as the crimson background against which the transplanted flame of Greek drama flickered and died out.

The forms of theatre which survived the competition of circus and arena were those which provided the greatest amount of amusement with the least possible effort of attention and imagination. The Roman mime was exactly suited to the purpose and flourished accordingly. The mime was a short scene from everyday life in which two or three actors carried on a merry and obscene dialogue on the foibles of the day. Local types and local celebrities were caricatured and the eternal absurdities of man came in for their full share of attention. These vignettes of domestic life were acted without mask or cothurnus and the nimble performers were dancers, musicians, gymnasts, and clowns in one. For such performances women were much in demand. The professional entertainer, the dancer, the courtesan, merged into the *mima*, and the profession took its appointed place among the despised but necessary vocations, all suffering under a like *infamia*. The legal and social position of actors in Rome was hardly better than that of the slaves, in spite of the fact that certain actors won fabulous wealth and power under the Emperors. The restrictions were levelled particularly against the women, who were classed as prostitutes, and could not contract legal marriages with patricians or engage in any other trade than that to which their birth had condemned them; nor could the daughter or granddaughter of an actress break away from the harsh restrictions of the law.

Within these professional limits, however, some of the *mimæ* won enviable riches and spectacular, if temporary, power. So popular were certain of these actresses that the city fathers paid fabulous sums to have them appear in the entertainments offered for the delectation of the Roman populace. Even a movie star to-day would not scorn the two hundred thousand sesterces — approximately fifty thousand dollars — which Dionysia received for her appearance on a single occasion. Other actresses were so popular, and presumably so gifted, that they held their position long after any physical charms could account for their success. Galeria Copiola made what we may presume was her last appearance on the stage at the age of one hundred and four, and the *mima* Lucceia was not far behind her with a hundred years to her credit.

Inscriptions exist which prove that certain talented actresses became *archimimæ* or leaders of a troupe, and in this capacity they not only directed the company of which they were the stars, but wrote the plays as well. The avenue of greatest wealth and influence, however, lay in the favour of the mighty. Roman history is rich in legends of these actress-courtesans, adored by the populace and protected by the great. There is the story of Cytheris the dancer, beloved of Mark Antony, who rode in triumph through Italy in a chariot drawn by leopards. Acte, one of the most faithful of Nero's mistresses, was a mime. She is supposed to have been converted to Christianity by Saint Paul himself, for which she was banished from Rome. She returned, however, when Nero was dying, the only one among his followers who remained with him to the end.

If the mime was the favourite theatrical diversion of the populace, the aristocracy had adopted a somewhat different form of entertainment which was to supplant the last vestiges of the classic drama during the years of Rome's greatest opulence and final disintegration. The pantomime is the one original contribution of the Roman genius to the multifarious arts of the theatre, and it developed, in the Imperial City, to a degree of perfection and dignity never achieved before or since. The Roman pantomimist was an actor and dancer in one, holding the stage alone and interpreting, through gesture, movement, attitude, and costume, a whole drama in which he assumed successively all the rôles required. His dance was accompanied by music. Occasionally an assistant sang or chanted in recitative the tale that was being unfolded, but to the great pantomimists these aids were merely embellishments of their performance and were not needed to make the story they acted intelligible. Their art was complete in itself, and was cultivated to such a point of perfection and subtlety that certain of the great pantomimists were said to be able to describe abstract ideas and philosophic concepts in their dance.

Curiously enough, it is through the pantomimists that the Greek myths and even the tragedies of the Golden Age were kept alive in Imperial Rome. Reducing words and music to a secondary plane, these masters of gesture and movement danced the story of the mad Hercules, of Ajax and Agamemnon, of the Fall of Troy and the curse of Atreus, while enthralled multitudes, gathered from the four corners of the earth, watched and understood the silent language of the dance. For though the pantomime was at first the plaything of the wealthy, it became in the end the delight of the people as well. The mob went mad over its favourites. Pylades and Bathyllus, the most famous pantomimists of their time, divided Rome into warring factions, and the former had to be banished in order to restore peace. The enormous power, wealth, and back-stairs influence of these actor-dancers is part of the gorgeous pageant of the crumbling Empire.

There were women as well as men pantomimists, women who held the stage alone, as did the men, and impersonated masculine rôles as men for so many generations had interpreted feminine parts. By the fourth century of the Christian era, women pantomimists were to be found in all parts of the Empire, drawing crowds to the theatres and holding their own as independent artists. The rage for pantomime was so great that even women of birth and position learned the art, taking part in Imperial feasts, as later during the Renaissance ladies and even queens took part in court pageants and masques.

The Roman theatre presents a picture of decadence

rather than a record of achievement, and certain learned scholars have gone so far as to lay this degeneration at the feet of the women who were first allowed to perform on its comic stage. They maintain that the women corrupted and debased a noble art, forgetting in their wrath that this noble art has always had a double manifestation, growing as heartily in the gutter as in the temple; forgetting also that Rome preferred the gutter variety and that it flourished accordingly. The first actresses were undoubtedly a ribald lot. They came from the lowest strata of society, and their performance was in keeping with their extra-theatric profession, as well as with the tastes and prejudices of the crowd. The mob that had the right, on certain days, to force the actresses to strip themselves naked on the stage could not expect, as it certainly did not demand, anything very subtle and delicate in the way of art.

To say that the atmosphere of the Roman arenas was contaminated by the appearance of women on the stages erected in their midst is an absurdity. The corruption existed in the whole social fabric of the time, and the excesses of the *scenicii*, men as well as women, were a manifestation of those conditions and not the cause of them. The women, particularly, were held down by the conditions of their enforced servitude. They could not, even if they desired, escape the slavery into which they were born and in which they were reared. There was no way out except through the favour of the rich and powerful, and even that was not enough to change their legal standing. It was not until the advent of the Empress Theodora, in the fifth century after Christ, that any effort was made toward improving the outlook of the women in the theatres.

Theodora's career is as spectacular as it is unique. Many dancers, mimes, and actresses had been powerful favourites in the unofficial harems of the Roman Emperors, but she alone among them all won to the height of

THE EMPRESS THEODORA

From a Byzantine mosaic of the sixth century in the
Church of San Vitale, Ravenna

A ROMAN DANCING-GIRL
From a terracotta of the Roman period in the
Metropolitan Museum of Art

legal spouse and empress. Her career began, if we are to
believe her malignant biographer Procopius, in the lowest
ranks of public entertainers. Her father was bear-keeper
in the Imperial Circus of Constantinople and she herself
appeared in the arena at a tender age. Thrown on her own
resources by the death of her worthy parent, she soon won
the favour of the mob by her gifts of mimicry and her obscene dancing. Procopius' sketch of her subsequent career, until she met and fascinated Justinian, does more justice to his gifts as a writer of pornographic literature than
to his sincerity as an historian, for all the evidence shows
that from the time she married the Emperor until her
death, Theodora was a faithful wife and a wise counsellor
to this most well-meaning of law-givers. Justinian made
her joint ruler with himself over the Empire of the East,
attributing his laws to her sage advice and including her
in all the foundations he made for the public good. It was
for Theodora's sake and in order that she might legally
marry Justinian that the harsh laws against the class to
which she belonged were finally abrogated. In the words
of the edict promulgated about A.D. 521 'a glorious repentance' was left open to the 'unhappy females who had
prostituted their persons in the theatre,' and by renouncing their calling they could become the legal wives of
Roman citizens.

The terms of the edict show what a new influence was
working in favour of the oppressed classes in the decadent
Roman Empire. The Christian Church, avowed enemy
of the theatre, was at the same time the one refuge and
comfort of its unfortunate denizens. Where the Roman
law showed no mercy, the Christian Fathers held out a welcoming hand. In exchange for servitude and repression,
it offered the comfort of hope and the glory of martyrdom to the despised and rejected of the pagan world. The
theatre, which can boast one Empress among its earliest
actresses, has also its noble army of saints and martyrs.

CHAPTER II
HROTSVITHA, A TENTH–CENTURY NUN
THE FIRST WOMAN PLAYWRIGHT

ALTHOUGH the early Christian Church welcomed to its bosom certain repentant actresses, it was on the whole the mortal enemy of the theatre. The war between Church and stage has been long and bitter, particularly in the early days when the theatre represented the last entrenched camp of paganism, and as such was the subject of virulent attack and condemnation. The Church desired nothing less than the complete annihilation of its enemy, and in this, by the close of the fourth century, it had largely succeeded. It is therefore not a little diverting to find that the first woman of any importance in the history of the theatre in Europe is a Benedictine nun. From the darkest of the dark ages of the theatre, as well as of Western civilisation, the work of only one playwright has come down to us intact. The six plays of Hrotsvitha of Gandersheim stand alone, bridging the gulf between Seneca and the *Representatio Adæ*, between the Latin tragedy of A.D. 65, and the French mystery play of the twelfth century of the Christian era. Whatever plays were written and acted, whatever playwrights, actors, and impresarios flourished during these centuries, Hrotsvitha's comedies alone have survived in their complete and original form. Hrotsvitha the Nun, devout daughter of the Church that sought to destroy the theatre, Hrotsvitha, 'German religious and virgin of the Saxon race,' Hrotsvitha, the 'strong voice of Gandersheim,' confined in a remote convent and following the rules of a strict religious order, is yet the first woman of the theatre, the patron saint of the motley followers of Thalia and Melpomene.

The curious anomaly that has placed this devout and dedicated nun of Europe's darkest period in the hierarchy of notable playwrights of all time, grows only more interesting as it is more closely studied. Every circumstance of time and place, of surrounding atmosphere, of education and of outlook would, at first glance, make such a phenomenon seem impossible, so impossible, indeed, that historians of the drama have almost unanimously dismissed Hrotsvitha as, artistically, a 'sport,' without literary or spiritual issue, and therefore of slight importance. Other scholars, more pedantic than accurate, have classed her plays as forgeries, solving the problem presented in her work by denying that she had ever existed. Unfortunately for those who prefer simple classifications and sweeping statements to the vagaries of actual events, this last assumption is untenable.

The manuscript of Hrotsvitha's collected writings, discovered by Conrad Celtes in the Benedictine monastery of Saint Emmeran, Ratisbon, in 1492 or '93, and now reposing in the Munich Library, is authentically of the tenth century. Celtes published his find in 1501, embellishing the book with woodcuts which have been attributed to Dürer. The most interesting of these pictures is the frontispiece, which shows Hrotsvitha presenting her manuscript to Otto II, with the Abbess Gerberga leaning protectingly over the kneeling nun. Not to be overshadowed by his protégée, Celtes included a companion picture of himself, in which he in turn is shown in the act of presenting the first printed edition of Hrotsvitha's works to his own liege lord. The most important modern edition of the plays is that of Charles Magnin, who, in 1845, published the plays in the original Latin with a complete French translation and a biographical and critical study of Hrotsvitha's works. There are several recent English translations of the plays, so that Hrotsvitha has at last come into her own. Her existence has not only been established beyond a doubt, but her curious and delightful contribution to the literature of the theatre has become part of the heritage of the stage. With the venerable scholar Henricus Bodo, first commentator on the writings of the Nun of Gandersheim, we who read her plays for the first time will be tempted to exclaim, 'Rara avis in Saxonia visa est!'

In order to appreciate fully the strength of that impulse for expression in dramatic form which must have impelled Hrotsvitha in her choice of so extraordinary a medium, we must realise what sort of world surrounded her and appreciate some of the handicaps with which she was burdened. She lived at the parting of the ways, a time of stress and strain between the collapse of the old order and the birth of the new. Europe, beaten upon by Northmen, Magyars, and Saracens, had at last repelled these marauders and won a respite from invasion. The crumbling Roman Empire had fallen apart, and a Saxon Emperor ruled a turbulent and disorganised band of feudal barons in the West. With the increasing power of the Christian Church, the last vestiges of the theatre in Italy had disappeared. It had split into its component parts, and bands of mimes, jugglers, dancers, and buffoons earned a precarious livelihood by travelling from place to place entertaining bored women and war-worn, brutish lords in the great halls of their feudal castles. The Roman theatre buildings themselves, scattered throughout Italy and Southern France, had been turned into donjon keeps — fortified castles for the protection of each man against his neighbour. The old order of the Roman world was destroyed and a new order had not yet come to take its place.

The Church itself was distracted with schisms and heresies, and its fight against paganism, in the theatre and elsewhere, was hardly more bitter than its internal conflicts. Wars, famines, and plagues completed the sufferings of the unfortunate lower orders, creating a universal chaos that has made this period seem to historians the most miserable that has afflicted the Western world. In such troubled and violent times, the convents and monasteries, which were growing up throughout Europe, were almost the only centres of culture and education that existed. The Christian Church, while doing its utmost to discredit the iniquitous literature of the pagans, was at the same time beginning to preserve it, and to act as guardians of the precious manuscripts which, in Europe at least, were all that remained as witness of past intellectual glories.

The fate of the women of the Dark Ages was necessarily harsh. A period which depended almost exclusively on its fighting men for survival had little interest in the development of the more peaceful arts and small time for the amenities of living. A woman at the time when Hrotsvitha lived was, in the eyes of men, a weak and foolish creature, useful only for the transmission of property, and the production of offspring. In the eyes of the Church, she was something more sinister than this. The venom with which the Church Fathers attacked the theatre was only surpassed by the vitriolic intensity with which they damned the female of the species and all her natural functions. Only one hope of redemption was held out to the unfortunate creature who through Eve's original weakness had brought sin and sorrow into the world. She must renounce this mundane existence and all its so-called pleasures, and vow herself to an eternal chastity, a virginity in this world mitigated by the hope of a spiritual union with the Beloved Bridegroom in the world to come.

The alternative careers which presented themselves to a woman such as Hrotsvitha in the year of grace 950, were strictly limited. She must either consent to be married off by her nearest male relative to some strong-armed warrior-baron who would acquire her property and her person simultaneously, and who would exercise a complete and unquestioned control over her whole future existence, or she might enter a religious order, where the questionable privilege of serving an earthly lord would be exchanged for the sure joys of a heavenly dedication. More compelling still, the convent gave her an opportunity for immediate intellectual development, the companionship of men and women keenly interested in the things of the mind, and the peaceful security of an ordered existence, nowhere else to be found. Monastic life, though physically restricting, was along certain lines intellectually liberating, and offered many of the inducements that college and a career hold out to the young girl of to-day.

The Abbey of Gandersheim would be particularly attractive to an eager and enterprising mind such as Hrotsvitha's. It was an oasis in a turbulent world, a centre of light and learning, of hope and peace, in the midst of danger and damnation. Founded in 850 by Ludolph, Duke of Saxony, it had already in Hrotsvitha's day acquired a unique literary and aristocratic tradition. Its abbesses were drawn from the imperial family of Saxony and held their fief directly from the King. They provided men-at-arms for their overlord, struck coins bearing their own image, and exercised all the rights and privileges of feudal barons. The close connection between the Imperial Court and the Abbey of Gandersheim brought it into the full current of the intellectual development of the day, and there is little reason to doubt that Hrotsvitha entered it the more eagerly because she knew that there she would be under the guidance of nuns who were as famed for their learning as they were for their piety.

Exactly when Hrotsvitha entered the Abbey of Gandersheim is not known, nor is there any record of her life before she took the veil. The dates of her birth and death, her family name, and all the details of her life are equally obscure, but in the brief forewords with which she enlivens her collected writings, we have a vivid impression of this extraordinary nun whose fate it was to play so unexpected a rôle in the history of the theatre. In thus inaugurating the delightful custom of writing prefaces to her plays, Hrotsvitha has given us what knowledge we have of her personality and her methods of work. She tells us that she was older than the Abbess Gerberga, who was born in 940, and from certain references in the texts of her poems, it is evident that she lived into the first years of the eleventh century, probably entering the convent about 960 when she was in her early twenties. She was undoubtedly of gentle birth, for Gandersheim was an aristocratic institution, welcoming the daughters of barons and lords, and presided over by an imperial princess. Moreover, her plays show familiarity with the amenities of life in the world beyond the cloister, and her education itself in an almost illiterate age attests her social standing. If, as her biographers believe, she was twenty-two or three when she took the veil, she had perhaps already experienced some of the joys and sorrows of that world which she renounced in her vows, but which, as her writings testify, she never entirely forgot.

On entering the convent, Hrotsvitha began her studies under the 'learned and gentle novice-mistress, Rikkarda,' but evidently she soon outstripped her teacher, for it is the Abbess Gerberga herself who introduced her to the classic literature which was to inspire her most famous work. She had other teachers as well, very possibly some learned monks and clerics from neighbouring monasteries; but it was in secret, and in those quiet moments which must have been difficult to secure in the carefully apportioned and supervised routine of a nun's existence, that she began her writing. 'Unknown to all around me,' she explains in the preface [1] to her first poems, 'I have toiled in secret, often destroying what seemed to me ill written, and rewriting it. . . . Up to the present I have not submitted the work to any experts, much as I needed their advice, for fear that the roughness of the style would make them discourage me to such an extent that I might

---

[1] The quotations from Hrotsvitha's prefaces and plays are taken from *The Plays of Roswitha*, translated by Christopher St. John.

give up writing altogether.' Though young 'both in
years and learning,' Hrotsvitha showed already a notable
self-reliance. Even in this preface, her humility, the
proper attitude of a woman and a nun, is mitigated by her
very just sense of her own deserts: 'Although [Latin]
prosody may seem a hard and difficult art for a woman to
master, I, without any assistance but that given by the
merciful grace of Heaven, have attempted in this book to
sing in dactyls.' The grace of Heaven is, of course, an inestimable blessing, and a nun must under all circumstances give credit to God for what there is of good in her
work, but Hrotsvitha lets us see between the lines, and
there we find a conscientious and hard-working artist who
is justly proud of her efforts and of the products of her pen.

Hrotsvitha's first work was a collection of poems in
praise of the Virgin Mary and of a number of saints and
martyrs of the Faith. Most of the poems are founded on
the tales and legends of the Greek Church, the sources of
which were at first accepted wholeheartedly by Hrotsvitha, but which were beginning to fall under the ban of
certain elements in the Western Church. Hrotsvitha,
however, had a sufficiently good opinion of her own work
to preserve these poems even when the authenticity of
their sources was questioned, proving once again her independence of judgment and decision of character.

The Martyrdom of Saint Pelagius is the most interesting among these early poems because it illustrates the sort
of contact with the outside world which was possible even
in a convent. This tale was told to Hrotsvitha herself by
an eye-witness of the event, a Spaniard who came from the
very town where Pelagius met his death. It is not surprising that martyrdoms and miracles, with all the horrors
that attend them, should seem subjects of intense interest
and importance to the poetess of Gandersheim, when
travelling strangers could regale her with first-hand descriptions of such events. It is illuminating also to note
in passing that the artistic necessity of contrasting good

with bad was already present to the young nun, who did not hesitate to describe the criminal advances that were made to the beautiful young man Pelagius by his Saracen captor. His unwillingness to submit to such 'abominable practices,' or to accept the life of ease which would have accompanied such submission, makes his death all the more edifying. Young as she was when she wrote these poems, Hrotsvitha showed none of that ignorance which later ages have often mistaken for innocence. She knew the ways and the weaknesses of the flesh as well as the strength of the spirit, and no false prudery interfered with her frank descriptions of scenes and events which to a modern mind might seem somewhat Rabelaisian. The mediæval point of view, as shown in its legends as well as its art and literature, had a tendency toward realism of detail rarely equalled even to-day.

The only other poem of particular interest in this first effort of the young poetess, is the *Fall and Conversion of Theophilus*, in which she tells a tale later to become the root legend of Germany's greatest drama. The story of Theophilus is one of the most popular in mediæval literature and concerns the priest who sells his soul to the Devil in order to obtain worldly advancement. Ruteboeuf, one of the earliest French dramatists, made use of it in his one extant play, and as the basis of Goethe's *Faust*, it has become a classic of world literature.

With this collection of poems, Hrotsvitha established herself definitely as the poet laureate of Gandersheim. Her superiors were well pleased with her accomplishments, and from this time forward her fame as a scholar and a poet spread among the learned and accomplished prelates and laymen of the Saxon Court. To her was entrusted the task of writing a panegyric to the Ottos, and her *Carmen de gestis Oddonis* is important even to-day as an historic document and is quoted in the Encyclopædia Britannica. It was written at the instigation of the Abbess Gerberga and is dedicated to her by Hrotsvitha in a charming preface in which she describes herself as 'one of the last of the least of those fighting under your ladyship's rule.' Singled out for the honour of recording the deeds and accomplishments of the Imperial House, Hrotsvitha had won for herself a position of distinction. Her fame had spread beyond the convent walls and her audience was no longer restricted to her fellow nuns. The panegyric of the Ottos was read by the Court and commented on by Archbishop William, one of the leading prelates of the day, while the plays are definitely submitted to the judgments of 'certain learned and virtuous men, patrons of the book.'

Her prefaces show that Hrotsvitha thoroughly appreciated the recognition she had won, though she never lost sight of what one might term the religious amenities. Her feminine tact was not blunted by her years of conventual life, and she could turn a complimentary phrase with a skill only comparable to that of the preface writers of a later and more sophisticated age. Her own words alone can do justice to the delicate balance she maintained between justifiable pride and graceful humility, between self-assurance and a disarming modesty. The Preface and Epistle which precede the most interesting of her productions, her six plays, is an excellent example of her style:

'To think that you, who have been nurtured in the most profound philosophical studies, and have attained knowledge in perfection, should have deigned to approve the humble work of an obscure woman!' she exlaims in her epistle to her patrons, and then, mindful of an even higher authority, she adds: 'You have, however, not praised me, but the Giver of grace which works in me, by sending your paternal congratulations and admitting that I possess some little knowledge of those arts, the subtleties of which exceed the grasp of my woman's mind. Until I showed my work to you, I had not dared to let any one see it except my intimate companions. I came near abandoning this form of writing altogether, for if there

HROTSVITHA PRESENTING HER BOOK TO THE EMPEROR

From the frontispiece (attributed to Dürer) of the first edition of
Hrotsvitha's works, printed by Conrad Celtes in 1501

COMEDIA TERCIA CALLIMACHVS

CALLIMACHUS AT DRUSIANA'S TOMB
From the first edition of Hrotsvitha's works

were few to whom I could submit my compositions at all, there were fewer still who could point out what needed correction and encourage me to go on.... I know that it is as wrong to deny a divine gift as to pretend falsely that we have received it. So I will not deny that through the grace of the Creator I have acquired some knowledge of the arts. He has given me the ability to learn — I am a teachable creature — yet of myself I should know nothing. He has given me a perspicacious mind, but one that lies fallow and idle when it is not cultivated.... That my natural gift might not be made void by negligence, I have been at pains, whenever I have been able to pick up some threads and scraps from the old torn mantle of philosophy, to weave them into the stuff of my own book... that the creator of genius may be the more honoured since it is generally believed that a woman's intelligence is slower. In the humbler works of my salad days, I gathered up my poor researches in heroic strophes, but here I have sifted them in a series of dramatic scenes and avoided through omission the pernicious voluptuousness of pagan writers.'

So for the greater glory of God, and with much 'sweat and fatigue,' Hrotsvitha fashioned the six plays which have brought her a kind of immortality she may not have foreseen, but which, judging by the glimpses we have of her personality, she would have been far too human not thoroughly to have enjoyed.

In telling us what she does of herself in her prefaces, Hrotsvitha unfortunately stops short of certain vital details. She attributes her interest in the dramatic form to her readings from Terence, but she fails to say what other influences led her to adopt so un-Christian a vehicle for her highly Christian teachings. She speaks of showing her productions to her companions, but does not tell us in so many words whether they performed the plays in the great hall of the Abbey of Gandersheim or possibly even in the church itself, or whether her comedies were purely literary exercises for her own entertainment. In conse-

quence the learned scholars have disagreed violently on
these points, in the end leaving the decision open to the
reader who cares to study the plays with sympathy and
imagination. One of the most careful students of Hrotsvitha's work, Charles Magnin, whose 1845 edition restored some of the invaluable stage directions, omitted
by Conrad Celtes in his first transcription of the manuscript, is convinced that Hrotsvitha's plays were acted.
The assumption that they were not performed is based
largely on the fact that no other plays, religious or secular, have come down to us from tenth-century Europe.

The earliest dramatic dialogue recorded in the theatrical history of the West is the Easter trope, the *Quem
Quæritis* described in the *Concordia Regularis* of Saint
Ethelwold, and dated about 965 or 975. This is nothing
more than an adaptation of the liturgy, the first step
toward the dramatic presentation of religious teaching
and far indeed from the elaborate plots and characterisations of Hrotsvitha's comedies. The first authentic mystery play, the anonymous *Representatio Adæ*, did not
appear until two hundred years after her day. It has
therefore seemed much simpler to many scholars to de-
cide that Hrotsvitha was merely doing an exercise in
Latin composition than to believe that she could have
been moved to write and probably stage real plays at a
time when no one else was doing it. This conclusion over-
looks two very important factors, the influence of the
Greek Church and the Greek tradition on a remarkably
enterprising and independent spirit, and the dramatic
viability of the plays themselves.

When Hrotsvitha entered the Abbey of Gandersheim,
Otto I was still on the throne, but Otto II was Emperor
during most of her lifetime. This Saxon prince was deeply
interested in the intellectual development of his country.
He turned to the older civilisations and particularly to
Constantinople as to the seat of culture and refinement,
and the Hellenistic influence was brought to his Court by

ambassadors and delegates from the East. In 972, he married Theophano, daughter of the Eastern Emperor Romanus II, and this Greek princess assumed an important position in the social and political life of the Saxon Court. The Abbey of Gandersheim was so intimately connected with the Court that when it was decided that Sophia, eldest daughter of Otto and Theophano, must take the veil, the reluctant princess was sent to Gandersheim. Sophia did not wish to become a nun. She had an eye for more worldly honours and a mind capable of government. When her brother Otto III came to the throne, he summoned her to his side to help him. Later Sophia returned to the fold, became abbess in her turn, and undertook various measures to prove her equality with other princes of the Church.

While Sophia was still a novice and a young nun, the Empress Theophano often visited the Abbey, and Hrotsvitha, accredited bard of the Imperial family, was undoubtedly granted special privileges which brought her into contact with the Greek princesses and their attendant train. From such sources she would have learned at first-hand the fascinating story of the war waged in Constantinople between the Orthodox Church and the theatre. In her remote Saxon convent, where such a thing as a play had never been seen, Hrotsvitha must have listened avidly to the accounts of spectacle-loving Constantinople told by the homesick exiles who had followed their princess into the barbarous North.

The tradition of the Greek Church at this time showed two distinct and contradictory attitudes; that epitomised by Saint Chrysostom, who in the fourth century poured out the vials of his wrath and of his sublime eloquence on all that remotely concerned the stage, and that typified by the writing of Gregory Nazienzen and the Apollinari, who, when Julian the Apostate prohibited the teaching of the Greek classics to the followers of Christ, attempted to preserve the Greek literary forms for their people by rewriting the Old Testament as an Homeric epic, and the New along the lines of the classic drama. Other devout Christians made similar attempts with even less success if we can judge by the fact that, of the large body of these Christianized Greek tragedies, only a few fragments have survived.

In Hrotsvitha's day many must still have been in existence, though it is very doubtful that she ever saw them even in manuscript. We do not even know whether she could read Greek, but her constant use of Greek tales and legends as sources for her plots proves her familiarity with the literature of the Greek Church. Though she could not by any possibility have seen a play acted, the mere existence of these Byzantine dramas was enough to encourage her in her efforts. Her failure to acknowledge in her preface so venerable a precedent as that created by these Christian dramas is easily understood when we glimpse the tangled web of heresies and schisms with which the whole history of the early Church is overlaid. It was safer to recognize the pagan Terence as her prototype than to refer to the Christian sanctions of the theatre, tainted as they were by the black heresy of Arius and the triumphs of the hated Iconoclasts.

Hrotsvitha, however, must in her own mind have found ample justification for looking with tolerance upon the drama. The Empress Theophano could have told her of the astonishing truce that had been called in the age-long battle between Church and stage. One of the most extraordinary incidents in the whole history of the Church is the compromise brought about in the year 990 by Theophylactus, Patriarch of Constantinople, a member of the Empress' own family. This reverend prelate, uncle of Romanus II, Theophano's father, and head of the Orthodox Church, actually introduced the theatre into the bosom of the Church itself, permitting professional actors, actresses, and dancers from the Hippodrome to perform in Saint Sophia, and countenancing all sorts of dramatic amusements, even to the wildest buffooneries. Theophano herself loved the stage. Her father had been a devotee of the Hippodrome, her son Otto III attempted to reëstablish the theatre in Italy, and her influence may in some measure account for the curious turn taken by Hrotsvitha's genius.

It does not require too wild a flight of the imagination, to picture the nuns of Gandersheim eagerly preparing to welcome their royal guest with a form of entertainment particularly dear to her heart and one of which she had been completely deprived since her departure from Constantinople. The Abbess Gerberga would not have been unwilling to show the foreign Empress that Saxony could produce a poet worthy of respect and that the resources of Gandersheim were equal to the task of presenting so sophisticated a form of entertainment as a drama. What more appropriate theme could have been chosen for the diversion of a Greek princess than Hrotsvitha's first play, *Gallicanus*, which sings the praises of Constance, daughter of Constantine, and reflects, in the story of the conversion of Gallicanus, the more famous conversion of Constantine himself, first of Christian Emperors and founder of the Empire in the East.

Hrotsvitha's avowed purpose of glorifying the 'laudable chastity of Christian virgins' is here clothed in a panoply of royal pomp. The scenes laid in the court of Constantine, the crowded battlefields, the streets of Rome, the audience hall of Julian the Apostate, offered ample opportunities for the display of all the beautiful vestments, the colourful copes and chasubles, the treasures of silk, embroidery, and plate with which the sacristy of a wealthy convent would be supplied. Possibly the armour needed for the contending forces of Romans and Scythians was contributed by the knights-at-arms attached to the Abbey. With what ardour the young nuns and novices would have thrown themselves into the task of making costumes and learning their parts! If we judge the tenth

century by later mediæval custom, the scenes presented
before the audience gathered in the Hall of the Abbey, or,
as Philarète Chasle believes, in the nave of the Church itself, would not have been devoid of dignity, even of a certain splendour. Hrotsvitha's first effort in dramaturgy is
not as skilful as her later plays, but no one who has accepted Shakespeare's sketchy battle scenes, nor the de-
tached and episodic structure of his chronicle plays, need
scorn Hrotsvitha's naïve introduction of two contending
armies on one stage, or her shorthand method of deciding
the fate of a tremendous encounter in twenty-five lines of
dialogue. *Gallicanus*, for all its faults, would have been an
effective pageant to unroll before a queen.

Hrotsvitha, in all her plays, follows with pious faith the
details of the legends which she dramatises, but her originality is evident in the skill with which she succeeds in
infusing personality into the lay figures of her tales. Constantine, whom she makes weak and vacillating in order
to bring out the strength and even the holy guile of his
daughter Constance; Julian the Apostate, who bids his
soldiers remind the Christians of their own teachings
about renouncing worldly goods while they are stripping
them of all they possess; John and Paul, almoners of Constance, who are not above a little judicious prevarication
while they go about the Lord's work — all these have
a distinct character of their own. In Constance we see the
outlines of a real individual, modelled on the lines of those
'royal personages,' Gerberga, Theophano, and Sophia,
whom Hrotsvitha had the privilege of knowing intimately.
Constance, receiving the daughters of Gallicanus and
offering a fervent and thoroughly orthodox prayer for
their salvation, might be the Abbess herself receiving a
distinguished postulant; just as the arguments between
John, Paul, and Julian the Apostate reflect the pious and
at the same time scholastic disputations so typical of
mediæval theology.

Hrotsvitha's plays must necessarily be approached

with sympathy and understanding, for they are expressed in an idiom alien to our modern point of view. They are all short — running from five to six hundred lines of concentrated dialogue broken into scenes of varying length by the transcribers of the original manuscript. At first glance, they seem naïve, crude, two-dimensional. Everything appears on one plane with little attempt at rounding out of contours. Especially is this true of *Gallicanus* and of the two martyr plays, *Dulcitius* and *Sapientia*. In them Hrotsvitha has been absorbed in her didactic mission. They are preachments rather than plays, and yet even here her native dramatic instinct has not been completely subdued; a character, a scene, a bit of dialogue comes out with startling clarity. *Dulcitius* is particularly interesting in that it contains the one intentionally comic scene in Hrotsvitha's plays.

The legend turns on the strange hallucination that overcame the Roman Governor, Dulcitius, when he attempted to rape three Christian maidens committed to his tender care. Making his way into the Palace kitchen, where he thinks the prisoners are confined, he embraces the pots and pans under the illusion that he is indulging in a night of love, to the immense amusement of the maidens themselves who watch the proceedings through a keyhole. The dramatic effect of having his would-be victims recount to each other the grotesque antics of the demented Governor, while the sound of crashing pans off stage emphasises the excitement, is excellent. Dulcitius' reappearance, covered with soot and his clothes in rags, making futile attempts to convince his own soldiers of his identity, is cleverly worked out. The scene is obviously meant for visual presentation and is a striking example of Hrotsvitha's eye for stage effects.

In the heroic virgins of *Dulcitius* and the other martyr plays, Hrotsvitha has painted a variety of religious fanatic for whom she had apparently very little sympathy. They have none of the royal dignity of Constance, the wisdom of Sapientia, the charm of Drusiana, Mary, or Thaïs. Whether consciously or not, Hrotsvitha presents the women who have been touched by sin far more sympathetically than she does the immaculate virgins who defy their tormentors and fly straight to heaven in a blaze of unfelt torments and complacent glory. The three martyrs of *Dulcitius* have all the objectionable characteristics of the type, but they are saved from complete smugness by their amusement over the Roman Governor's absurd misadventure. Dulcitius, it is to be remarked, disappears suddenly from the story, the laughter he has provoked making him unsuitable as an instrument for really impressive martyrdom. His successor in the office of executioner dispatches two of the maidens in short order, but with the third, Irena, he argues at length, and is, of course, worsted in dialectics as he is frustrated in his design of humiliating and defiling her.

Hrotsvitha's preoccupation, in all her plays, with the glories of virginity must be taken as the hall-mark of her profession. In a community of dedicated nuns it was natural, indeed inevitable, that this aspect of their tribute to God should be presented in all its beauty and nobility, and that all its ramifications should be of palpitating interest. Undoubtedly also, Hrotsvitha obtained a certain release for her own emotional suppressions by elaborating these pictures of carnal dangers and the pitfalls of the flesh. These scenes, wherein holy virgins, refusing advantageous offers of marriage, are dragged off to brothels to be 'abominably defiled,' or are attacked by brutal soldiers and escape only by miraculous intervention, are the product of a mind that may have denied, but has not forgotten, the 'sinful lusts of the flesh.' Hrotsvitha's plays illustrate very vividly the process of psychic compensation which is so striking a feature of mediæval monastic literature.

In *Dulcitius*, as in her last play, *Sapientia*, Hrotsvitha gives expression to a vein of sadism which is also associated with certain aspects of repression. She positively revels in the lurid and suggestive details of her torture scenes in a way which has led some critics to brand these plays as completely unactable. When we remember the enthusiasm with which such scenes were presented in later mediæval mystery plays, as evidenced by the records, and by such pictures as that of the martyrdom of Saint Apollonia by Jean Fouquet, Hrotsvitha's excursions into the horrific are less surprising. We are to-day more squeamish about physical manifestations of the sort on our stage, but the nuns of Gandersheim were nourished in a sturdier school. They were suckled on tales of torture and martyrdom, and the more boiling oil, fiery furnaces, severed limbs, and bleeding wounds a tale provided, the greater the thrill. Hrotsvitha was not unwilling to write penny-dreadfuls of the sort, nor could a more edifying and intimately comforting spectacle be imagined than that of these pure young girls taunting and defying Emperors and all the strength of embattled masculine paganism while their faith prevented them from feeling the pain and ignominy to which their bodies were subjected. We may turn with repugnance from the scenes in which Sapientia's children are scourged by the centurions, but we should not in our disgust forget that one of the most popular scenes ever presented on the American stage was that of the scourging of Uncle Tom, as well as, curiously enough, the death and ascension of little Eva, a child almost as objectionable in her way as any of Hrotsvitha's smug young heroines.

Again and again, even in these two martyr-plays, which seem to us the least actable of Hrotsvitha's works, little strokes of dialogue vividly suggest the stage picture, as in the opening of the third scene in *Sapientia*, when Antiochus says to the Christians, 'That is the Emperor you see there, seated on his throne. Be careful what you say to him'; or, in another scene when Sapientia is encouraging her horde of infant martyrs, 'Oh, my dearest little ones, My beloved children! Do not let this narrow prison sadden you.' In a phrase or two, Hrotsvitha sets the stage, and one need only imagine the attending groups of nuns, dressed as courtiers, executioners, Roman matrons, followers, or slaves, rounding out the scenes with the action suggested in the text, to realise that the plays are eminently actable.

Dulcitius is the only play containing obviously comic scenes, yet all of them, even the most terrible, are redeemed from sadness by the faith which animates their author. To understand Hrotsvitha's spirit, it is necessary to remember that Catholicism, even mediæval Catholicism, with all its demonology, its horrors and damnations, was essentially a happy religion. The promise of future blessedness compensated for much present suffering, and the little martyrs could giggle like any other children, though in the presence of an executioner. 'What are you muttering there?' one of the latter exclaims in exasperation. 'Behave yourself and do not laugh!' The constant complaint of their persecutors is that the Christians are laughing at them, making fools of them. Not only do the Christians triumph by their holiness, but they outargue and outwit their tormentors at every turn.

Hrotsvitha makes use of these opportunities to air her own scholarly accomplishments, and we find discourses on mathematics and music interjected into the most unlikely situations. She feels it necessary, however, to make some apology for these excursions into what the Emperor Hadrian in one of her plays brands as 'intricate and unprofitable dissertations.' 'It would be unprofitable,' Hrotsvitha's Sapientia answers, 'if it did not lead us to appreciate the wisdom of our Creator, Who in the beginning created the world out of nothing... and then, in time and the age of man, formulated a science which reveals fresh wonders the more we study it.'

The Sapientia who formulates this apologia for the pur-

suit of knowledge may well be taken as representing the
Nun of Gandersheim in her later years. Hrotsvitha's intellectual hunger is so evident, her eagerness to know and
learn so palpable, both in her plays and prefaces, that we
cannot fail to see in such sentiments as these her own ex-
cuses for enthusiasms which in a woman and a nun of the
Dark Ages needed some measure of explanation. The
stately, nobly born, and extremely intelligent Sapientia is
Hrotsvitha in the full flower of her maturity and success,
devoting her life to the service of God, and the creations
of her genius to his everlasting glory.

A more tender and humanly touching Hrotsvitha is
revealed in her fourth play, *Abraham*. It is not a martyr play, nor is it overburdened with too many 'threads
and scraps from the torn mantle of philosophy.' In a
series of swift and straightforward scenes it tells the
story of Mary, niece of the hermit Abraham, who at the
tender age of eight dedicates herself to Christ. After
many years spent in solitary prayer and meditation under
the care of Abraham, she is seduced by a passing stranger.
In shame and horror she flees from the hermitage and
abandons herself to a life of sin. Abraham follows her,
and by his love and his exhortations brings her back to
God.

The scenes in the brothel where Abraham, disguised as
an ordinary traveller, has gone to find his niece, are
handled with extraordinary delicacy and charm. At first
Abraham is shown talking to the innkeeper, asking for
food and lodging and for the company of the beautiful
girl with whom he is 'already in love' from the descriptions he has heard of her. Mary comes in, but does not
recognise her spiritual father, who with an effort conquers
his emotions and continues to play his part. Hrotsvitha's
treatment of this scene is particularly sensitive, and
though it is almost impossible to capture the quality of
her writing in a few lines, this, and the following recognition scene give some idea of the sincerity and directness of

her style, as well as her ability to convey profound feeling in a few lines. The innkeeper greets her boisterously — 'Luck comes your way, Mary! Not only do young gallants of your own age flock to your arms, but even the wise and venerable come to you.'

MARY: It is all one to me. It is my business to love those who love me.

ABRAHAM: Come nearer, Mary, and give me a kiss.

MARY: I will give you more than a kiss. I will take your head in my arms and stroke your neck.

ABRAHAM: Yes, like that!

MARY: What does this mean? What is this lovely fragrance, so clean, so sweet? It reminds me of the time when I was good.

ABRAHAM (aside): On with the mask! Chatter, make lewd jests like an idle boy! She must not recognise me or for very shame she will fly from me.

MARY: Wretch that I am! To what have I fallen! In what pit have I sunk!

ABRAHAM: You forget where you are! Do men come here to see you cry?

INNKEEPER: What's the matter, Lady Mary? Why are you in the dumps? You have lived here two years and never before have I seen a tear, never heard a sigh or a word of complaint.

MARY: Oh, that I had died three years ago before I came to this!

ABRAHAM: I came here to make love to you, not to weep with you over your sins.

MARY: A little thing moved me, and I spoke foolishly. It is nothing. Come, let us eat and drink and be merry, for, as you say, this is not the place to think of one's sins.

After eating supper, they go into the bedroom where the scene continues:

MARY: Look! How do you like this room? A handsome bed, isn't it? Those trappings cost a lot of money. Sit down and I will take off your shoes. You seem tired.

ABRAHAM: First bolt the door. Some one may come in.

MARY: Have no fear, I have seen to that.

ABRAHAM: The time has come for me to show my shaven

head and make myself known! Oh, my daughter, oh, Mary, you who are part of my soul! Look at me. Do you not know me? Do you not know the old man who cherished you with a father's love, and wedded you to the Son of the King of Heaven?

MARY: God, what shall I do! It is my father and master Abraham!

ABRAHAM: What has come to you daughter!

MARY: Oh, misery!...

ABRAHAM: Why have you thrown yourself down there? Why do you lie on the ground without moving or speaking? Get up, Mary, get up, my child and listen to me!

MARY: No, no, I am afraid, I cannot bear your reproaches.

ABRAHAM: Remember how I love you, and you will not be afraid.... The mercy of Heaven is greater than you or your sins. Let your sadness be dispersed by its glorious beams....

And so on, until Mary is convinced of God's love and forgiveness and returns to the desert, riding on Abraham's horse, 'that the stony road should not hurt her delicate feet.'

With *Paphnutius*, the play immediately following *Abraham*, Hrotsvitha handles the same theme, that of the conversion of a harlot, in an entirely different manner. *Paphnutius* is the story of Thaïs, the first dramatic presentation of this old and still popular legend. In it Hrotsvitha shows her increasing ability to differentiate character and the art with which she can develop her material. When the hermit Paphnutius goes to Alexandria in the hope of saving a lost soul by converting the famous courtesan Thaïs to the true faith, he, too, like Abraham, dons worldly attire, and, armed with piety and the necessary gold pieces, ventures into a house of sin in pursuit of his worthy purpose. Both plays are surprisingly, if naïvely, realistic, for both hermits boldly demand the most intimate favours of their would-be converts, and Hrotsvitha does not hesitate to introduce her godly men into the bedchambers of these prostitutes. When Paphnutius demands of Thaïs that she take him into a secret room, she shows him her bedroom. 'How would you like a bedchamber fragrant with perfumes, adorned as for marriage? I have such a room. Look!'

The dramatic effect of both conversions is, of course, greatly heightened by the fact that they occur at the very moment when these erring women are engaged in their evil trade — but, though the scene is the same, the whole treatment is radically different. Abraham is throughout the gentle old man, disguising his emotion with difficulty and finally revealing himself in words of kindness and gentle exhortation. Paphnutius, on the other hand, makes a very creditable lover. Young and handsome, he woos Thaïs in words he must have learned elsewhere than in his desert hermitage, but when he begins to admonish her, all gentleness disappears. Fire and brimstone, terror and grief, are the lot of one as confirmed in evil, as hardened and as profligate as Thaïs the Harlot. Hard as Mary's life of penitence, prayer, and fasting may seem to us, it has not the revolting cruelty of the fate to which Paphnutius condemns the unfortunate Thaïs.

Here again Hrotsvitha's eye for realistic detail spares us no aspect of the plight in which Thaïs found herself when she was condemned to pass what remained of her life walled into a narrow cell which had no opening save one tiny window. She shrinks with fastidious disgust from the filth which, to the mediæval ascetic, was far nearer godliness than the perfumed cleanliness of a decadent Roman civilisation. It is no wonder that the unfortunate penitent died shortly after her release. But Thaïs' end is all the more edifying because of her great penitence — and this picture of physical suffering was no doubt considered highly edifying by Hrotsvitha's contemporaries, whatever it may seem to us to-day. Evidently also Hrotsvitha's surprising excursions into houses of ill fame were forgiven by her spiritual pastors and masters in view of the good work she was accomplishing in these unholy places. As her preface proves, she justified her treatment of such subjects by the moral effects of their teachings, but when we read the plays themselves, we cannot help thinking that Hrotsvitha enjoyed these voyages outside the convent walls, and that in her heart of hearts she loved the sinners she painted far more than she hated their sins.

Hrotsvitha must have found some difficulty in justifying all her expeditions into forbidden territory, for this surprising nun was bold enough to write at least one love-story. In the preface of the plays, she shows herself fully conscious of the dangerous ground she was treading. 'One thing has... embarrassed me and often brought a blush to my cheek,' she tells us. 'It is that I have been compelled through the nature of this work to apply my mind and my pen to depicting the dreadful frenzy of those possessed by unlawful love and the insidious sweetness of passion — things which should not even be named among us. Yet if from modesty I had refrained from treating these subjects, I should not have been able to attain my object — to glorify the innocent to the best of my ability. For the more seductive the blandishments of lovers, the more wonderful the divine succour and the greater the merit of those who resist, especially when it is fragile woman who is victorious and strong man who is routed with confusion.'

Safely ensconced behind this laudable and appropriate excuse, Hrotsvitha proceeded to write the first romance of modern literature, her third play, *Callimachus*. The curious external resemblances between *Callimachus* and *Romeo and Juliet* are no less striking than the atmosphere of passionate romanticism which emanates from the whole. The plot concerns the fatal love of Callimachus for Drusiana, wife of Prince Andronicus. Drusiana had dedicated herself to God, renouncing 'even that which is lawful,' her husband's bed, and, rather than break her vows of chastity, she prays for death to deliver her from the tempting importunities of her lover. She dies at once, and is buried, but Callimachus' passion follows her into the grave. The scene at the tomb of Drusiana, when Callimachus, aided by the faithless servant Fortunatus, finds himself in the presence of his dead love, strikingly prefigures the famous climax of Shakespeare's tragedy. The deaths are almost as numerous, too, for both Callimachus and Fortunatus are killed by miraculous intervention. The resurrection of all three, and the repentance and conversion of Callimachus is the religious dénouement needed to justify Hrotsvitha's bold attempt at romantic drama and is of less importance than her obvious preoccupation with her love-story.

Hrotsvitha's characterisations, embryonic as they are, show her originality. Drusiana, unlike the strong-minded saints of the martyr plays, sure of their faith and of their ultimate victory, is conscious of her own weakness in the face of temptation. Touched by the ardour of Callimachus, she is afraid that she will be unable to resist him, and, determined neither to rouse the anger of her husband against him nor fall from the grace she has obtained, she prays for death. In the few lines that are allotted to her, from her first scene with Callimachus, where she attempts, rather pathetically, to put off his advances, to her final act after her resurrection, when she restores to life the villain who betrayed her dead body to her lover, the character of Drusiana is consistently gentle, loving, and tender — as far removed from the colourless heroines of the Latin theatre as it is from the heroic figures of Greek tragedy.

The distracted husband, Andronicus, is also, traditionally speaking, a creation of Hrotsvitha's own imagination. Certainly the husbands and fathers of Latin comedy established no precedent on which to model this forbearing and kindly gentleman. One wonders even more where, among the barons and fighting lords of the Dark Ages, his prototype could have been found. His love for Drusiana never wavers, though she has left his bed, and though he

knows that she has died in order to escape the importunities of another man. His devotion and faith are so great
that it is he, rather than the Apostle John, who is made
the mouthpiece for the moral of the tale. Standing over
the dead bodies of Callimachus and the servant, he medi-
tates on the heavenly revelation which he had just received: 'What astonishes me most,' he says, 'is that the
Divine Voice should have promised the resurrection of
[Callimachus] who planned the crime and not of him who
was only an accomplice. Maybe it is because the one,
blinded by passion of the flesh, knew not what he did,
while the other sinned of deliberate malice.' Hrotsvitha
had not forgotten the words of One whose understanding
was so great that He could say of a certain sinner, 'Her
sins, which are many, are forgiven, for she loved much.'

In the character of Callimachus, Hrotsvitha gives a
vivid outline sketch of an experienced worldling, not unlike
the dashing Romeo. In the first scenes of the play he talks
to his friends, in the tenth-century equivalent of Euphu-
ism, a scholastic splitting of phrases that only half-veils
the intensity of his ill-advised passion. His relations with
Drusiana show him to be as thoughtless of her happiness
and safety as Romeo himself. He pursues her even into
the grave, and here we see the Benedictine nun handling
with extraordinary delicacy and understanding a situation as bold, one might almost say as lurid, as anything the
Elizabethans could have invented. Hrotsvitha was evidently so moved by a strong sympathy for the miseries of
frustrated love that she did not hesitate to present it in all
its intensity. Callimachus' outburst over the dead body
of Drusiana has an authentic ring of passion: 'O Drusiana,
Drusiana, I worshipped you with my whole soul! I
yearned from my very bowels to embrace you! And you
repulsed me, and thwarted my desire. Now you are in my
power, now I can wound you with my kisses, and pour out
my love upon you.'

Strange words to echo in a convent hall, bringing suddenly to the surface the troubled and violent stream of imprisoned feeling. Hrotsvitha's intense and passionate nature is revealed for a moment only, to be quickly covered by the accustomed mantle of sober piety. But Callimachus' conversion and frenzied repentance is merely another phase of an intense emotional experience.

'I came here for an evil purpose,' he exclaims after his resurrection, 'but the pangs of love consumed me. I was beside myself.' And John answers him: 'What mad folly possessed you, that you should dare think of such a shameful outrage to the chaste dead!' Callimachus can only repeat: 'I was mad!... I am overwhelmed by the thought of my abominable crime. I repent with my whole heart and bewail my sin.... Oh, hasten then to help a man in dire need — give me some comfort! Help me throw off the grief that crushes me! Show me how a pagan may change into a Christian, a fornicator into a chaste man! Oh, set my feet in the way of truth! Teach me to live mindful of the divine promises.'

His plea is not in vain. For all his black sin, Callimachus is forgiven. The note of peace after the storm rings like the quiet tolling of the Angelus, reminding the nuns of Gandersheim that they have found a refuge from the 'dreadful frenzy of passion.' The Judge who could forgive Callimachus because he loved too greatly could be counted upon to 'search the heart and reins and reward or punish fairly.'

The plays of Hrotsvitha, after long years of neglect, have recently been studied with great interest and attention, and have even been acted in English both in London and New York with varying degrees of artistic success. The impossibility of recapturing an atmosphere as alien to us as that of mediæval Christianity will always make their presentation peculiarly difficult. Few indeed are the playwrights who have actually survived their own day unless, in addition to possessing dramatic gifts, they have been poets of such high order that the hungry generations have listened in awe to their music. Hrotsvitha was not a great poet. She was an acute observer, an avid scholar, an adventurous and enterprising soul. To enjoy her style one must have a taste for the phrase that suggests rather than describes, for a simplicity which is at once naïve and full of wisdom. Like the early painters, her work is stiff, clearcut, often harsh, and occasionally crude, but none the less vital for all its shortcomings. Her plays are all brief, her characterisations often no more than outline sketches, yet in the quick strokes with which she defines an individual she shows a master's hand. Her comedies have a vivacity, a directness of approach, and, in spite of much that is incredible, an essential veracity which gives them permanent value.

If it is true, as the scholars tell us, that Hrotsvitha had no imitators or successors, she nevertheless foreshadowed a new dramatic dispensation, where love, human and divine, were to reign supreme, and where the romantic ideal of individual freedom was finally to replace the Greek conception of inescapable fatality. Working alone in her remote Saxon convent, where plays and players had never been seen, surrounded by a social order barely emerging from barbarism, this Benedictine nun cherished in secret the wavering flame of a great tradition, pouring into it the new oil of the Christian religion and handing it on, sweetened and strengthened by her care, to later generations of those who know and love the theatre.

CHAPTER III

THE COMMEDIANTE APPEARS

THE FIRST ACTRESSES IN ITALY

IN spite of Hrotsvitha's shining example and the proof her works afforded of women's intrinsic capacity for dramatic achievement, the theatre of the Middle Ages, as it emerged from the oblivion into which the break-up of the Roman Empire had plunged it, was as hostile to women as that of ancient Greece itself. The Church, having attacked and destroyed the pagan theatre, took possession of the idea it contained and re-created a theatre in its own image. Hrotsvitha's desire to use 'the seductive sweetness' of pagan drama for the greater glory of God was the seed from which an entirely new dramatic impulse developed. In the very heart of the Church itself, the despised and anathematised theatre came to life once again.

It came to life, however, vigorously denying women a share in its activities. Women were not allowed to speak in church even for the praiseworthy purposes of exhortation and prayer; how much less would they be tolerated as performers in its sacred mysteries. In a woodcut dating from the twelfth century, a group of women are shown suffering extreme torment in a flamy hell for the nefarious sin of having raised their voices in church. Silenced and forced to cover their heads for greater modesty, excluded from the performance of any sacred office, and relegated to a properly subordinate position, there was no possibility of women taking part in religious plays, except when they were performed in the seclusion of their own world of the convents. In the churches and cathedrals of mediæval Europe, it was a clerk or deacon, a choir-boy or priest, who, 'donning white garments and a white silk veil,' enacted the part of the Virgin, of Mary of Magdala, or of Eve herself. Not until the Renaissance had shaken Europe from its lethargy and aroused man once more to an appreciation of his intellectual heritage did the theatre throw off its religious preoccupation and its consequent restrictive attitude toward women.

The influence of the Renaissance itself on women's entrance into the theatrical world was more general than particular. It lay in the reversal of the mediæval attitude toward women, in the liberating and stimulating atmosphere of the times, rather than in any direct effect on stage customs. As a matter of fact the Revival of Learning — the first flowering of the Renaissance — was again hostile to their presence on the stage because of its preoccupation with the classic tradition, its desire to reproduce the Greek and Latin plays as nearly in their original form as possible. But even though this scholarly attitude put yet another stumbling-block in the way of women's conquest of the theatre, the whole movement of the times made possible her eventual triumph. Where once she had been considered the source of all evil, she now became, in theory at least, a messenger of light.

Dante's mystic idealisation of Beatrice was metamorphosed during the following centuries into a practical and purely pagan theory of inspiration, which accepted the flesh-and-blood women of the Renaissance as appropriate vehicles for the transmission of the divine fire. No longer outcast from the world of the mind, nor apologetic, as was Hrotsvitha, for daring to adventure into realms held for centuries as the exclusive property of men, the women of the Renaissance cultivated all the arts and some of the science of the period. They were expected to take an intelligent, if always gracefully subordinate, share in the intellectual activities of men, and were looked upon as leaders in the effort toward an increasingly polished and cultivated social life. In this world where women were thought of as sources of inspiration, the position of the actress was already prepared and only awaited her arrival.

The theatre played no small part in the dissemination and popularising of the new culture which was born of the rediscovered classic knowledge. It was one of the most exciting finds of the scholars in the stirring days of the revival of learning, and it played an important rôle throughout the Renaissance. With the rediscovery of Plautus in 1429, of Vitruvius in 1486, and of Aristotle, that Bible of the theatre, in 1498, the riches of the classic theatre were unfolded to an enthusiastic and delighted company of learned young princes, prelates, warriors, and priests. At first the plays were acted in Latin in the true classic tradition by young men and boys, but very soon they were translated into Italian, songs and dances performed by women were added, and the young poets, inspired by the Latin plays, began to try their own hand at this new and diverting game. Ariosto's *Cassaria*, Cardinal Bibbiena's *Calandria*, and Machiavelli's *Mandragola*, all of which appeared in the early years of the sixteenth century, were among the first and most famous of the early Italian plays.

The staging and performance of these comedies, whether Latin or Italian, was one of the chief amusements of the ducal and princely courts. All over Italy theatres were built in the palaces and performances given on the most splendid scale. The Dukes of Mantua and Ferrara, the Medici in Florence, the Pope in his gorgeous and worldly Court at Rome, vied with each other in the magnificence of their display.

Typical of these splendid performances was a fête given at Urbino during the carnival of 1513, when Cardinal Bibbiena's *Calandria* was performed to the accompaniment of elaborate pageants and *intermezzi* celebrating the return of the Duke of Urbino from the war and the delivery of Italy from foreign oppression. Count Baldassare Castiglione, himself the perfect courtier and gentleman of his

famous book *Il Cortegiano*, superintended the staging of
the plays. His letter, written just after the festivities, is
rich in details of scenery and staging:

'Our comedies have gone off very well,' he says in part,
'most of all the *Calandria* which was represented in truly
magnificent style.... The scene was laid in a very fine city
with streets, palaces, and towers, all in relief, and looking
as if they were real, the effect being completed by admirable paintings in scientific perspective.... The first *intermezzo* was a *moresca* by Jason, who appeared on one side
of the stage dancing in antique armour, looking very fine
with a splendid sword and shield. On the other side came
two bulls, so lifelike that several spectators took them for
real animals, breathing fire through their nostrils.... The
second interlude was a very beautiful chariot of Venus
with the goddess seated and holding a lighted taper in her
hand. The car was drawn by two doves, who certainly
seemed alive, and who were ridden by two Amorini with
lighted tapers in their hands and bows and quivers on
their shoulders.... The fourth *intermezzo* was a car of
Juno, also ablaze with light. The goddess, wearing a
crown on her brow and carrying a sceptre, appeared
seated on a cloud which encircled the chariot, and surrounded by numberless heads blowing the winds of
heaven. This car was drawn by two peacocks so beautiful and lifelike that I could hardly believe my eyes,
and yet I had seen them before and had myself given
directions how they were to be made.'

And so, with much dancing and singing in glorification
of ideal love, the festa came to an end. Venus put aside
her diaphanous draperies, Juno laid down her sceptre and
her crown. As the two girls hurried into their ordinary
clothes — deep red or dun-coloured cloth with snugly fitting bodice and wide, heavy skirt — as they adjusted the
gold clasp that held their white chemisette in place, and
arranged their bit of jewelry to best effect, they may have
commented on the play of which they had heard snatches

while, crowded behind the scenes, they waited to go on in
their wobbly painted chariots. It was the first time that
they had been able to understand the words spoken during the innumerable performances in which they appeared as singers, dancers, or mythological personages.
Usually they had to do much tedious standing around
while elegant youths recited interminably in Latin. This
time they had understood the Cardinal's words; some of
the jokes had been really funny — but how absurd to expect any one to take Messer Lodovico, even in his girl's
clothes, for a woman! He looked and spoke like a boy,
and when he was dressed as a boy, no one could possibly
remember that he was supposed to be a girl masquerading! It spoiled the plot, or so Venus and Juno had the
boldness to whisper in each other's ears, and they began to
think that, as plays were being written in a language they
could master, perhaps they themselves might have a
chance.... But at this point they were rudely awakened
from their dream by His Serenity's major-domo, who
wanted no loitering about the place and sent them pack-
ing.

The same idea was forming in the minds of the elegant
ladies who had watched the play from their vantage-point
in the Great Hall. They did not see why their dashing
brothers, lovers, or husbands should have all the fun of
this newly discovered toy. They could read and learn by
heart both Latin and Italian, they could sing and dance as
well as, if not better than, the men. They loved the
theatre as passionately as any one, and very soon they
were taking part in the more select and aristocratic performances. The daughters of Ercole d'Este performed
the *Adelphi* of Terence on the occasion of a visit of Pope
Paul III to Ferrara, and in 1539 we find another princess
of the Este family appearing in a Latin comedy for the
delectation of her elders. When the *Danza di Venere*
was produced at Padua, the daughter of the Marchioness of Soragna played the part of Amarilla, but on the

whole their share was chiefly decorative. They appeared ornamentally in the pageants and masques, while the acting was still done by young men, especially in the classic rôles. We hear of a certain reverend prelate, the Cardinal Inghirami, who was known as Phædra long after he had become a Prince of the Church because of his superlative performance of that impassioned rôle. Little by little, however, the prejudice against women's appearance on the stage was being broken down. As new comedies were written for 'modern' tastes, and as the interludes became more elaborate and demanded an increasing number of women for their performance, the line of demarcation between actress and *figurante* becomes less and less clear.

The phenomenal rage for interludes increased the demand for women on the stage. No play was complete without *intermezzi*, no festivity could be undertaken unless poets, painters, and architects were on hand to fabricate these intricate ballet-pantomimes in celebration of some idea or event. The greatest artists of the day, Mantegna, Raphael, Peruzzi, and the rest, were called upon to paint scenery and plan elaborate effects. Even religious plays, such as the *Sacre Rappresentazione* of Florence, were diversified by allegorical ballets which took place on the same stage and at the same time as the religious plays, performed by boy actors. The stage directions of one of these performances gives a picture of the kind of episode that was introduced into the middle of a solemn Judgment scene:

'Now goes the King to Rome,' the text reads, thereby, we are to suppose, clearing the stage of actors, 'and you meanwhile make four women, naked, or clothed in flesh-coloured cloth, rise waist-high from the sea, with tresses to the wind, and let them sing as sweetly as may be.'

Or again: 'In the interval you will cause three women, well-beseen, to issue from a cave, one of them attired in white, one in red, the other in green, with golden balls in their hands, and with them a young man,' who together perform a dance — the masque of Hope, in a scene that brings vividly to mind the groups of graceful dancing figures set against a meticulously painted landscape of grottoes, woods, and hills by the imperishable brush of a del Cossa, a Botticelli, or a Mantegna.

In an account given by Isabella d'Este of the wedding festivities on the occasion of the marriage of her brother Alphonso to Lucrezia Borgia in 1502, women are mentioned among the actors gathered in her father's palace to perform Latin comedies for the assembled notables. She does not specify, however, whether they acted in the plays or only in the dances and interludes that embellished them.

'My father brought in all the actors,' Isabella wrote to her husband, the Marquis of Mantua, who was not able to be present. 'He showed us the costumes which had been prepared for the five comedies, to prove that the dresses had been made on purpose, and those worn in one comedy would not be used again. There were in all, one hundred and ten actors, men and women, and their clothes were of cendale and camlet. The leader of the troupe appeared in the character of Plautus and explained the argument of the five plays.... About six o'clock the play began. Neither the verses nor the voices struck me as very good, but the Moresche dances between the acts were very well danced and with great spirit.'

In a later letter Isabella told her husband that Ariosto's *Cassaria*, which was also given on this occasion, was 'lascivious and immoral beyond words,' and that she would not allow her ladies to attend it.

Here we find a very definite influence exercised by the women of the Renaissance on the theatre, quite aside from any share they may have taken in the actual performances. They formed an important, perhaps the most important, element of the audience, and their effort was on the whole in the direction of greater refinement and culti-

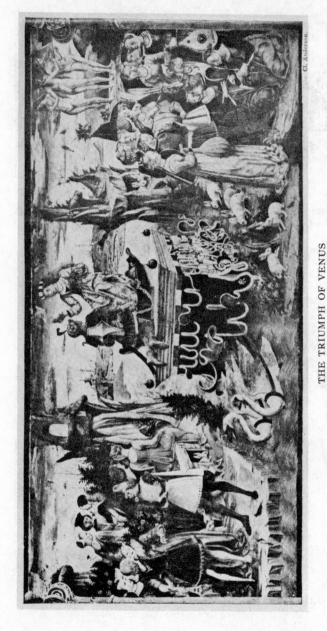

THE TRIUMPH OF VENUS

Fresco in the Schifanoia Palace at Ferrara by Francesco del Cossa

Trattenimento che dano ogni giorno li Ciarlatani in Piazza di S. Marco al Populo
d'ogni natione che matina e sera ordinariamente, vi concore &c &c
Giacomo Franco Forma con Privilegio

MOUNTEBANKS IN THE PIAZZA SAN MARCO, VENICE
Engraved by Giacomo Franco, 1610

vation. A diarist writing in Venice in 1522 describes a scene at the theatre:

'There were about sixty ladies sitting on the stage, the elders in hoods, the young girls, with their charming coifs, all dressed in the best taste. The ladies became angry on account of what was said on the stage, as the whole conclusion was nothing but obscenity, filth, and cuckoldry, so that the next night another comedy had to be substituted, which being "honneto" was well received and loudly applauded.'

While the Church was busy developing a theatre from which women were excluded, and the High Renaissance itself, for all its general liberating atmosphere, still clung to the classic tradition that denied them a place on the stage, women were slowly invading the theatre by the road which led from the street and market-place. Forbidden to play in church, they played in the gutter; denied the company of the scholarly poet-actors in the revival of Greek and Latin plays, they joined the charlatans and mountebanks in the piazza and cracked ribald jokes for the delight of gaping crowds. The records of the mediæval stage contain fleeting allusions to these earliest of strolling actresses, these *joculatrice*, *tornatrice*, jugglers, singers, dancers, and buffoons, distant descendants of the forgotten Roman mimes and fellow wayfarers with the fools and fun-makers of mediæval Europe. We know practically nothing of them except an occasional name, such as Matill' Makejoy and Adelina Ioculatrix among the English minstrels, an agreement entered into by the 'Menestreus et menestrelles, jongleurs et jongleresses,' of Paris in 1321 in the French records, and certain early wood-blocks and illuminations in manuscripts which prove that there were women in the earliest guilds of professional entertainers even though they were not yet recognized as real actresses.

As time went on and the craze for spectacular displays and pageantry spread over all Europe, these women un-

doubtedly took part in the performances that were staged
on every possible occasion. From Sicily to the Nether-
lands they sang and danced in the triumphal processions
with which the worthy citizens of the feudal towns welcomed the advent of a new ruler, or celebrated the wedding festivities of a local princeling. As we have already
seen, they took part in the interludes with which plays,
both sacred and profane, were enlivened, but they were
chiefly to be found on the platforms raised in market-
place and fairground, singing ballads, dancing and recit-
ing verses, walking on the tight-rope and playing tricks
with the zanies and fools who like themselves were attendants of the quacks and nostrum-sellers who flourished on
the gullibility of the people.

These mountebank performances sometimes rose to the
dignity of farcical playlets in which women took an active
part, as Coryat shows in his famous description of the
mountebanks of Venice, written in 1608. 'Some that are
women,' he writes, 'and there were diuers also among
them, are attyred according to that person they sustain.'
Their chief rôle in these performances was to sing and
dance, and as *cantatrice* certain among them gained an
enviable reputation during the Renaissance. As early as
1492, a Farsa was given before the Prince of Calabria in
Naples in which 'an actress representing Joy sang to her
own accompaniment on the viols, while her followers
played the flute and the rebec.' Machiavelli, writing to
his friend Guicciardini, recommends the *cantatrice* La
Barbera to his attention and protests that 'she engaged
his thoughts a deal more than did the Emperor.' This
famous lady travelled from one court to another carrying
with her her own troupe of dancers and performing allegorical interludes to fit whatever play was being given
at the moment. Another young girl was famous for her
acrobatic dancing. A contemporary reports that she
'laboured like Hercules in the Moresche dance' to the
admiration of all beholders and to her own lasting fame.

This was probably the 'Signora Angela who jumps so well,' admired by the Duke of Mantua's secretary. Singing and dancing were, indeed, so popular with all classes of society during the Renaissance that they almost overshadowed the plays themselves. As we have seen, that very critical and cultured lady, Isabella d'Este, preferred the interludes given at her father's Court to the Latin and Italian dramas which they embellished.

The transition from singing and dancing, the arts of pure entertainment, to straight acting, came therefore very gradually. When women began to act on the Renaissance stage, their chief function was still to look pretty and to sing and dance — requirements which continued for many years and which are not without their distinct merit. They probably made their initial appearance as actresses in the company of Andrea Beolco, known as Il Ruzzante, the first Italian writer of genuine folk-comedy. With Ruzzante and his zestful, earthy, dialect plays, produced between 1520 and 1542, and performed, as many authorities believe, by women, real feminine characters begin to emerge from the Latinate penumbra of the pseudo-classic plays. Ruzzante's peasant wives and sweethearts are nothing if not racy. It would demand the verve and freedom acquired on the mountebanks' bench to present them with proper spirit, as well as proficiency in the arts of singing and dancing for the more pastoral moments. Beolco's company was not regularly organised or fully professional. His actresses, like his actors, were gathered and trained for special occasions, selected from among the local *cantatrice* and dancers, and taught to perform the dialogue as well as the songs and ballets with which his plays inevitably close. Other companies had actresses also, as we see by the mention of a pastoral comedy presented by a group of young men and girls of Sienna at a dinner given in honour of the young Federico Gonzaga in 1512.

As the century wore on, the mention of women on the

stage becomes more and more frequent. In 1533, a classic play was given in Switzerland wherein it is directed that 'the Lady Lucrece and her servants, men and women, shall be perfectly chaste, modest, and bashful, decently attired in black, without luxury.' Grazzini's famous song, supposed to have been written about 1540 and often referred to as containing the earliest mention of the *commedia dell'arte* characters, speaks of the women of the troupe waiting with the other actors to appear before the audience assembled in the Great Hall:

> Lovers, women, braggart captains
> In the hall are guarding treasure...

Finally, at Lyons in 1548, a performance of the *Calandria* was given in honour of Henry II and Catherine de' Medici in which 'de plus excellens comediens et comedientes d'Italie' appeared and gave great delight, particularly the actresses, 'who were very beautiful, spoke very well, and were full of grace.' The chief authorities on the subject, Bartoli, Riccoboni, Cecchini, and d'Ancona, give dates between 1550 and 1564 for the first appearance of professional actresses in Italy, but it is evident that for some time before this they had been slowly climbing up on to the stage from the lower strata of theatric life.

The phrase *commedia dell'arte* indicates an important development in dramatic affairs, for it means that this comedy was performed by members of a guild or *arte*, who devoted their whole time to acting, and were, therefore, strictly speaking professional, as distinguished from the occasional or amateur actors who had taken part in most of the court performances. These actors and actresses came, as we can see from their names and characteristics, from just such mountebank companies as Coryat describes. They were recruited from the various districts and principalities of Italy, bringing their local costumes, dialects, and personalities to the formation of that unique creation of the Italian stage — the *commedia dell'arte*

all' improvizzo. The aristocratic Renaissance stage, for all
its gorgeous investiture, for all the glamour of the great
names of painters, architects, and poets who contributed
to its splendour, developed no important playwrights and
fostered no original dramatic form. The most distinctive
expression of Italian dramatic genius was born at the very
opposite extreme of the social scale. While princes and
poets gave imitations of Plautus and Terence on the
magnificently decorated stages built in palaces and ducal
halls, the real Italian theatre was coming to life in the
market-place. It developed rapidly in the open air and
under the stimulating and noisy approval of the people,
until it in turn reached the courts, became the pet of the
aristocrats, and finally the chief recreation of all the mon-
archs of Europe. And of this theatre for every one, this
spontaneous, lusty, and thoroughly professional theatre
of the *commedia dell'arte*, women were from the very beginning an integral part. They started anonymously as
members of the strolling groups of players who wandered
over Italy, but little by little we begin to learn more
definite details concerning them.

The Roman girl Flaminia is the first professional actress
of whom we have any definite record. As early as 1565,
she had already achieved a marked success. We hear of
her from Leone de' Sommi, who was an actor as well as a
manager of theatrical companies and the writer of one of
the earliest essays on play production and the arts of the
theatre. 'Among the many accomplished persons who
play perfectly in this age of ours,' he writes in terms that
are nothing if not enthusiastic, 'especially remarkable
has always seemed to me the acting of a young Roman
woman named Flaminia, who, besides being adorned
with many fair qualities, is adjudged so rare in this profession that I think the ancients never saw nor can there
be seen among the moderns anything better than she on
the stage, for one does not seem to see a concerted imitation of an action, but something which really happens un-

expectedly, so much she changes her gestures, voice, and colouring according to the variety of incidents.'

Flaminia was not alone in her glory. Vincenza Armani was her contemporary and rival. They acted together on occasions and divided the towns where they appeared into warring factions, each actress having her loyal and vociferous supporters ready to come to blows with any one who denied the superiority of their particular idol. If we are to judge by the far from dispassionate panegyric written for her after her death by one of her numerous lovers, Vincenza must have outshone even the talented Flaminia, for no human being could have rivalled such perfections.

'In cooking, in embroidery, nay, in painting with the needle she far outstripped the Arachne of fable and Minerva herself,' wrote Valerini in 1570. 'Before she finished the third lustre of her age, she perfectly possessed the Latin tongue, admirably explaining all its peculiarities, and read and wrote so easily and correctly in Latin and her native idiom that the very discoverer of orthography could not have done better. A wonderful speaker, a sublime musician, herself a composer of madrigals and of the music for them which she sang herself; an exquisite player on many instruments, a sculptress in wax of the most skilful, ready yet thoughtful in talk and a remarkable actress. She played in three different styles, in comedy, tragedy, and pastoral, observing the proprieties of each so exactly that the Academy of the Intronati of Siena, which cherishes the cult of the drama, often said this lady spoke better extempore than the most finished writers after much thought.... Every one avoided arguing with her [in the academic debates], for if at times she argued on the side of falsehood, she made it seem the truth to those who heard her.'

Vincenza was, indeed, so popular that when in the course of her professional tours, she arrived in a town, cannon were discharged in her honour and she was received with every mark of respect and enthusiasm. It is evident from other contemporary comments on her acting that she materially contributed to the development of her art, and her general culture was such that she has been called the Bernhardt of her time. Her sculpture has not survived, nor her painting — whether with needle or brush — but a few of her poems can still be studied, and show a certain warmth and spontaneity which raises them above the level of the average literary product of the day.

Her life was not without its adventures, for Vincenza was a young woman of spirit and independence. It is related that a certain Federico de Gazuola attempted to carry her off by force on one occasion. 'He came posthaste to Mantua to steal away the actress Vincenza for his solace,' as the chronicler tactfully expresses it, 'but the little wretch hesitated to abandon all at once the position won by so many years of labour. After feigning disdain, she went to him boldly enough, dressed as for riding away, then suddenly turned her back, daring him and cursing him, he being destitute of any weapon but the tongue for a retort.'

The recorder of this incident did not approve of such independence in a mere actress, and evidently Vincenza's fiery disposition was in the end fatal. She died young, supposedly of poison, leaving the field clear for the gathering band of her sister actresses.

By this time several *commedia dell'arte* troupes had been organised and almost every court had its band of actors skilled in improvisation. Harlequin, Pantaloon, the Doctor, and the Captain were known and loved and laughed at by high and low alike and were beginning to travel beyond the borders of Italy. Every first-class company had its leading lady, its *prima donna innamorata*, chosen for her beauty and grace, who played without a mask and realised in her own person the sprightly and untrammelled heroines of the improvised scenarios. When the companies began to travel, the presence of women in their midst caused much excitement in those countries where the innovation was as yet unknown. England was particularly hostile, as we can see by a contemporary writer who exclaims that the Italians who appeared at a court fête in 1592 were 'a sort of squirting baudie comedians that have whores to play women's parts and forbeare no immodest speech or unchast action that may procure laughter.' In Spain, too, there was much opposition to the introduction of women into the theatre. A Jesuit priest, writing in 1589, denounces the custom in no uncertain terms: 'The low women who ordinarily act,' he exclaims, 'are beautiful, lewd, and have bartered their virtue, and with gestures and movements of the whole body, and with voices bland and suave, with beautiful costumes, like sirens they charm and transform men into beasts and lure them the more easily to destruction as they themselves are the more wicked and lost to every sense of virtue.'

The efforts of the Church to stem the tide were, however, unavailing. The virus had been brought by the Italian actor and manager Ganassa when he led his company, including women, to Spain in 1579. When, ten years later, Drusiano Martinelli arrived with his company, Spanish actresses were already well established in their new-found territory. Efforts were made to stop the Italian women from appearing, not only on moral grounds, but also for the good reason that the Italian companies were destroying the trade of the local troupes. In a petition which has survived till this day, Drusiano and his companions go on record as to the value of women in their company. They protest that they are helpless without their actresses and that they cannot act at all unless the women are allowed to perform. A special permit was at last issued, licensing the married women to act because they are under the 'protection' of their husbands. This is rather amusing in consideration of the fact that Angelica

Martinelli was their leading lady, and Angelica was a fairly notorious character.

Unlike Vincenza, Angelica did not turn her back on her importunate lovers. She is reputed to have been courted by Vincenzo Gonzaga and by his father the Duke at one and the same time. The latter made himself ridiculous by adorning his cap with coloured ribbons and streaming feathers to fascinate the charming Angelica. That wily lady was able to manage the situation to the complete satisfaction of every one, including her husband Drusiano Martinelli, who complaisantly signed himself as 'Madonna Angelica's husband' in his letters to his patron Duke. One of the stipulations in the permit which finally allowed Angelica and her sister actresses to play in Madrid was that they should not appear in men's clothing — a limitation which, if lived up to, would have proved fatal to almost every *commedia dell'arte* situation, where no plot is complete without this kind of disguise. Probably the prohibition was ignored, as is usually the case with inconvenient rules of the kind, and it may safely be supposed that if Lope de Vega went to see Angelica and her companions, as he assuredly did, he was regaled with the choicest and most spirited variety of Italian improvised comedy. Lope de Vega's heroines undoubtedly owe something to the presence of these lively and accomplished Italian actresses in the Spanish capital.

The conquest of France by the women of the *commedia dell'arte* began, as we have seen, as early as 1548, when an Italian company played with such success in Lyons. The Court of France, dominated for many years by the all-powerful Catherine de' Medici, was always cordial to the Italian comedians. Catherine brought up her children to a warm appreciation of the arts and graces of her native country. The nursery of princelings gathered at Saint-Germain, which included no fewer than six future kings and queens in its number, gave performances for the amusement and edification of the elders. Nor did the taste for things theatrical diminish as time went on. The popularity of the *commedia dell'arte* with the Valois Court is vividly attested in a painting by Paul Porbus which hangs to-day in the Bayeux Museum. This canvas, executed in 1572, shows Ganassa and his troupe, including several actresses, playing a sort of royal *commedia* scene with Charles IX and his Court. Here we see the King himself and the dashing Duc de Guise in a mock quarrel over the kneeling *innamorata*, the King's brother of Alançon standing beside the Queen Mother, Catherine de' Medici, the Duc d'Anjou, later Henry III, watching from the background, while other notables of the Court follow the proceedings with interest.

This glimpse of royalty at play, mixing familiarly with the *commedia* masques, with Pantaloon, Harlequin, Zanni, and their women, is in striking contrast to the brooding dangers of the time. It was painted while the Italian comedians were at the French Court helping to entertaiṇ the great company of distinguished guests gathered there to celebrate the marriage of Marguerite de Valois and Henry of Navarre — that marriage which was expected to bring peace to a distracted country by uniting a Catholic princess, sister of the King, to a Protestant prince, leader of the Huguenot forces in France. Paris was crowded with Huguenot nobles who had at last been persuaded to trust themselves within the King's domain. Pageants and celebrations had marked the festivities preceding the betrothal, which took place on August 17, 1572. On the 18th, Ganassa was paid 'the sum of seventy-five livres tournois... to him and his companions in consideration of the pleasure they had given His Majesty during the marriage celebrations.' Six days later, the players were awakened from pleasant dreams of success and home-going by the sound of the tocsin ringing ominously in the early morning quiet. In a few hours the streets of Paris were literally running with blood, the Seine choked with corpses of murdered Huguenots. The wedding feast had turned to massacre and 'Saint Bartholomew' had become a synonym for brutal treachery and violence.

Charles IX, who had played the young lover in the *commedia* scene with so much spirit, who adored pageantry and disguisements and the gaieties of court life, did not long survive that bloody day's work. He died in 1574, and his brother, Henry III, who had in the mean while been elected King of Poland, was sent for posthaste. That young man, only too eager to escape the rigours and barbarities of his distant court, slipped out of his Cracow palace by the back door, and made his way to France in a leisurely and circuitous manner. We find him in 1574 in Milan and later in Venice, enjoying 'nine days of enchantment,' as he termed it, in that marvellous city. He was entertained by the Doge with a splendid ballet in which two hundred noble Venetian ladies, arrayed in robes of white gauze looped with diamonds, danced with such ravishing grace as to elicit rapturous admiration from the King. He also attended several performances by Ganassa's company, the *Gelosi*. He was delighted with its 'magnifico' and succumbed to the fascinations of its leading lady, that 'sweet siren' Vittoria Piissimi. The company made so deep an impression on the King that two years later he asked that the *Gelosi* should be sent to France. The journey to Blois, where the French Court was then sojourning, was attended by various difficulties for the unfortunate comedians. They were captured by the Huguenots on their way northward and held for ransom, but finally reached their destination in safety. Later, they went to Paris and there fell foul of the local comedians who acted under the monopoly held by the Confrérie de la Passion. But in spite of the hostility of the French actors, the Italians triumphed and the craze for *commedia dell'arte* continued its sway in France.

Not a little of the success of the Italians was due to the charms of Vittoria, who was reputed irresistible, both on and off the stage. In the end her international triumphs made her impatient of restraint. Returning to Italy in 1578, she broke away from the *Gelosi* and established a company of her own, which flourished for some time under the patronage of the Duke of Mantua. A fascinating and beautiful woman, Vittoria had an enthusiastic following, and received her due share of flowery verbal tributes. 'Exalted above all praise was the divine Vittoria,' a contemporary writes of her. 'She metamorphosed herself in the scene before our very eyes — a great magician of love, whose words light up the passions in a thousand heart.'

Like her namesake and prototype, the heroine of Scala's comedy *The Portrait*, a play included in the repertory of the *Gelosi* and probably written for her, Vittoria was of a lively and unconventional disposition, indulging off the stage as well as on it in that freedom of speech and action so vividly described in the *novelle* of Boccaccio and in the comedies of the day.

With Diana Ponti, the leading lady of the *Desiosi*, a poetess and actress of repute; with Sylvia Roncaglia, most famous of soubrettes who played Columbines and serving-maids and could improvise in three languages; with the 'beautiful and too tender' Lidia Bagnacavello and the growing band of Caterinas, Silvias, Beatrices, and Lavinias, whose presence is recorded in the early *commedia* companies, the stages of Italy would seem to have been fully supplied with actresses. Yet so rooted was the prejudice against them, so ingrained the habit of having boys play women's parts, that for years after their actual triumphs on the stage the controversy regarding their presence continued to rage. In 1588, Pope Sixtus V stopped the performances of the *Desiosi* until they had substituted boys for women. The ban against actresses held good in the Papal States for two hundred years, though we hear of occasional illicit performances being given, such as those sanctioned by a certain Cardi-

nal Lancelotti, who ran a theatre of his own in Rome in
which a band of actresses, trained by the Cardinal himself, played all the rôles, including those of men. Even as
late as the eighteenth century, we find the papal prohibition still theoretically in force. One of Casanova's
pleasantest adventures concerns a certain Bellino, who
proved to be a woman masquerading off stage as a man
in order to act women's parts on it, while even Goldoni
did not see women on the stage until he went outside the
bounds of the Papal States. 'There was a troupe of
comedians at Rimini,' he writes, 'whom I found delightful. It is the first time that I saw women in the theatre
and I find that they decorate the scene in a most piquant
manner. Rimini is in the legation of Ravenna; women
are allowed on the stage and one does not see, as one does
in Rome, beardless boys or boys whose beards are just
growing, taking the parts of young girls.'

If the Pope disapproved, the more intelligent actors
and managers eventually welcomed the change brought
about by the introduction of women. Niccolo Barbieri,
who was at one time a member of the *Gelosi* and knew its
actors and actresses intimately, gives some cogent reasons for the suppression of boy actors, who became as
great a menace to good manners and good morals as the
women were at first supposed to be.

'It is more natural that women should perform their
own parts,' he writes in his *Supplica*, published in 1634.
'They are able to dress themselves, and as they are respectable, they set a good example instead of creating
scandal.... The boys don't even know how to put on the
clothes that don't belong to their own sex, so they have
themselves dressed at home by their women or their
rattle-brained servant-maids, who joke and flirt with
them. Those whom age and responsibility have not
sobered may easily become vain and silly, for once they
are dressed up as women these children proceed to show
themselves off in town, talking and fooling with every

passer-by and arriving at the theatre dishevelled and untidy. Then their friends or directors must start in and do the work all over again, comb their hair, freshen their make-up, arrange their collars, fasten their ribbons, and adjust their clothes. At that, one must be glad that they arrive in time at all. Then they must be flattered and cajoled to give them courage — altogether it is enough to exhaust the patience of any one who has charge of them.'

The advent of actresses proved on the whole of great advantage to the theatre, even though the first *commedianti* of Italy were hardly what would be called a sober and serious-minded lot. They were, in fact, only just emerging from the ranks of the oldest profession in the world and had scarcely differentiated their occupation from that of the ballad-singer, the dancer, and occasional entertainer of the market-place and banquet-hall. A few rose to positions of fame and affluence comparable to those of the great courtesans of Rome and Venice, but it remained for one of their number, the famous Isabella Andreini, to establish the actress as a respected and respectable member of this new profession. Isabella opened the theatre as a career to women who were truly gifted in that line. She established a standard of ordered and decent living in the profession and broke, once for all, the age-old tradition of a womanless and one-sided stage.

A COMMEDIA DELL'ARTE TROUPE AT THE COURT OF CHARLES IX
From a painting by Paul Porbus, 1572

ISABELLA ANDREINI
From an engraving by A. Locatelli after the portrait
engraved by Raphael Sadeler

CHAPTER IV

ISABELLA ANDREINI

ISABELLA ANDREINI, '*bella di nome, bella di corpo, e bellissima d'animo*,' was the flower of the pioneer players of Italy as well as the first distinguished actress of the European theatre. Coming at a time when the stage had just been opened as a career for women, she leaped at once to the heights of professional achievement. She stands at the head and front of her profession, a lovely figure of the *cinquecento*, clothed in the double glamour of the dying Renaissance and the newly developed *commedia dell'arte*, that lusty, earthy child of the market-place and mountebanks' bench which was one of the fore-runners of the modern theatre.

Isabella is fascinating to us to-day, not only because she was a pioneer actress and innovator in her profession, but because she took part in the creation of that world of pure theatre, that actors' world of movement and improvisation which had so great an influence on the European stage. Stately and beautiful, learned and virtuous, Isabella was at the same time a true child of the theatre. She could dance and sing, she could play hilarious comedy, and hold her own in the crudest farce. Her talents were multifarious, but, unlike most of her contemporaries, her virtue was above reproach. Among the madcap lot, the street-singers, tight-rope dancers, prostitutes, and rogues who flit in and out of the records of the sixteenth-century theatre, Isabella stands out as the first serious professional actress of her day.

She brought a new quality to the theatre, her learning, her grace, and her personal charm adding beauty and lustre to the high-spirited antics of the *commedia dell' arte* scene. When she came on the stage, dressed in brocaded silk or *cendale*, her waist close-nipped in the long pointed bodice of the time, which the Virgin Queen then ruling over England had rendered so popular, her full skirts billowing about her, and her little head, set off by its cap of pearls, framed in snowy ruff or rising free from a square-cut neck, Isabella was the very personification of the Renaissance ideal of feminine grace. We can see her to-day in a painting which hangs at the Carnavalet in Paris, holding a pair of gloves in her right hand, her left raised to her breast in a gesture of slightly shocked withdrawal. The portraits of Isabella are, on the whole, far from satisfactory; there are two woodcuts in the early editions of her works and a medallion struck in her honour after her death — none of which does justice to the beauty so often sung and so much admired by poets and kings of her day, but this canvas, inadequate as it is, shows her in her accustomed setting, surrounded by the masks who were her companions and servitors, and shining with warm radiance, even in the veiled dimness of a dusty and uninspired painting.

Isabella was born in Padua in 1562. Her first appearance on the stage was at the age of sixteen, when she became part of the company of the *Gelosi*, then performing in Florence. It was at the moment when the troupe had lost its leading lady, Vittoria Piissimi, so that the young débutante was able to step at once into Vittoria's vacant place. From that time on to the day of her death she was *prima donna innamorata* or first lover in this band of supremely gifted and popular comedians. When Isabella joined the company, it had already acquired its international reputation, having been to France and Spain under the leadership of Ganassa. Now, in 1578, with Flaminio Scala at its head, it could boast one of the leading scenario writers of the period as its director. Its Pantaloon was none other than the 'magnifico' who had delighted Henry III during his visit to Italy, its

Zanni, Graziano, and Francatrippa were all so excellent in their particular line that a contemporary poet wrote of them with warm enthusiasm: 'The voices, actions, and gestures of these players are so charming that they amaze the people and make them almost split their sides with laughter. I do not believe that any actors in the past, whether in Rome or in Athens, ever performed so charmingly and gracefully on the ancient stage.... Hence even more than they the *Gelosi* shall be honoured in future centuries.'

The leading actor of this company was a certain young man of talent and experience, Francesco Andreini, who had already won recognition and fame in his profession. His accomplishments included proficiency in six languages, a pretty talent for verse, unusual facility in improvisation, and a gift for scenario writing. Moreover, he could boast as many adventures as a hero of romance, having at one time been taken prisoner by the Turks, escaped from their galleys, and wandered about in strange lands. When Isabella joined the company, Francesco promptly fell in love with her and was not long a-wooing. They were married the same year, and their mutual devotion through a quarter-century of conjugal and professional partnership is as unusual as it is engaging.

For ten years after their marriage we can trace the travels of the Andreini family from Florence to Venice, from Venice to Ferrara, Mantua, Bologna, Milan, and back again to Florence. They were welcomed in all the courts of Northern Italy, and their reputation grew with the years. Their family also, for Isabella had in all seven children, four girls and three boys, in whose advent, care and ultimate fate she took a lively interest. All four of her daughters, according to one historian, became 'holy Virgins of God in convents at Mantua.' One of her sons also felt the call and became a monk at Vallombrosa, while another adopted the profession of arms. Her eldest son, Giovanni Battista, born in 1579, followed in his parents' footsteps, becoming in time 'first lover' of their company and later a writer and director of repute.

In the mean while Isabella's professional career was not allowed to suffer. She and her husband took an active part in the development of improvised comedy, co-operating with Scala in perfecting the *commedia dell'arte* style. Together they brought the scenarios, which till that time had been largely buffoonery and horseplay, to a 'definite form with all good rule' as Scala's biographer tells us. The comic stunts, the time-honoured *lazzi* of Harlequin, Zanni, and the rest, always remained the chief attraction of the *commedia*, but little by little an elaborate framework was evolved to support these slapstick diversions. When the companions of the mountebanks were taken from their original setting and brought into contact with cultivated people in ducal halls and palaces, lovers such as Isabella and Flavio, played by Scala, were introduced into the action, young men and women speaking Tuscan, in contrast to the dialects of the stock characters, and wearing the fashionable clothes of the day, while their graceless attendants were standardised by mask and costume into the familiar figures of Pantaloon, Graziano, or Pulcinello.

The enthusiasm among cultivated people for Latin comedy and the classic rules, together with other influences, not least among them the presence of decent women such as Isabella on the stage, tended to develop the *commedia dell'arte* into an intricate, though always rough-and-tumble, comedy of intrigue. Its outstanding characteristic remained, of course, the fact that the dialogue was improvised on the spot by the actor and not written out by the author. Isabella and her companions had, therefore, to be trained and experienced performers with a high degree of technical skill. Each was assigned his or her part in a play some time before its performance. On the day it was given, an outline of the plot was nailed up in the wings, and with an intrepidity breath-taking in this day of endless word-perfect rehearsals, the actress stepped out on the stage and spoke and acted as the exigencies of the plot required.

The Italian actors learn nothing by heart, Gherardi, who was himself a *commedia* actor, tells us in his book on the Italian theatre. 'For the acting of a play it is enough for them to have seen the subject a moment before going on the stage. In fact, the greatest beauty of their pieces is inseparable from the action, the success of their plays depending entirely upon the actors, who embellish them more or less according as they themselves possess more or less wit and according to the good or bad situation in which they find themselves when acting.'

A form of theatre such as this bred not only a particular kind of play, with its stereotyped characters and situations, but a particular kind of actress as well. Type-casting was not merely a managerial habit, it was an obvious necessity. Men and women alike played one part all their lives, but they could play it differently at every single performance. They remained forever the lovelorn heroine, the sprightly serving-wench, the old man, the perennial dupe, or the knavish valet, but they adjusted the part to every change of bill and to every new plot evolved by their scenario writer. Each individual actor or actress, if sufficiently gifted, was able to give the rôle of his election a characteristic form, so that it bore forever the imprint of his personality. In this way Francesco Andreini created the bombastical Capitano Spavento della Valle Inferna of prodigious eloquence and microscopic courage, developing him from the braggart captain of tradition, Dominico Biancolelli evolved Harlequin to such a state of perfection that he was always known by that name, and Tiberio Fiorilli was known as Scaramouche.

Isabella Andreini's contribution to the *commedia dell' arte* gallery of characters was the beautiful, sprightly, loving, and usually virtuous heroine who from that time forward bore her name. A free-spoken and lively lass, this Isabella of comedy takes an active part in the intricate imbroglios in which the *commedia dell'arte* clan is eternally involved. Always enamoured of the handsome and usually worthless hero, she pursues her intrigue with unflagging energy and ready wit, disguising herself as a man, feigning madness, duping her ridiculous old lover, husband, or father, quarrelling with her rivals, beating her servants, and berating her enemies, yet preserving a certain elegance and charm in spite of her violence. Her conduct is almost always technically above reproach, though her conversation is nothing if not unconfined, nor is she in the least dismayed by the merry obscenities of her serving-wench, and the motley crew of masks by whom she is surrounded. In the end she invariably marries the Ottavio or Oratio of her fancy, but before that happy event occurs, she must weather a perfect storm of confusions, misunderstandings, and jealousies.

The situations evolved for such a type character as this were so well foreseen that Isabella, though improvising her dialogue, could have on hand an assortment of appropriate speeches with which to cap an important moment. Sometimes these bits of dialogue were adapted from classic sources, sometimes they were paraphrases of popular poetry. Petrarch and Boccaccio were drawn on for inspiration, and every actor had his memory stored with appropriate sayings. The more gifted among them concocted their own speeches, and published these flowers of rhetoric in book form, for the edification of their successors and the greater glory of their names. Isabella Andreini composed many speeches of the kind, adapted to every emergency, by which a *commedia dell'* *arte* heroine might find herself confronted — tirades of love rejected, love triumphant, expressions of grief, joy, hope, and despair, moral disquisitions and edifying reflections of all kinds. Almost all these *concetti* turn upon the theme of love, and smack of those learned disputations indulged in with so much enthusiasm by the poets and humanists of the Renaissance literary Academies.

Isabella's skill as a *commedia* actress was shown by the success with which she introduced her set speech into the pattern of the plot, but these effusions, like the tirades of French tragedy, delighted the audience whether they were appropriate or not, and were greatly admired for their own literary merits. They served the same purpose in the rôle of the heroine or hero as the comic stunts or *lazzi* in that of the masked characters, giving an opportunity for a display of histrionic fireworks independent of the harsh exigencies of plot. The brief stage direction, 'Isabella despairs as a despised lover,' would give her an opportunity to indulge in some such outburst as the following:

'I renew the tortures of Tantalus and long for the food and drink of love which are not given me.... My days fleet on with the months and the seasons. The sun changes the trees, alternating with his sister in giving light, my sorrow alone remains the same. That neither changes its character nor its place, nor gives way to pleasure. Yet what do I say? My grief changes only too much; from ill it goes to worse, from cruel and bitter to unspeakable and unbearable... so that now my harsh laments weary town and village, mountain and valley, rivers, seas, meadows, woods, and even tireless Echo herself....' But apparently not the public, which loudly applauded such rococo flights of fancy!

Or, on another occasion, giving way to a mood of philosophic pedantry as an interlude between Harlequin's antics and Captain Spavento's *bravura* passages, she might remark to an impatient suitor: 'You say that love is a mode of behaviour of the soul, that the soul is eternal and that therefore Love will be eternal. I admit that the soul is immortal, but Love is only one of its attributes.... Since it is not credible that an attribute of the soul is, like it, eternal, why do you wish me to believe this? Love in others, moreover, is fed on hope and happiness, yet you say he is fed in your breast by despair and pain.... Every one follows, you add, his own good, and you alone your own enemy, desire your harm and seek it.' Such a burst of eloquence from his lady-love would undoubtedly startle a juvenile lead of to-day, but the elegants of the Renaissance had a different standard, and Isabella Andreini was proud to air her learning on the stage, and add the laurels of literary achievement to her personal successes as an actress.

In her extreme youth, Isabella had tried her hand at dramatic composition. Her pastoral *Mirtilla*, though not published till 1588, was written, she tells us, when she was so young that she could scarcely read. It is an insipid poetic effusion, differing very little from the multitude of its kind produced during the later Renaissance, but it shows that Isabella had a distinct aptitude for verse, as well as an excellent education. Rasi, one of the leading authorities on Italian theatre history, in commenting on her poems says that she rises on occasion to great heights; he praises the fluency and harmony of her lines, as well as the clearness and simplicity of her style. At the time of her death, she was preparing her *Lettere* for publication. The book, with a dedication by her husband, came out in 1607 and was republished in six fairly large editions before 1647.

In 1589, eleven years after Isabella joined the company, the *Gelosi* were in Florence for the festivities given on the occasion of the marriage of Ferdinand I de' Medici to Christina of Lorraine. Isabella and her companions entered into a sort of dramatic tournament with another *commedia dell'arte* company headed by Vittoria Piissimi. On this occasion she played in *La Pazzia*, which a contemporary describes as a 'comedy by Isabella Andreini of the *Gelosi*,' saying that it was played superlatively well, especially with 'genius and eloquence by Isabella.'

Whether this play was actually written by Isabella or not, it was one of her chief vehicles, her war horse, and gives an excellent idea of her comic vein. It is included in Flaminio Scala's volume of scenarios, and shows how far the art of scenario writing had been carried at this time. Scala prided himself on his adherence to the classic rules of the drama. The unity of time and place are carefully observed in the midst of a hodge-podge of conventional action and situation typical of the now fully crystallised *commedia dell'arte* style.

Isabella's *La Pazzia* is a lively tale concerning a Turkish princess, turned Christian and brought home by the hero to become his wife. It details her misadventures, her quarrels with his former sweetheart, her madness, feigned and real, brought about by his inconstancy. The cast shows the whole company of the *Gelosi* in action. Scala himself as the hero, Francesco Andreini in his favourite rôle of swashbuckling captain, Flavio and Flaminia as second lovers, and all the train of masks in attendance: Pantalone as Oratio's father, Gratiano as the Doctor, called upon to cure Isabella of her madness, Pedrolino, Arlecchino, Ricciolina, and Franceschina as impish attendants on the leading characters and prime movers of the piece. The mad scenes so freely provided in the plot were a favourite device of the Italian comedians for provoking laughter. Isabella, raving about the stage and 'doing her insane tricks,' was a figure of fun, and the situation gave her ample opportunity for displaying her comic gifts. In her lines she burlesques her own serious disquisitions, indulging in all sorts of puns and garbled classical allusions, while she raves, tears her clothes, pummels the doughty captain who trembles before her, and generally provides the kind of horseplay so dear to the heart of the *commedia* audiences.

It is always difficult to recapture the secret of an actress's fascination, but we can learn something of Isabella's quality when we realise the kind of plays in which she appeared, and the type of histrionic talent popular at the time. The *commedia dell'arte* method of improvisation required not only the high-spirited fooling of such comedy mad scenes as those in *La Pazzia*, but very special dramatic gifts as well. Isabella had these gifts in abundance. She was endowed with a quick and sensitive response to situation, an alert intelligence and a ready wit, as well as an excellent memory. A good memory was, as a matter of fact, as essential to the players of improvised comedy as to the ordinary actor, for though the dialogue was invented on the spot, the peripatetics of the day's plot must be kept in mind, the new relationships between familiar characters accurately remembered, and the appropriate set speech for use at a critical moment instantly available. With a new scenario for almost every performance, with a partner improvising his lines and changing his business as the mood struck him, with an audience often disorderly and always vocal, an actor of the *commedia dell'arte* could not loaf through his part. Coöperation between the members of the cast was essential, and the great and sustained success of the *Gelosi* was probably due in no small measure to the harmonious relations existing between its leading members.

We have but to glance through the pages of Scala's volume of scenarios to realise how colourful and varied were the plays in which Isabella appeared. Here we see her indulging in a bout of fisticuffs with a rival; there, dressed as a man, she is in danger of being killed in a duel; again, in the inevitable night scene, she is mistaken for a courtesan and finds herself in a desperate scrape. Her life is nothing if not active and full of adventure, even though everything takes place, in true pseudo-classic style, on one spot in the 'comicall' street scene, described by Serlio in a phrase which sums up the essentials of all *commedia* plots: a scene 'whereof the houses must be made as if they were for common or ordinarie people... but specially there must not want a brawthell

or bawdy house, and a great Inn and a church, such
things of necessity to be therein.'

Isabella's repertory was not limited to comedy. She
played every variety of theatre — 'comedies, tragedies,
pastorals, spectacular pieces, interludes, and other de-
vices,' as her husband tells us, not excluding *opera miste*, a
weird combination of every style, very popular at the
time. As Fellide or Amarilla in the pastorals, she sang and
danced through an imaginary Arcadia, clothed in pseudo-
classic style and discoursing of idyllic love and of the
beauties of nature as imagined by scene-painter and machinist. Scala was an enthusiastic creator of allegorical
shows and pageants so that Isabella, in addition to her
other functions, had many opportunities of appearing as
a goddess, a grace, or a nymph, in all the splendour of
costume and décor that the *cinquecento* adored.

When the *Gelosi* performed at Court, whether in Mantua, Ferrara, or Paris, the settings were as lavish as a
generous patron could provide. For these occasions all
the elaborate resources of the Renaissance theatre were
brought into play, and such items as 'one practicable
moon, two live babies, one beautiful ship, and an earth-
quake' are mere details on the list of properties required.
At the performances for the general public, where the
mise-en-scène was provided by the players themselves, the
settings were far less imposing. The smaller *commedia
dell'arte* troupes often played on temporary platforms,
raised in market-place or hall, with a simple painted
back-drop, such as those shown in Callot's spirited draw-
ings, for scenery. Isabella and her companions had to be
as ready to adapt themselves to changes in setting as to
improvisation in dialogue, with the result that their acting became famous for its flexibility, verve, and resource-
fulness.

The *commedia* companies improvised tragedies as well
as the more familiar and typical comedies, and in these
impressive concoctions Isabella was particularly effec-

tive. Her natural dignity, as well as the somewhat severe
cut of her profile, as shown in the medal struck in her
honour, fitted her for the portrayal of the noble and excessively high-minded ladies in distress in which the more
serious scenarios abound. Her own written effusions
were particularly appropriate for the spacious moments of
tragedy and gave her an opportunity for acting in the
grand manner, as a contrast to her comedy style. The
Gelosi took their good where they found it, acting written
as well as improvised comedies and tragedies, so that Isabella had the whole body of Italian dramatic literature to
choose from. The comedies of Machiavelli, Bibbiena, and
Ariosto were at her disposal, and contemporary poets and
writers produced endless neo-classic dramas for the actors
of the day to perform. On the whole, however, the reputation of the *Gelosi* rested on the *commedia all' improvizzo*
rather than the *commedia sustenuta*, or *erudita*, as it was
called.

This may have been due to the fact that the quality of
the Italian written drama was not arresting, for though
Italy of the Renaissance was enamoured of the theatre
and a pioneer in its technical arts, it produced few plays
that have stood the test of time. Her poets contributed
little to dramatic literature, though her stage-folk created
a world of pure theatre which was for years the delight
and inspiration of Europe. Italy provided the actors and
the stage, while Spain, England, and, later, France produced the dramatic literature which such an actress as
Isabella would have revelled in. At the very moment that
Isabella was making the best of the material at hand and
giving butterfly life to the ingenious fancies of her own
brain, Lope de Vega was writing his innumerable comedies in which Isabellas without end figure so charmingly, and across the Channel another poet was creating
rôles which would have been particularly fitted to her
talents. Shakespeare's high-spirited heroines, prone to
disguise themselves in doublet and hose, agile of wit and

ready of tongue, yet chaste and honourable withal, might have been created for Isabella herself. Rosalind was written in 1599, just when Isabella was at the height of her powers; Shakespeare's Isabella of *Measure for Measure* in 1604, the year of her all too early death.

But Isabella needed no playwright to justify and sustain her art. She was of those who create theatre by their mere presence on the stage, by a turn of the head, an inflection of the voice, a gesture of welcome or dismissal. She was, as Gordon Craig says, among 'the Great Persons, the wonder of their age and of their calling.' Honours flowed in on the fair Isabella, who had, by the close of the century, become the leading actress, not only of Italy, but of all Europe. The strenuous routine of her professional career was interrupted by such pleasant episodes as her election as Laureata to the distinguished Accademia degli Intenti of Padua. She was given the name of *Accesa*, and her election was fêted and sung throughout Italy. Tasso and Marino wrote sonnets in her honour, and she was praised by all the poets of her day. She carried on a flowery correspondence with various lords and princes, in which she exhibited a wealth of learning and philosophy. The Duke of Mantua stood sponsor for her son, and she dedicated her *Mirtilla* to the Duke of Savoy. In Rome, Cardinal Aldobrandini, patron of the arts and lover of the theatre, gave a festival in her honour, on which occasion her picture, crowned with laurel, was given a place of honour between the portraits of Petrarch and Tasso. In 1599, she went to France for a brief engagement and again, in 1603, we find the *Gelosi* playing at the French Court.

On this visit, Isabella stood at the summit of her career, smiled upon by fortune and deeply loved and admired by all who knew her. She had achieved a great personal success, but more than that she had made an important contribution to the stage. By combining in her art the finest qualities of the high-born educated amateur with the ex-

perience, skill, devotion, and gusto of the professional
entertainer, she had brought a new note into the professional theatre. Her contemporaries recognised her superiority to the other actresses who were making their initial
essays at about the same time. Garzoni wrote of her, as
early as 1587: 'The graceful Isabella Andreini, the most
brilliant ornament of the stage and theatre, as praiseworthy for her virtues as for her beauty, has rendered so
illustrious her profession that as long as the world shall
last, and down to the end of time, the name of the famous
Isabella Andreini will be held in veneration.'

Isabella's last appearance was in Paris. In spite of their
great success at the French capital, the Italian players
never stayed long away from home. The spring of 1604
saw them starting southward. One of the many poetic effusions written in Isabella's honour expresses the sorrow,
not to say the shocked surprise, of her admirers at her
decision to leave France. It was written by the poet de
Ryer, and is perhaps more admirable for its feeling than
for its versification. Freely translated into English two of
its verses run something like this:

> I cannot think that Isabella
> Is indeed a mortal woman.
> Rather is she some young goddess
> Clothed in human form to tempt us,
> Steal away our souls and senses,
> Through the joy of sight and hearing.
>
> Deathless spirit whose perfections
> All of France will be adoring
> Endless years after your death —
> (Paris is worth Italy!)
> Your admirers all adjure you,
> Do not leave us here bereft!

The poet little thought that he would soon be called
upon in reality to mourn poor Isabella's untimely end.
In spite of de Ryer's protests, she started southward in

good spirits carrying a letter from Marie de' Medici to the Duchess of Mantua, in which the Queen graciously says that she is happy 'in being able to assure Your Highness that during the time Isabella Andreini has dwelt here, she and her company have given full satisfaction to the King, my lord, and to me, and for this reason I recommend her to you with all affection.' Isabella was further armed with a note from the King himself to the Governor of Lyons, in which 'Ysabelle, comediente, et sa companie' were put under his immediate protection.

While in Lyons, Isabella, who was enceinte, was taken suddenly ill, and on June 11, 1604, in her forty-second year, she died. Her husband was inconsolable, and never again appeared on the stage, and the company of which she had for so long been the moving spirit did not survive her loss. Her son, Giovanni Battista Andreini, known on the stage as Lelio, was at the time of her death the young lover of the company. He, too, left the stage for a while, but later returned and organised a new company under his own management, calling it *I Fideli* as faithful followers of his mother's tradition.

The municipality where she died rendered every homage to Isabella's memory. She was buried with pomp and circumstance. Worthy citizens of the merchants' guilds carried torches at her funeral, the flags of the city were borne in procession, and all Lyons mourned her passing. A long Latin epitaph recording her excellencies and her services to art, marked by its presence in a Christian church the full acceptance of an actress by that sworn enemy of the stage: *Religiosa, pia, musis amica et arti scenecæ*, Isabella Andreini, the first actress of Europe rests in peace, having won position, glory, and renown in a new profession and set a shining example to all her successors in those qualities of 'Virtù, Fama ed Honor,' of which her company had ever been the jealous guardians.

CHAPTER V

FROM SALTIMBANQUE TO TRAGÉDIENNE

THE PIONEER ACTRESSES OF FRANCE

WHILE Isabella and her compatriots triumphed on the stages of Italy, Spain, and France, winning their laurels as the first European actresses, France was rapidly developing her own players, who were soon to rival and eventually to outshine their Italian forerunners. France, indeed, can claim priority in the matter of admitting women to her stage, though the Italian actresses, particularly Isabella Andreini, achieved distinction earlier. The French attitude was more liberal than that of Italy in permitting women to take part in the mediæval mystery plays. When the religious drama finally emerged from the interior of the church and was presented in the open by groups of laymen organised for the purpose, it joined hands with the forms of secular entertainment already in existence in which women had from time immemorial taken part. The presentation of the religious plays became more gorgeous, taking on the colour and movement of pageantry, while the interludes, sometimes allegorical, sometimes farcical, which were added, were completely non-religious, not to say profane. They were purely professional in character, performed by men and women dancers, jugglers, *farceurs*, and other entertainers already flourishing in the highways and byways of France.

The theory that the farce existed in itself before the mystery play developed, and was not merely the product of its lighter moments, is upheld by certain modern students, and is supported by such references as that contained in an ordinance of the time of Charlemagne, dated 813, in which the priests are enjoined to avoid the *farceurs*. There exist also descriptions of dances performed

THE SALOME OF THE ROUEN CATHEDRAL

The tympanum over the door of Saint John in the Rouen Cathedral showing the dance of the daughter of Herodias

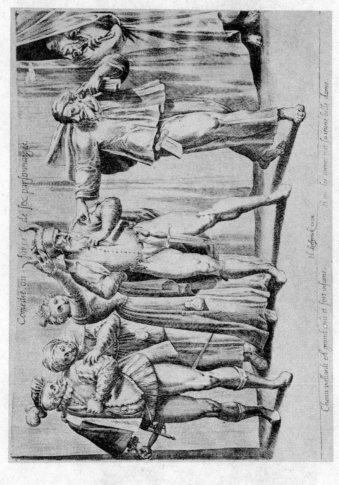

A SIXTEENTH-CENTURY FRENCH FARCE

From the Recueil Fossard in the National Museum of Stockholm

by professional *saltimbanques* and *jongleresses* which are
distinctly dramatic in character — a dance of *Hérodiade*
done to the accompaniment of a text — half narrative,
half dialogue, and even more elaborate performances in
which the reading of a long poem is interrupted by singing, dancing, and pantomimic action to give it variety.
These forms of lay entertainment, to which women were
essential, were fitted into the current of a mystery play
and provided those moments of relaxation so much
needed in its sombre length. The French, like the Italians, were fond of dancing, particularly of a violent and
acrobatic kind, and we can see to-day, in the charming
relief that adorns the façade of the Cathedral at Rouen,
how a twelfth-century *saltimbanque* interpreted the rôle
of Salome. This little figure, heels over head in an attitude more astonishing than seductive, represents very
vividly the type of athletic dancing popular at the time.

When women were first allowed to appear in the main
body of the mystery plays and not merely in the interludes and farcical entertainments, they were merely silent
figures on the scene. As early as the thirteenth century,
the most beautiful girl of Beauvais was selected to represent the Virgin Mary at a festival in celebration of the
Epiphany. She rode through the town on an ass, followed by the Bishop and clergy, entered the church, still
mounted on the richly caparisoned animal, and took part
in the service. As realism in the production of the religious plays increased, women were more and more in
demand for such rôles as that of Eve before the fall, and
of Bathsheba and Susanna taking their famous baths. In
both English and French mystery plays, Eve appeared
quite naked, as the texts indicate, nor would such a vision
in the least surprise audiences accustomed to the allegorical nymphs and sirens of pageantry.

One excellent reason why the women of the Middle
Ages did not take a larger share in the presentation of
religious plays was the fact that few of them were suffi-

ciently educated to read. They were, therefore, unable to learn the enormous quantity of lines given to the leading characters in these performances. They might also have found difficulty in sustaining the physical fatigue attendant on these gigantic undertakings, which as time went on became appallingly long and unwieldy, some running to nine or ten days' acting time. The records show, however, that there were a few women who did have the required learning, as well as the necessary endurance, to undertake a leading part. The chronicler of Metz, recording a performance of the *Mystère de Sainte Catherine* in 1468, tells us that: 'The personage of Saint Catherine was performed by a young girl, about eighteen years old, who was the daughter of Dédiet the glazier, and she did her duty very well indeed, to the pleasure and delight of everybody. Though this girl had 2300 lines in her part, she had them all at her fingers' ends, and this girl did speak so quickly and so pitifully that she made several people cry, and pleased everybody. And for this reason the girl made a rich match with a nobleman belonging to the hired troop of Metz, named Henri de Latour, who fell in love with her because of the great pleasure he took in her playing,' thereby setting a precedent which has been followed ever since, and ending, we are to presume, the brief career of the first actress of whom we have any record, the first woman, as far as we know, ever allowed to raise her voice in public in a religious play.

Not until 1535 do we again find any definite account of a woman taking part in a *mystère*. In that year a girl of Grenoble, Françoise Buatier, played the part of the Virgin Mary to the great admiration of all beholders, and at about the same time five girls of Valenciennes were permitted to appear in a religious play given there, but the custom never became general, perhaps on account of its possible abuses. In Spain, where by the end of the century women were appearing constantly in these holy rôles, the results were not always edifying. 'The representation of the most pure Queen of the Angels has been profaned by them,' Lupercio exclaims in a memorial on the theatre addressed to Philip II in 1598, 'and so true is this that in presenting a *comedia* of the life of Our Lady in this capital, the actor who played the part of Saint Joseph was living in concubinage with the woman representing Our Lady, and this was so notorious that many were scandalised and laughed when they heard the words which the most pure Virgin replied to the Angel's question: Quomodo fiet istu, etc. And in this same *comedia*, arriving at the mystery of the birth of Our Saviour, this same actor who played the part of Joseph reproved the woman because she looked, as he thought, at a man of whom he was jealous, calling her by a most vile name which is wont to be applied to evil women.' Perhaps it was as well that in France only a few of the more spiritually minded young girls were, as far as we know, allowed to take part in the religious plays.

As the influence of the Italian Renaissance penetrated into France, a new theatre began to develop, quite aside from religious drama and native farce. In this theatre of the humanists, women had even greater difficulty in winning a foothold than in the more flexible and inchoate theatres of church and market-place. It was limited almost exclusively to the universities, where Latin plays were mounted and performed as part of the curriculum, and were acted entirely by men and boys. At Court, however, where, as we have seen, Catherine de'Medici reigned for many years, the enthusiasm and interest in the classic revival was enormous. The performance of French and Italian translations of Latin plays was one of the major diversions of the Court, and added the necessary touch of culture to the gorgeous pageants staged for the delectation of the Queen and her *entourage*.

The royal family itself took part in the plays as well as in the masques which, in France as in Italy, were part of the performance. On one occasion the Princess Marguerite and her brother of Anjou, the future Henry III, performed a tragedy in French at Fontainebleau before the assembled Court. But though royal ladies might occasionally appear in amateur performances of this sort for their own amusement, the public stage was still in a rudimentary form of development, fed by the coarsest of farces and not far removed from sheer witless buffoonery and horseplay. Until recently, women were supposed to have been completely excluded from this professional stage, but in 1888 an important and illuminating document came to light which disproves this sweeping assumption. It shows that as early as 1545, before Flaminia had won her reputation in Italy, or Spain had produced any actress of note, before England had even seen an Italian comedian on the stage, and while Germany was still in the dark ages theatrically speaking, France had one, and by implication probably many more professional actresses.

This document, the contract of Marie Fairet with her manager Antoine l'Espéronnière, is the first of its kind yet discovered in the history of the European stage. With it tangible evidence takes the place of inference and conjecture, and the first professional actress makes her entrance into the theatrical world. She arrives on the scene in a rather startling fashion, equipped to turn cartwheels or do handsprings, like the little Salome of the Rouen Cathedral, as well as to act in regular plays, including the classic repertory. Marie was evidently a variously talented young woman, whose distance from an Adrienne Lecouvreur, a Sarah Siddons, a Bernhardt, or a Duse is measured as much by the modesty of her honorarium as by the agility of her *soubressaulx*. The terms of this first agreement between an actress and a manager are precise enough to give some idea of the theatrical conditions which greeted this pioneer of the stage.

The contract was signed at Bourges in 1545, three years before the first Italian company, including women in its

number, played the *Calandria* before Henry II and Catherine de' Medici at Lyons, and seven years before Étienne
Jodelle produced the first classic tragedy in French and
inaugurated the new school of the French tragedy. In it
Marie Fairet, or Ferré, sometimes described as the wife
of the town crier, Michel Fasset, agrees with Antoine
l'Espéronnière, 'player of histories, to help him to play
during the time indicated as much and as often as he
chooses in the art of playing ancient pieces of Rome, con-
sisting of several moral histories, farces and *soubressaulx*.'
Furthermore, the said Marie promises to do all this 'in
such a way as to give joy and recreation to all present, in
order to earn, amass, and obtain money from those persons who wish to see the play, for and to the profit of the
said l'Espéronnière,' for which she is to receive, besides
board and lodging, the magnificent sum of twelve livres
Tournois a year, or approximately twelve modern dollars.
This amount, even in Marie's day, could hardly be considered excessive, but the wily manager, apparently conscious that Marie's charms might bring her in revenues
other than those supplied by himself, further stipulates
that should any one during her engagement give her
clothes or money, then 'Gailharde, wife of said l'Espéronnière, should receive one half thereof.'

From this contract it is evident that the travelling
French actors, even such a small and inconspicuous band
as this of Bourges, were already acting plays derived from
Latin sources, wisely adding thereto a judicious mixture
of farce and horseplay for the greater delight of their
largely untutored audiences. Though there can be little
doubt that Marie's art in these 'anticailles de Rome' was
not of a very elevated variety, her existence is important
as illustrating the transition period between the lower
forms of entertainment and the beginning of straight acting. Marie was probably not the only professional actress
of her day, for, though no other documents survive and
we know of no other actresses then or for many years

later, the wording of her agreement does not indicate that it was unique or unprecedented. There were probably other companies and other actresses wandering about France at this time, a supposition reënforced by an engraving of the period, which shows a young woman taking part in a comedy scene, a young woman, who, though probably not Marie herself, may very well have been a sister actress performing at about the same time.

The period in which Marie made her appearance on the French stage has always been considered the lowest point in French acting. Italy was already beginning to boast companies of comedians whose performance was so much admired that they were in demand in all the capitals of Europe. All things Italian were looked upon by the cultivated French as superior to native products and the local troupes were given little encouragement. For years the Italian comedians received subsidies from the French Crown, to the detriment of the French actors. There was undoubtedly a certain amount of snobbishness in this attitude, for in some branches of the art the French actors were even better than the much-admired Italians. Girolamo Ruscelli, the Italian writer, travelling in France in 1554, witnessed the performance of a French company and was very much impressed by its proficiency: 'In France they have been presenting farces silently,' he writes in his memoirs quoted by Ricoboni. 'Without uttering the smallest word in the world and depending entirely upon gesture, they yet convey their meaning so admirably and with such complete satisfaction to the audience, that I, for my part, do not remember ever to have witnessed a performance that gave me more pleasure — and it is amazing that Italy, always so forward to introduce any sort of creditable work, should up to now have failed to take any steps to do the same.'

But whatever skill in pantomime the particular group of actors praised by Ruscelli may have achieved, the general run of French players, including such women as were of their number, were little better than rough-and-tumble *farceurs*. 'They were nearly all rascals,' says Tallement des Réaux of these early actors, 'and their women lived in greatest licentiousness; they were common property, even among the members of the company, to which they did not belong.' Marie Fairet's contract proves conclusively that on the last point, Tallement, writing in 1657 from tradition rather than documentation, was incorrect. As early as 1545, women were evidently professional actresses and in that sense members of the company. But Tallement's general impression of the manners and morals of these early bands of roving players was undoubtedly quite accurate. The whole profession was at a low ebb. Only one permanent theatre existed in Paris, that of the Hôtel de Bourgogne, which was leased by its owners, the Confrères de la Passion, to various groups of professional actors. The members of the Confrérie held a monopoly of theatrical productions in Paris, though after the edict of 1568, which confirmed their patent, but prohibited the performance of religious plays, they no longer attempted to act themselves. From that time forward, the stage of the Hôtel de Bourgogne was given over to native farce, which, toward the end of the sixteenth century, became so coarse that women could not appear in it at all — or even attend the play. The lines allotted to the soubrettes, nurses, and old women were in particular so indecent that even the easy-going women connected with the theatre refused to appear in these rôles and the parts were taken by men. The custom continued long after women were thoroughly established on the stage. At the Hôtel de Bourgogne a man called Alizon was famous for his performance of old nurses and foul-mouthed harridans, and even in Molière's company two men specialised in such old women's parts as that of Madame Pernelle in *Tartuffe*, and Madame de Sottenville in *George Dandin*.

Paris suffered severely under the domination of the

Confrères de la Passion, who in the exercise of their monopoly would permit no native drama to be given outside the Hôtel de Bourgogne, and who were, themselves, incapable of fostering anything but farce. The true French theatre, driven out of the capital, was taken up by travelling companies, such as that of l'Espéronnière, and very probably these companies continued to include women. One or two casual references in journals and stories of the day confirm the belief that, if we knew more about these inconspicuous groups of players, who in their wandering and uncertain existence fostered the growth of French tragedy and prepared the way for the Golden Age of the French theatre, we should find a number of pioneer actresses among them. Scarron's *Roman Comique*, written in the middle of the seventeenth century, refers to this early period, and the strolling company which he describes contains a number of worthy and efficient actresses. When the troupe of Valeran Lecomte was playing in Bordeaux in 1598, it could boast an actress of considerable talent. 'She was a very beautiful creature,' a contemporary tells us, 'and when she appeared as a queen or princess, nothing was lacking in her impersonation except birth itself. By her expression, her gestures, and her speech you would have thought her a true queen. She was particularly lovely when she played exquisite and languishing parts. She was loved by Valeran, but retired from the stage when her husband died.'

Valeran was one of the more enterprising and progressive of the early actor-managers of France. He succeeded in getting a foothold in Paris, and there introduced the works of Hardy, the first writer of French plays actually adapted to the theatre, who had been poet-in-ordinary to his troupe in its provincial wanderings. He also introduced women to the Parisian stage, the two reforms going hand in hand, for whatever may be said of the manners and customs of the first actresses, their presence on the stage of the Hôtel de Bourgogne did much to improve the general tenor of the performances there. It is in Valeran's company that we first hear of Marie Vernier, wife of the actor Mathieu Le Fébure, called Laporte. Mademoiselle Laporte, for it was by the title 'Mademoiselle' that all actresses were designated, whether married or single, 'Madame' being reserved of the nobility and gentry — Mademoiselle Laporte invaded the stage of the Hôtel de Bourgogne in 1610, though her professional career began before this. She is supposed to have acted farce as well as the heroines of tragedy and the more appealing rôles of lover, wife, or mistress usually reserved for the women of the company. In all these undertakings she acquitted herself with great success. In 1619, she and Laporte retired from the stage, as we learn from an act of rehabilitation, granted by Louis XIII, wherein the loyal inhabitants of Sens are adjured to forgive her and her husband the errors of their youth, and to permit them, in spite of the fact that they had once been actors, to enjoy, the privileges of citizenship in the town in which they had elected to spend their old age.

Mademoiselle Laporte and her sister actresses of the early days were faced with a very serious rivalry when they made their début on the stages of Paris and the provinces — a rivalry which was to continue for many years and which undoubtedly did much to improve their style and strengthen their technique. The Court, and in consequence all fashionable Paris, was under the spell of the Italian actresses. Isabella Andreini's memory was still green, and her successors were no less popular. They acted at the Hôtel de Bourgogne alternately with the French companies and stood high in royal favour. Catherine de' Medici had inaugurated the cult for Italian acting, which Marie de' Medici, wife of Henry IV, continued through her years as Queen and Regent of France. It was not until Richelieu came into power that the French theatre received the support and encouragement which court favour and royal patronage could give.

In the mean while the French actresses were learning their profession, developing hand in hand with the poets and playwrights who were preparing the way for the Golden Age of the theatre.

Mademoiselle Laporte, before retiring to Sens, probably tried her hand at some of the seven hundred tragedies, tragi-comedies, and pastorals fabricated by Hardy for Valeran's company, while a little later Mademoiselle Le Noir and Mademoiselle La Villiers created the 'pitiful and *précieuses*' heroines of the period between 1625 and 1635. Mairet is supposed to have written a number of his tragedies for Mademoiselle Le Noir, who, like Mademoiselle Laporte, was the wife of an actor, and had served her apprenticeship in the provinces as a member of the troupe of the Prince of Orange. In 1625, she appeared before the Court as Thisbé in Théophile's *Pyrame et Thisbé*, one of the important plays of the moment, which, with Racan's *Bergeries* and Mairet's *Sophonisbe*, actually inaugurated the great days of French tragedy. Her chief claim to fame, however, is that she probably played the leading rôle in Corneille's first play, *Mélite*, in 1629. Her husband, Le Noir, was with Mondory when that perspicacious actor discovered the young advocate of Rouen, who was later to become the great and only Pierre Corneille, and bought his first comedy. The tremendous success of *Mélite*, after its first three performances, must have been a satisfaction to the actress who created its heroine, and Mademoiselle Le Noir shared the triumph which established Corneille, Mondory, and her husband in their successful careers, and inaugurated the best years of the Théâtre du Marais, which now boldly rivalled the Hôtel de Bourgogne. Five years later, however, this happy combination was broken up by order of Louis XIII, who transferred Le Noir and his wife to the Hôtel de Bourgogne troupe, which was the King's own company, and left Mademoiselle La Villiers in power at the Marais.

La Villiers or Devilliers, generally known in the theatre

by his stage name of Phillipin, was a comedian in Mondory's troupe, and his wife gained a great following and was much applauded as leading lady, playing opposite Mondory in all the important tragic rôles of the time. It was rumoured that Corneille wrote his first tragedy, *Médée*, in order to provide her with a rôle which would give scope for her talents, just as later Racine is supposed to have created Phèdre in order that La Champsmelé might have a vehicle fit for her tragic powers. Whether this is true or not, it is almost certain that Mademoiselle La Villiers created Chimène on one of the greatest first nights in history — the night when Corneille's masterpiece *Le Cid* set the high-water mark of French tragedy and was greeted by wild applause from the public and equally violent disapproval on the part of the formalists. While the Academicians raged against it and Corneille's enemies vented their spleen in floods of controversial literature, *Le Cid* continued to fill the theatre, and Chimène's heroism and anguish to entrance the public.

Le Cid is perhaps the noblest example of the Love and Honour tragedy. In it Corneille for the first time tried his hand at this favourite theme, and his magnificent alexandrines carry the endless struggle between duty and passion into a realm of pure beauty, which touches us even to-day when we are completely out of sympathy with the whole school of poetry, acting, and play-writing of which it formed a part. It is easy to imagine how stirring *Le Cid* must have been to those who heard it for the first time, how Rodrigue, compelled by honour to kill his beloved's father, and Chimène, forced, equally against her heart's desire, to seek Rodrigue's death, moved audiences to wild delight. Chimène has always been a favourite rôle for actresses of mettle; how much more exciting must it have been to create the part on its first presentation! Mademoiselle La Villiers played daily before the most distinguished audiences in Paris. 'I wish you were here,' Mondory writes enthusiastically to his friend Balzac, 'to

enjoy the pleasures of the day, especially to see the fine
new comedies which are being given — particularly *The
Cid*, which charms all Paris. He is so handsome that all
the ladies are in love with him, even the most indifferent.
The crowd at our doors has been so great and our space so
small that the remotest corners, which used to serve as
niches for page-boys, have been honoured by the presence
of gallants wearing the "cordon bleu." The stage has
glittered with decorations of the highest order, while the
benches in the boxes hold those who ordinarily are seen
only in the Halls of Gold, seated on chairs covered with
the fleur-de-lys of France.'

What a triumph for Mademoiselle La Villiers, and how
she must have gloated over her rivals! Unfortunately, we
know so little about her that we cannot follow her career
very far. She is sometimes confused with another actress
of the same name, and just as we focus her as the leading
interpreter of Corneille's heroines, we find another actress,
Mademoiselle Baupré creating Camille in *Les Horaces*,
produced in 1640, and so lose sight of the original Chimène forever. Mademoiselle Baupré has come down to
us more clearly, thanks to two lively anecdotes recounted
of her which set her a little apart from her nebulous sisters.
It is she, who, unconscious of the privilege she enjoyed in
creating some of the greatest rôles in the French theatre,
took Corneille to task for raising the standard — and the
prices of play-writing. 'Monsieur Corneille has done us a
great wrong,' she is reported to have said; 'we used to be
able to get plays for three écus which were made for us
overnight. The public was used to them, and we made a
lot of money. Now Monsieur Corneille's pieces cost us a
great deal, and we earn very little with them.' Apparently Mademoiselle Baupré was not impressed by the
rolling periods of 'le grand tragique,' and looked back
with regret to the good old times when such tinsmiths as
Hardy were fabricating plays to order for the company,
and incidentally dying of starvation in the process.

Mademoiselle Baupré had other weapons with which to defend herself besides her sharp tongue. Tallement des Réaux describes a duel between this fiery young woman and Mademoiselle Beauchâteau, her rival in love as well as in art. The duel took place on the stage, the opponents duly armed with rapiers fell upon each other with murderous intent. Before they could be separated, each had inflicted wounds on the other and were 'covered with blood.' Unfortunately, we are not told who was the victor, winning the disputed cavalier by her skill in sword-play.

Mademoiselle Beauchâteau was the wife of the leading actor at the Hôtel de Bourgogne, and it is hard to associate the interpreter of the grandiose heroines of high tragedy with the blood-stained young tom-boy of Tallement's anecdote. Yet it is Mademoiselle Beauchâteau, who of all this early group survives most vividly as an actress, immortalised by Molière's swift parody of her artificial and saccharine methods of declamation. She and her husband were for years shining examples of the early style of tragic acting, stilted, sweetly sentimental, and entirely removed from reality or feeling. In his *Impromptu de Versailles*, after scoring Beauchâteau, Molière turns his mockery on the actress. 'Don't you see how natural and full of passion her acting is?' he exclaims. 'See what a smiling face she keeps through her deepest affliction!' And so, sweetly simpering over her blood-and-thunder lines, Mademoiselle Beauchâteau makes her exit, giving place to Mademoiselle des Œillets, who was, we are told, 'a marvel on the stage, for though she was neither young nor good-looking she was one of its chief ornaments.' Mademoiselle des Œillets had a very real talent, and for years held her own as the leading actress at the Hôtel de Bourgogne, interpreting Corneille and Racine and preparing the way for the great days of French acting.

The professional standing of the first French actresses

was by now thoroughly established. They formed an accepted part of the organizations both at the Hôtel de Bourgogne and the Marais — the two established theatres. They shared in the profits of the companies, though, according to Chappuzeau, the earliest historian of the French theatre, they rarely attended the play readings and were kept as much as possible from the management of theatre affairs. There were 'little difficulties' involved in the casting of the women's parts, Chappuzeau tells us, 'for, as there is not one among them but wishes to remain perennially young, they are not eager to play the Sisygambis parts. The poet's art consists in creating mothers in the prime of life and in giving them sons who will not convict them of being more than forty. To tell the truth, in the theatre as elsewhere, there is much difficulty in controlling women, and men give less trouble.'

Chappuzeau's remark explains why we find men acting women's parts on the French stage for so long, even after the parts had become sufficiently decent for women to interpret them. Vanity, rather than any question of morals or custom, kept them for a while from undertaking what would now be called character parts. Mademoiselle Beauval, of Molière's company, was one of the first women to undertake these rôles, replacing Hubert, who had usually played them. Corneille was very much in favour of having women play his nurses and old women rather than men in masks as was still the custom, but it was some time before the gay ladies of these early days, who had with some difficulty won their way on to the stage, would consent to dim their beauty and diminish their charm by appearing as old and unattractive women.

For it must be admitted that, though these first actresses had gained deserved praise for their portrayal of the noble and virtuous heroines of tragedy, they had not achieved any particular reputation for sobriety of conduct in their private lives, and the stage was still for them the best way of shining before a brilliant and profligate court. Curiously enough, the Italian comedians, whose liberty of speech and action on the stage was such as to shock the fastidious taste of the French public, were far better behaved off stage. 'There is a greater difference between the characters of the Italian and French comédiennes than between our opera and theirs,' writes the Marquis d' Argens in his letter on the theatre of his day. 'The Italian actresses are inspired by sentiments unknown to our own; they share the honours of civil society; they are encouraged by the respect in which their talent is held, and, since their profession includes nothing which is not brilliant, they are careful not to render themselves contemptible by debauchery.... Our French actresses, on the contrary, seem to wish to profit by the idea which we have of them; they avail themselves of the advantage of being regarded as libertines, and, since their art exposes them to contempt, they cease to be restrained by sentiments which would be useless.'

Du Tralage, writing somewhat later, repeats the same accusation, and draws up a list in which he separates the good from the bad. The Italians are almost all on the right side of the ledger, while the French actresses come in for many sharp raps. Much might be said in their defence, not least of all the effect of that contemptuous attitude of society as a whole which the Marquis d'Argens so justly condemns. The customs and arrangements of the theatres were also greatly to blame for the general demoralisation of these early actresses. Even as late as 1639, men and women dressed and undressed in the same tiring-room, where they were further harassed by the presence of impudent and pretentious gallants, whom they did not dare send about their business. Even while they were playing, the actresses were not free from the importunities of these bewigged and beruffled cavaliers, who sat on the stage throughout the performances, conversing with each other and with the actresses, and making themselves generally conspicuous and intolerable. If the ladies were not polite and responsive, these charming gentlemen would settle themselves in full view of the audience and take their revenge by talking, coughing, or hissing just when the unfortunate actress was about to break into her best tirade. It required no little charm, ingenuity, and talent for these first actresses to hold their own against the distractions provided by a mob of glittering and noisy courtiers banked on either side of the stage, nor is it surprising that these same lordlings found the women of the theatre easy prey.

The actresses were, however, beginning to resent the attitude so generally taken in their regard. As their position became more assured, they asserted their rights both in and out of the theatre. In 1635, Scudéry provided them with one means of answering some of their critics. The first act of his *Comédie des Comédiens* gives vivid glimpses of affairs behind the scenes at the Hôtel de Bourgogne, and in the words of the leading lady, Mademoiselle Beausoleil, the actresses were able to express their opinion of their tormentors. 'They think the farce a picture of our life,' she exclaims resentfully, 'and that we act on the stage only what we do off it; they think the married women among us must needs belong to the whole company. They imagine we are common property like the sun and the elements. There is not one among them who does not fancy he has a right to annoy us by his importunities.'

It was to be many years before the reputation of the French actress was as good as that of her Italian sister, but in the mean while she was outdistancing her on the road of professional success. The dynasty of great French players was about to begin, founded on the work of these pioneers and opening with the careers of Madeleine and Armande Béjart, the first actresses of whom we have any detailed knowledge. However critical their contemporaries may have been of the manners and customs of the first actresses of France, they were all loud in praise of their personal fascination, and histrionic talents. The rapid development of the French theatre during the first quarter of the seventeenth century, though not to be attributed to these charming ladies, was undoubtedly assisted and accelerated by their presence, and their co-operation made possible the spectacular flowering of the Golden Age of the French theatre. They were on the whole a refining, as well as a stimulating influence, and to them should go some of the credit for the great days which made France for many years the centre of theatrical life and the inspiration of the world.

CHAPTER VI

MADELEINE AND ARMANDE BÉJART

MOLIÈRE'S MISTRESS AND HIS WIFE

THE history of the French theatre and the history of
women's participation in its development go almost hand
in hand. The stage of Æschylus, Sophocles, and Euripides had, as we have seen, no actresses, Terence and
Plautus knew them not, and Shakespeare's lovely heroines were impersonated by beardless boys; but when
Corneille, Racine, and Molière lifted the French theatre
to the highest pinnacle of its achievement, the group of
actresses whose careers we have briefly followed were at
hand to play their variously tragic and lively heroines.
It is as the contemporaries and interpreters of the greatest playwrights of their country that the French actresses
achieved their first important successes on the stage.
Theirs was the inestimable privilege of coming into their
own in the Golden Age of French drama and of being able
to create all its greatest rôles. More than half a century
passed before Shakespeare's plays were acted by women,
but Molière wrote his comedies with the actresses of his
company in mind and created his most engaging and
sprightly heroines for no less a personage than his own
wife. Two women of the theatre dominated his existence:
Madeleine Béjart, who first attracted him to the theatre,
and the debonnaire and much-maligned Armande, whose
singular fate it was to be passionately loved by the master
of modern comedy and to be hated almost as passionately
by the great army of his idolaters.

Armande Béjart, the actress, has always been overshadowed by Armande Béjart, the faithless wife of a
great and suffering genius, just as Madeleine Béjart is
known more generally as Molière's mistress than as an

excellent actress and the competent head of a company of strolling players, but both Madeleine and Armande are important on their own account, representing as they do a transition period in the French theatre and crystallising in their widely divergent careers the experiences of the whole group of early actresses. Madeleine, the competent and versatile trouper from the provinces, Armande, the darling of the Parisian public, each is strikingly individual and at the same time typical of her kind. Their intimate connection with Molière, and their influence on his career, give them in addition a glamour reflected from his genius and make it possible to follow their careers in greater detail than can be done in the case of any other actress of this earliest period. The two Béjarts emerge from the crowded background of the seventeenth-century stage distinctly characterised — vividly alive. In spite of the smoke screen of calumny and misrepresentation that has been thrown around them, in spite of the obscurity and confusion that surrounds many details of their lives, Madeleine and Armande can be clearly discerned at the head of the graceful procession of French actresses, the one resourceful, talented, capable, and wise, the other, light-hearted and light-headed, witty, capricious, but inescapably alluring — two sides of the medal representing the eternal Thespian, two aspects of that engaging creature whose equivalent is not to be found in English, *la comédienne française*.

In the records of the city of Paris appears an item indicating that in the year 1636 a certain Madeleine Béjart purchased and occupied a tiny house in the Cul-de-sac de Thorigny, in the old quarter of the Marais, not far from the theatre where at that very moment Mondory was producing *Le Cid* with such success, and Mademoiselle La Villiers was enchanting the town and Court with her irresistible Chimène. This Madeleine was the daughter of one Joseph Béjart, Sieur de Belleville, and of his wife

Marie Hervé. The Béjart family was poor, but prolific, and Madeleine's girlhood was spent in helping to care for the ten or twelve younger brothers and sisters whose successive appearance made heavy inroads on whatever income Joseph might derive from his occupations as 'huissier audiencier à la grande maîtrise des eaux et forêts de France, siegeant à la table de marbre du palais' — a governmental appointment more impressive in sound than in revenue. How Madeleine at the age of eighteen achieved a house of her own is not known, though it can be surmised when we find that two years later, in July, 1638, she gave birth to a daughter Françoise, whose paternity was freely acknowledged by Madeleine's accredited lover, Esprit Rémond de Moirmoiron, Baron de Modène, a dashing young sprig of the nobility whose roving affections had for a time been arrested by the fresh and vigorous charms of the youthful Madeleine.

The baptismal record of this baby indicates clearly the pleasantly casual attitude of the times toward such affairs of the heart as that with which Madeleine's career begins. The child was held at the font by Madeleine's own mother, Marie Hervé, who evidently looked with entire complaisance on its somewhat irregular advent into her family, while the other sponsor was the infant's own half-brother Gaston, the eight-year-old legitimate son of the Baron de Modène. By way of completing the picture, the boyish godfather, being too young to appear himself, was represented at the font by Jean-Baptiste Tristan l'Hermite, brother of the playwright of that name, who was later to see de Modène flirt with his wife, and finally take his daughter, another Madeleine, as his second wife. Family complications of the period were not limited to the Béjart-Molière tribe.

Whether Madeleine's affair with de Modène, by removing the possibility of a sober bourgeois marriage, forced her to take up the stage as a career, or whether, as seems more probable, she had already been attracted to the theatre by the opportunity it afforded of earning money, seeing the world, and breaking away from domestic responsibilities, can never be known. It is evident, at any rate, that she made her choice of a stage career early, for at the age of eighteen she was already recognised as a personage in the theatrical world of the day, and this in spite of the fact that she was not connected with either of the established theatres. Tallement des Réaux in his invaluable contemporary 'Historiettes' tells us that she was considered a far better actress than either the Hôtel de Bourgogne or the Marais could boast and that her talents as a tragedienne were generally recognised. At this time she was in the full flush of her vigorous youth, a handsome girl with red-gold hair and an engaging presence, never distinguished for beauty, but full of vitality and allure. She had won friends among the poets and dramatists of the day, wrote verses and plays, and laid the foundations of those intimate connections with the theatre which were later to be of so much service to Molière.

The great Rotrou, whom Corneille called his father in dramatic art, did not disdain Madeleine's poetry, even publishing some laudatory verses from her pen as the dedication of his tragedy, *L'Hercule mourant*, when it was printed in 1636. As we have seen, she was on intimate terms with Jean-Baptiste, brother of the playwright François Tristan l'Hermite in whose lurid tragedies she and Molière later attempted to take Paris by storm. The atmosphere in which Madeleine served her theatrical apprenticeship was one of extraordinary literary activity. The avalanche let loose by Théophile, Racan, and Mairet was flooding the Hôtel de Bourgogne with pseudo-classic tragedies. Alexandrines dripped from every poetaster's pen. The classic rules were the subject of the most impassioned debate, the most poisonous feuds. Under Richelieu's protection the French theatre was coming into its own, outdistancing at last its Italian rivals who had for so long basked in the sun of royal favour. A dozen writers of distinction, precursors and contemporaries of Corneille, were composing for the theatre. Fashion also took a hand, and it was becoming a sign of elegance and culture to dabble in verse, to know the poets, and to attend first-nights of the new tragedies.

When Madeleine was not herself acting in Paris or the provinces, she undoubtedly went to the play with her friend de Modène or some other admirer. We can imagine her at the Hôtel de Bourgogne, waiting for the curtain to be drawn on the first performance of the latest tragedy and exchanging gossip and greetings with the crowd of friends and acquaintances gathered there. Perhaps she was accosted by one of those gadflies of the theatre, the typical first-nighter of every age and generation, who haunted the Hôtel de Bourgogne, as he haunts the theatres of to-day. 'He points out the great ones as they come in,' a pamphleteer of 1635 tells us, 'exclaiming so that all may hear: "There is Monsieur de Rotrou, or Monsieur du Ryer." Then he dashes off, and returns in a moment full of importance. " I beg your pardon for my incivility," he says, " I had to greet Monsieur de Corneille, who arrived only yesterday from Rouen. He has promised that we shall go together to see Monsieur de Mairet. We will discuss the plan of *Cléopâtre* and five or six other subjects which the author has taken from Roman history and with which he hopes to create worthy companion pieces for his incomparable *Sophonisbe*.... I hear that they have just seen some of the verses of *L'Ulysse dupé*; that Scudéry is writing the third act of *La Mort de César*; that the *Médée* is almost finished. I think that Rotrou's *L'Innocente Fidélité* is his most beautiful production, though many believed he could not reach greater heights than he has already achieved. I hear that the author of *Iphis* and *Iante* is writing another *Cléopâtre* for the Royal Troupe. Chapelain has not

yet worked on his poem, *La Pucelle d'Orléans*, nor
Corneille on the one he is writing about a former Duke of
his country…"' and so on endlessly through the long list
of poets and playwrights who were friends and contemporaries of Madeleine Béjart.

During the seven years which followed her acquisition
of a house in the Marais quarter and preceded her meeting
with Molière, Madeleine acquired a wide and useful knowledge of theatrical life. She travelled through the provinces with various groups of players, occasionally acting
in Paris, but more often pursuing the arduous and uncertain fortunes of the strolling player. Of her more intimate
affairs during these years we know absolutely nothing,
though scandal, abhorring a vacuum, has filled the gap
left by history and provided her with innumerable lovers
to enliven her wanderings. 'She was the pastime of a
number of young men of Languedoc,' blithely remarks the
anonymous author of a libellous pamphlet. Such a statement is easily made and at this distance impossible to
refute, but there is no shred of factual evidence to support
it, and everything we know of Madeleine's character is in
direct opposition to the picture of easy and venal promis-
cuity that the phrase evokes.

Madeleine was far from being a puritan. She was warm-
hearted, passionate, and untrammelled. In her youth she
loved and lived with de Modène without benefit of clergy,
but to Molière and to Molière alone she gave her deepest
affection, lavishing on him, and on her brothers and sisters to whom she was sincerely and consistently attached,
the devotion of a lifetime. Though frankly indifferent to
conventions that had little weight either in the theatrical
world in which she lived, or that larger world of the Court
to which all society aspired, Madeleine possessed a stable
and vigorous character, capacity for hard work, and a
clear-headed sense of reality which made it possible for
her to maintain her equilibrium through the strenuous
years of her personal and professional connection with

Jean-Baptiste Poquelin, known to fame and history as the great and only Molière.

The exact time and place of the momentous meeting between the two is not known, though it has been the subject of profound researches, as well as the point of departure for much picturesque speculation. The important fact in the history of the theatre and of their individual lives is that, somewhere and somehow, they did meet, that Molière was at once charmed by the vivid and enthusiastic young actress, and that Madeleine was not indifferent. Madeleine's four years of seniority and her connection with the stage, far from acting as a barrier between them, only added to her glamour in the eyes of the impressionable young man, just finishing his studies and already looking with distaste upon his future prospects as *valet de chambre tapissier* to the King, and heir to a flourishing upholstery business. The year 1643 is memorable in the annals of the stage; memorable for such apparently unrelated happenings as the death of the obscure and prolific Joseph Béjart, who left his widow nothing but debts, and forced his children to try their hand once more in the precarious field of theatrical enterprise: memorable also because Jean-Baptiste Poquelin had just turned twenty-one, and, receiving from his father a part of the inheritance due him from his mother's estate, had proclaimed his emancipation from his inherited trade by renouncing his right of succession to the honours and titles of upholsterer to the King. The result of these two events was to take form in the signing of a contract in which the names of Madeleine Béjart and Jean-Baptiste Poquelin, the future Molière appear for the first time together, a partnership continued through many vicissitudes and sea-changes, until a certain sad February day, twenty-nine years later, when Molière's name stands alone on the document recording the death and burial of his lifelong companion.

With what high hopes the group of young people, including three members of the Béjart tribe as well as their mother, signed their first agreement is attested by the name with which they adorned their embryonic theatre. They had acted together before, calling themselves *Les Enfants de Famille*, but now, on the eve of a more serious endeavour, they baptised themselves *L'Illustre Théâtre*, and launched what they hoped was an organisation which would rival the two established theatres of Paris and bring honour, glory, and, not least of all, cash, to its founders. Madeleine was the leading spirit of the enterprise. To her was given the first choice of rôles, and her experience guided the beginners in their plans. The other members of the company were all richer in faith than in works. Ambition and good will were counted on for success rather than any recognised talent. In these virtues both Molière and the Béjart family abounded. Madeleine's mother was ready to back the venture with such money as could be raised by mortgaging her house and its contents. Molière put all and more than he had received from his father into the lease of a building, a covered tennis-court in Fossé de Nesle, which could be made into a theatre. With the signing of the contract, Molière became once for all a child of the theatre, deserting the ranks of respectable and humdrum middle-class business endeavour and joining Madeleine on the outer fringes of Bohemia. He gave Madeleine's house in the Cul-de-sac de Thorigny as his address when he signed the document, proving that at this date they had joined forces for better or worse both on and off the stage. By her enthusiasm and ambition, her love of the theatre, and her desire to shine on the boards, Madeleine had led her young lover into a career, which with all its trials and struggles was to be for him the vehicle of a transcendent achievement.

The two years that followed the founding of *L'Illustre Théâtre* were spent by Madeleine and the young people of the company in frantic efforts to obtain recognition from a completely unresponsive public.   In spite of money spent on improving their theatre building, in spite of heroic labours and unflagging enthusiasm on the part of the actors, all Paris stayed away from the tennis-court in the Fossé de Nesle, and even from that more desirable location on the right bank at the Port Saint-Paul which the ambitious actors later occupied. Madeleine was presiding genius of the theatre in the early day, and Madeleine, imbued with the spirit of her age, was enamoured of tragedy. Her passion was shared by Molière himself. The little house in the Cul-de-sac de Thorigny must have resounded with the rolling thunders of perfervid alexandrines as Madeleine and Molière rehearsed their parts in the lethal dramas of Magnon, du Ryer, and Tristan l'Hermite with which they began their dramatic career.

If Madeleine was a good tragedienne, she failed to make her lover acceptable in heroic parts, though he was to become in time the leading comedian of his day. Molière never was able to play tragedy, and Madeleine alone could not carry the burden of acting for the whole company. Things went from bad to worse with the Illustrious players and the ambitious heads of the company must have spent many anxious hours over their precarious situation. Madeleine used all her connections in the theatrical world to forward the interests of the troupe, obtaining plays from her various friends and even enlisting the interest of her ex-lover de Modène in the enterprise. The title of Troupe of His Royal Highness, which the company flaunted for a while, was probably obtained for it through the good offices of the Baron de Modène, who had at one time been gentleman-in-waiting to His Royal Highness the Duc d'Orleans.

De Modène may also have suggested to the Duc de Guise, whom he was then serving, that the members of Madeleine's company should receive a share of the magnificent wardrobe which the Duke distributed among the leading players of Paris. Clothes being the main item of theatrical *mise-en-scène*, the gift of the Duc de Guise to

the troupe of La Béjart was an even more valuable acquisition than the Duc d'Orléans' name. The clothes were
not only magnificent on the stage, but they could, in addition, be pawned when ready money was needed — which
was more than could be said of His Royal Highness's title.
The value of these costumes was so great that an indig-
nant actor, who had not been favoured in the distribution,
burst into verse on the subject. Mr. Chatfield-Taylor in
his 'Life' of Molière has a translation of this rhyme which
gives us an amusing glimpse of theatrical rivalries, and
proves that, in spite of their lack of success, the players of
the Illustrious Theatre were grouped with the leading
actors of the day and were considered their equals if not
their superiors:

> Already in the royal Troupe,
> Sir Beauchâteau, that popinjay,
> Lets his impatient spirit droop,
> Whene'er thy gifts he can't display.
> La Béjart, Beys, and Molière,
> Three stars of brilliance quite as rare,
> Through glory thine have grown so vain
> That envy makes me loudly swear
> I'll none of them, should'st thou not deign
> To grant me clothes as fine to wear.

But neither the Duke's cast-off clothing nor His Royal
Highness's economical patronage, neither Madeleine's
acting nor Molière's enthusiasm, neither a change in lo-
cale nor the engagement of a ballet-master to lighten the
horrors of tragic repertory, served to avert the doom impending over the Illustrious Theatre. Madeleine, Molière, and the rest of the Béjart contingent, after two years
of struggle which won them no better recognition than a
debtor's prison for Molière, decided to leave Paris and try
their fortune on the road.

Madeleine's former experience in travelling companies
made the move seem the practical solution of their pro-
blems. In the provinces they could mature their talents

and experiment with new material; they could be fairly sure of earning a living, and, with luck, secure enough money for another assault upon the capital. It took fifteen years of tenacious effort to accomplish this purpose; fifteen years which were, however, rich in experience and in theatrical education. The company travelled all over the South of France, acting in small towns as well as the larger cities such as Limoges, Toulouse, and Lyons, acquiring from time to time new actors and actresses and slowly building up a reputation which placed them in the forefront of the provincial companies. For a long time the players were known as the troupe of La Béjart, but little by little Molière took over the general management and direction, his growing authority and experience winning for him the position of leadership in the band. Madeleine remained, however, his chief support. She controlled the finances, ruled the household, and took the leading rôles on the stage until the advent of younger and prettier actresses relegated her to the equally essential but less decorative character parts.

These wanderings were strenuous, but not without their agreeable aspects. After the first years of hardship, the company made money and lived well. They obtained the patronage of the Prince de Conti, and through him were constituted official entertainers to the Estates or Parliament of Languedoc when it met at Montpellier or Pézenas. Ten years after the company left Paris loaded with debt, Madeleine Béjart as treasurer of the troupe was in a position to lend the government of Languedoc the sum of ten thousand livres, and we find such considerable sums as seven and eight thousand livres due them for their services to the States and elsewhere.

Such success as this implies was not achieved in a moment. The troupe that had left Paris in 1645 was hardly more than what Augustin de Rojas, a contemporary Spanish actor-author, describes as a *Boxiganga*—a troupe which had two women, six or seven men, and 'many vexations.' By the time that it had obtained the honorific title of players to the Prince de Conti, the vexations were, perhaps, as many, but money was plentiful. With capital out at interest, with regular employment, and a fairly ample income, the members of the Béjart-Molière troupe were no longer penniless vagabonds. They were in a position to dispense hospitality as well as to receive it, as the wandering poet d'Assoucy tells us in his casual, vivid manner. D'Assoucy was an impassioned gambler, as well as a singer and a musician, who wandered about France with his page boys and his lute and left a rambling account of his picaresque adventures. On one occasion he lost everything, including his shirt, in an all-night gambling bout at Avignon. 'But a man is never poor so long as he has friends,' he writes, 'and as I am esteemed by Molière and on friendly terms with all the Béjarts, I felt, in spite of the Devil, fate, and the whole Hebrew people, richer and more content than ever. For these liberal people, not satisfied with helping me as a friend, wished to treat me as a relative. As they were summoned to the Parliament of Languedoc, they took me with them to Pézenas, and I cannot say how amiably I was treated by the whole family. They say that the best brother tires of feeding his brother at the end of a month, but these people, more generous than any brothers, did not tire of having me at their table a whole winter.'

The table, to judge by d'Assoucy's admiring description, was excellent and plentiful. Over it presided Madeleine Béjart, regulating the affairs of the household, as of the company, with a steady and generous hand. With a wisdom as admirable as it is rare, she had consolidated her new position. No longer sufficiently young to take the rôles of ingénue and leading lady, she accepted secondary parts — the soubrettes, confidants, and strong-minded serving-maids — and carried them off with vigour and distinction. No longer able to hold Molière's roving fancy, she accomplished a still more difficult transition and, ceasing to be his mistress, became his loyal and devoted friend. Her practical good sense and strong clan instinct must have helped her to bridge the chasm between the ardent days of the founding of the *L'Illustre Théâtre* and the calmer realities of provincial success. The Béjart troupe, like the old *commedia dell'arte* companies, was really an enlarged nomad family. Madeleine's mother travelled with the company, while Joseph, Louis, Geneviève, and, later, the mysterious 'little one' Armande, were at Madeleine's side, both on and off the stage, until death or old age brought about the inevitable separations.

To this family nucleus of which Molière formed an integral part, several important additions were made during the years of provincial touring. Two leading actresses were acquired. One was the charming Catherine de Brie, the eternal ingénue, sweetly feminine and consolatory, who is supposed to have succeeded Madeleine in Molière's affections, and to have comforted him, intermittently, during his stormy married life. The other was the beautiful du Park, wife of Gros René the fat comedian, whose given name of Marquise fitted her haughty and resplendent beauty. Tradition has it that Molière loved her, too, but that she rejected his advances, as later she allowed both Pierre Corneille and his brother Thomas to languish in vain. The husbands of these two were members of the troupe as was also Charles du Fresne, who for a while headed the company and brought to it his mature experience as an actor. By March, 1653, when the company gave Molière's first play *L'Étourdi* in Lyons, it was in excellent shape, and won from Chappuzeau, who knew the theatre of his day thoroughly, the commendation that, though only a travelling company, it was 'well worth that of the Hôtel de Bourgogne which stayed in one place.'

Heartened by their provincial successes and fortified by the experience and money acquired during their exile from the capital, Madeleine and Molière were ready for a second attack on Paris. In July, 1658, we find Madeleine once more negotiating for a tennis-court which might be transformed into a theatre, while Molière made every effort to obtain a hearing before the King. It is amusing to see that on her business trips to Paris, Madeleine stayed with Poquelin senior, or at least gave his house as her residence. Perhaps this indicates that her share in leading Molière from the paths of virtue and upholstery had been forgiven her. Possibly father Poquelin's discovery that the red-haired siren of the stage was actually a capable business woman, who had successfully managed the finances of the company during their years of trial and experiment, contributed to the reconciliation which had already begun before Madeleine and Molière left Paris. At any rate, Molière's father gave his bourgeois blessing to the returned wanderers and was soon to have the pleasure of seeing his son make his bow before the 'Greatest King in the World.'

The all-important day arrived at last. Molière had secured the protection of the King's brother and a hearing before the King himself. With what agitation must the troupe, especially Madeleine, who had inspired its beginnings and nursed it through its years of growth, have faced the ordeal of playing at the Louvre. The performance took place on October 24, 1658, in the Salle des Gardes of the palace, now known as the Hall of the Cariatides, before Louis XIV and the assembled courtiers. The play chosen for this crucial evening was Corneille's *Nicomède*, followed, fortunately, by a little farce of Molière's own fashioning, *Le Docteur Amoureux*, which so delighted the youthful monarch that he confirmed his brother's decision to allow the players to call themselves the Troupe of Monsieur, Only Brother of the King, and, further, gave them permission to play in the theatre of the Petit Bourbon, alternately with the popular Italian actors who were installed there at the time.

Not a little of the success of the new company was due

to the charm and the accomplished playing of its actresses. For the first time the King saw tragedy played with a certain degree of sincerity and feeling. The training that Madeleine and Molière had given their company was not that of the Hôtel de Bourgogne, whose actors watched this first performance of the interlopers from the provinces with a scornful superiority which must have turned quickly to secret trepidation as they saw the King's interest and growing enthusiasm. The long battle between Molière and the exponents of the old order of sound and fury in acting had its beginnings on that famous evening when the players from the Hôtel listened to Molière's pleasant compliments addressed to them from the stage, but discovered, before the evening was over, that a rival had come to town. With the King's approval behind him, Molière had won his cause, and Madeleine, who could no longer aspire to personal triumphs on the stage, had the satisfaction of taking an active, if not a dominant, part in this final victory.

From this time forward, Madeleine fades into the background of theatrical history. Her gifts were preëminently those that made her of value on the road and during the apprentice years of Molière's theatrical training. In the reorganisation of the company which followed its installation in the Petit Bourbon, her function as business manager of the company was taken over by a new arrival — that excellent actor and worthy man La Grange, who became the *jeune premier* of the troupe, the handsome and accomplished young lover of Molière's plays. More important still, he started at once to keep his famous *Régistre* in which he noted all the business details of Molière's enterprises down to the most minute items of box-office receipts and company expenditures — a daily record which has proved an invaluable source of information concerning Molière's life and career.

With the return to Paris, Madeleine, queen of the road company and of Molière's destinies, becomes the solid

citizen her native common-sense had destined her to be.
We see her now and again through Molière's eyes as the
forthright, frank, and hearty Dorine of *Le Tartuffe*, or,
more clearly, as herself in that all too brief but extraordinarily vivid presentation of the members of Molière's company, his *Impromptu de Versailles*. In this glimpse of the
troupe at work, written for the amusement of the King,
Madeleine appears as the senior member of the company
talking to Molière with the freedom of long familiarity,
airing her opinions, giving him sound advice, and reminding him of a play he had once planned to write — as she
must have done in reality on many similar occasions.
Clear-headed, practical, full of common-sense and business acumen, Madeleine spent the last years of her life
in comparative affluence, accumulating a respectable fortune and keeping her friendship with Molière unimpaired,
through the storms and turmoils of his later years, until
the day of her death.

With Madeleine's eclipse, a new star rose on the theatrical horizon, a star whose brilliance was to dazzle the
Parisian audiences and completely bewitch the 'grand
comique' himself. And this new star, this sprightly, way-
ward, and mercurial creature so eminently suited to the
tastes of the sophisticated society she was soon to delight,
so fascinating and so fatal to Molière himself, was another
Béjart — Madeleine's younger sister? — Madeleine's
daughter? No one knows, or ever will know, unless the
baptismal certificate of Armande Grésinde Claire Elizabeth Béjart should miraculously come to light. Her importance, however, lies not in her birth, but in her being.
She brought a new element of joy and suffering into
Molière's life. She stimulated his genius for creative
writing, as Madeleine had stimulated his interest in the
theatre. For her, and in her image, he created his most
engaging heroines. She was the *satirique spirituelle* of
Molièresque comedy, the vivid, witty, independent,
sometimes cruel lady who flaunts her gay plumage through

his pages. She created the rôles of Élise and Elmire, of Lucile and Célimène to the entire satisfaction of their author and of the public, and this alone would prove her to have been an accomplished actress. Her contemporaries admired and praised her, even while they calumniated her, but posterity has been less kind, giving ear to the scandalous chronicle that has grown up around her and forgetting to appraise justly her talents as an actress or her true value as a human being.

Armande Béjart is preëminently a child of the theatre. The very confusion that exists as to her birth and parentage, the cloud that hangs over her early years, the agitations and ambiguities of her human relationships, and the tinsel eminence of her public career, reflect the struggles and uncertainties of a profession only just opening its doors to women. Had Armande not been an actress, a popular and courted actress, as well as the wife of a leading playwright and actor-manager, no one would have thought of questioning the validity of the documents that present her to the world as the daughter of Marie Hervé and of that 'good man' Joseph Béjart, deceased. It is thus that she appears on the marriage contract signed in February, 1662, by Molière, Armande, and various members of the Béjart family including the mother, Marie Hervé, *veuve* Béjart, and Madeleine herself. It is thus that she is written down in all the legal documents it was her fate to sign throughout her life. It is thus, too, that she appears in Madeleine's will in which she is made residuary legatee of her sister's estate, and which, signed by Madeleine three days before her death, might be supposed to contain the truth. If Armande was Madeleine's daughter, we must believe that Molière, the Béjarts, and all their friends and intimates subscribed to a long campaign of perjury, and that Louis XIV himself was hoodwinked by this fabrication. For the King put himself on record as Molière's friend and champion when he stood sponsor to Armande's first child, the little Louis who lived

SCENE FROM 'TARTUFFE'

From a print attributed to Jean Lepautre (1669?)
in the Bibliothèque Nationale, Paris

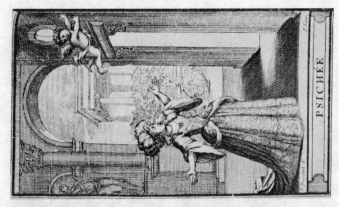

PSICHÉE

GEORGE DANDIN

ARMANDE IN 'GEORGE DANDIN' AND 'PSYCHÉ'
From the 1682 edition of Molière

only a few months, making this gesture of friendliness just after Molière's enemy, the actor Montfleury, had accused Molière of 'marrying the daughter after having loved the mother.'

So savory a bit of scandal about the all too successful poet-player could not, however, be silenced by the King's gesture of friendliness and respect. In Molière's time and during Armande's widowhood, the tale, embroidered with lurid details, crops up again and again, nor have the learned historians, for all their efforts to analyse the facts dispassionately been entirely unprejudiced. The weight of evidence, as derived from actual documents seems in favour of the rather tame theory that Armande really was what she and her family professed her to be — mother Béjart's youngest child, that 'little one not yet baptised,' who is mentioned in the legal papers drawn up in 1643 in which the recently widowed Marie Hervé renounced the inheritance of debt left her by her husband Joseph. The ingenious theory, that even at this early date Madeleine was trying to hide the identity of a love-child by passing her off as her mother's daughter, seems somewhat weak when we know with what perfect good-humour and friendliness her first child, Françoise, had been received into the world. It seems simpler to believe that Armande really was this unbaptised infant, especially as there is evidence that Marie Hervé was forty-six or seven years old and not fifty-three, as many historians believed, at the time of this mysterious baby's birth.

The strongest indication in favour of the assumption that Armande was really Madeleine's daughter and not her younger sister is contained in one of the most curious documents in all this curious and involved affair. This is the baptismal certificate of Molière's only daughter, the one child that survived its parents and lived on into another century, carrying in her name a challenge to the simple solution of her mother's birth. This second child of Molière and Armande was called Esprit-Madeleine, and was held at the font by Esprit Rémond, Baron de Modène, and his ex-mistress Madeleine Béjart! If Armande Béjart was really the child of these two, and if any effort was being made to hide the fact, such a public appearance together would seem the height of folly. Yet there they stand side by side, the broken-down nobleman who was at the moment living in the same house as the Béjart family and to whom Madeleine and Molière were giving pecuniary aid in his difficulties, and Madeleine, whose thrift and industry had brought her some degree of comfort as well as a highly respected position in the community. Does their presence prove their parental relation to Armande, or does it, on the contrary, indicate that they had nothing whatever to hide? Certainly, from our sober point of view, the baptismal records of the Béjart family offer food for surprised cogitation.

It may at any rate be safely presumed that, whatever her parentage, Armande was brought up under Madeleine's watchful eye. After passing her first years in the country with a foster-mother, and after acquiring a smattering of knowledge in a convent, she joined the company in its wanderings, completing what may well be called a liberal education under the guidance of Madeleine and Molière. She travelled with the troupe for several years before it came to Paris, appearing occasionally as a nymph or shepherdess, and learning the ways of the theatre and the thrills of the actor's life.

Armande's first appearance on the stage in a speaking part did not take place till the company was well established in Paris — about a year before her marriage, but not before Molière had contemplated that possibility. In the spring of 1661, he asked to be allotted a second share in the division of the company's profits in the event of his marrying. Shortly afterward, the name of Armande Béjart appears in the cast of *L'École des Maris* and still later in the same summer she played the rôle of Orphise in *Les Fâcheux*. In January, 1662, the marriage contract was drawn up, and finally Armande and Molière were married in the Church of Saint Germain l'Auxerrois on the twentieth of February. With that stroke of possibly undeserved good luck, Armande's professional career was firmly assured. She had married the head of a successful troupe, the actor-manager-playwright whose recently won position in Court and public favour promised many years of brilliant success to his company. To be sure, he was twice her age, a busy, harassed, sensitive, overstrung genius whose passionate intensity inevitably turned to jealous distrust and who may have been more exacting and difficult than his admirers will admit, but there is no reason to suppose that Armande did not have a genuine affection for him, even though she was, in the very nature of things, unable to make him happy.

It is impossible, in discussing Armande's career, to dis-associate the woman herself from the characters which were written for her performance. They are almost the only evidence we have concerning her personality and talents, and though too much weight should not be placed on the biographical significance of Molière's plays, there is no doubt at all that, as Grimarest, his first biographer, tells us, he put himself and the people around him into his plays. When Armande first came seriously into his life, Molière wrote and produced a play in which a charming young girl is wooed and won by a sensible, sympathetic, and broad-minded man several times her age. Armande is supposed to have played the Léonor of *L'École des Maris* in June, 1661, the summer before they were married. The part is small and could easily have been handled by a novice. Molière showed her, in the character of Ariste, all the advantages of the projected match, while as Sganar-elle, which he himself acted, he brought out and lam-pooned all the possible objections. Molière, as a good psychologist, may have hoped that Armande would eventually believe off the stage what she said on it, and that his own courtship would end as successfully as that of his hero.

The play was given at the Palais Royal which Molière had taken over and renovated a short time before. Every one in the company must have been conscious of the curious courtship implicit in the lines of the play, for Molière had already requested that second share, in case he took a wife, and evidently all his thought and energy were bent upon persuading Armande to take the step. Nothing can more vividly illustrate the strength of the tie which held the members of Molière's troupe together, and their genuine devotion to its leader, than the fact that Armande's advent did not disrupt the organisation. In this play Madeleine appears in the cast as Armande's serving-maid, while Molière's other ex-mistress, Catherine de Brie, takes the leading rôle.

Shortly after the production of *L'École des Maris*, Molière's company was called upon to take part in a lavish entertainment organised by Louis XIV's Minister of Finance, Fouquet. Forgetting that it is wiser for a Minister not to show more wealth and power than his master, Fouquet allowed himself to be carried away by his desire for display, to such good effect that he found himself, a few months later, under arrest, and spent the rest of his life in prison, repenting his depredations on the royal preserves. Molière's contribution to the festival arranged in the gardens of Vaux le Vicomte, took the form of a ballet-spectacle in which was embedded that series of caricatures known as *Les Fâcheux*, or the Bores. In this performance at Vaux, we find Madeleine and Armande again taking part, the former as a Naiad who appeared rising from a sea-shell, 'a Nymph, excellent in her art,' as La Fontaine tells us, and one who could still hold her own on the stage with her younger comrades and receive her due share of praise from poets, critics, and courtiers alike. Armande was the young Orphise, the one lady who was not a bore. Here, too, Molière had given her but a few lines, first steps on the stage for a beginning actress, but an opportunity, nevertheless, to appear before the King and to make her first impression on the courtly circles. Armande was not yet nineteen when she made her bow to the great world that centred about Louis XIV's throne. It was a hothouse atmosphere for an impressionable girl, and it is hardly surprising that Armande, who was to know no other life than that of the feverish, glittering court and the equally sophisticated capital, should not develop those virtues which privation and hard work had taught Madeleine.

Everything that touches Armande Béjart has a way of becoming tenebrous and confused. Some historians maintain that she did not act at all before her marriage and that her real début took place almost a year and a half later in *La Critique de l'École des Femmes*. Every one agrees, at any rate, that she did act in this, and that she created the rôle of Élise. From this time forward we have a clear record of her performances in Molière's plays, and we can trace the increasing reliance he placed on her powers as an actress and the very definite kind of part he created as best suited to her gifts. Élise is a witty, sparkling young creature with a quick, malicious humour and much worldly wisdom. She is a type derived from Armande's own personality and one which Molière draws and elaborates again and again — a young woman who, for all her gay, bantering independence and occasional sharpness of tongue, is at heart true and loyal.

On her next appearance at Versailles, Armande is presented to the monarch and his court under her own name and personality in the *Impromptu de Versailles* already quoted. Molière is still sufficiently in love with her, still sufficiently sure of himself and of her, to indulge in a little marital jesting at his own expense. There is a brief passage at arms between husband and wife, introduced by Armande, who interrupts Molière's discussion with Madeleine as to what they could possibly rehearse and perform on the short notice given them by the King, with the exclamation:

Do you want me to tell you something? You ought to write a comedy which you could act all alone!

MOLIÈRE: Be quiet, wife, you're silly!

ARMANDE: A thousand thanks, my dear husband! That's the way it goes. Marriage certainly changes people. You never would have said that eighteen months ago!

MOLIÈRE: Be quiet, I beg of you!

ARMANDE: It's a funny thing that a ceremony can deprive us of all our best qualities, and that a husband and a lover look upon the same person with such different eyes!

MOLIÈRE: What a lot of talk!

ARMANDE: Yes, indeed, if I were writing a comedy, I'd use that theme. I would justify women in many of the things they are accused of doing; and I would point out to husbands the danger that lies in the difference between their rough manners and the civilities of the gallants.

And with a toss of the head, almost visible across the centuries, Armande lapses into a discreet and wifely silence.

Some three months after this, Armande's first child was born, the little Louis for whom the Great Louis himself stood sponsor. For a while she remained out of the theatre, but by spring she was again ready to take up her professional career. She made her reëntry in all the beauty of costume and pageantry, the glamour and feverish excitement which accompanied a royal fête. Louis XIV, in the first exuberance of his passion for Louise de la Vallière, had determined to give her a festival which should outshine all Fouquet's splendours and dazzle the world at large with his magnificence. Molière took a large share in the organisation of the *Pleasures of the Enchanted Isle*, as the seven-day fête, officially dedicated to the Queen, was called, and in all of them Armande figured triumphantly.

For a moment the sun shone in all its splendour on the little actress, translated for a brief space into the dizzy world of the Court. She took part in the same pageant in which the splendid young King and his courtiers appeared; she displayed her beauty in Apollo's chariot dressed as the very symbol of the times, the Age of Gold.

She played the Princess herself in Molière's poetic fantasy *La Princesse d'Élide*, written for the occasion, and finally she created one of Molière's most engaging and kindly heroines, the young wife Elmire in *Le Tartuffe*. For the moment, too, the sun shone on Armande's heart as well. The calumnies that had been hurled at her head by her husband's enemies had been dispersed by the King himself when he stood sponsor to her son, still happily alive. Her husband had written a charming Princess part for her, where her gifts could be agreeably displayed. In *Le Tartuffe* he had for the first time confided to her the creation of a leading rôle in a play which was very near to his heart and which, as history has proved, was one of his masterpieces. And to crown it all, she was young and pretty and beautifully dressed. Surely, for a little while, Armande was happy and, let us hope, still anxious to make her husband so. Nine years later, in the inventory made of Molière's effects after his death, a faded memorial of these brilliant hours came to light — a certain citron-colored taffeta skirt and bodice, covered with gold and silver embroidery, which Armande had worn as the Princesse d'Élide in that distant and long-forgotten Enchanted Isle.

It would be pleasant to be able to see Armande in that citron-coloured dress. Unfortunately, no authentic portrait of her exists to-day. If she was ever painted by Mignard, who painted Molière and all the notables of the time, the canvas is lost. Mignard was an intimate friend of the Béjart-Molière tribe. He had known them from their early days and he is one of the executors named in Madeleine's will. He had seen Armande since she was a child and would have been able to fix on canvas something of her vivacity and charm. She was probably not as handsome as Madeleine, her features more irregular, her general effect piquant rather than beautiful. The versifiers of her time, however, were loud, if somewhat vague, in their praises.

O justes Dieux, qu'elle a d'appas
Et qui pourrait ne l'aimer pas!

Robinet warbles, while Mademoiselle Poisson, writing after her death says, more specifically and far more vividly: 'She had a mediocre figure; but her manner was engaging, although her eyes were small and her mouth large and flat. She did everything well, even to the smallest things, although she dressed most extraordinarily, in a manner always opposed to the fashion of the times.'

But the best description that exists of Molière's gay young wife is the one given by the poet himself in an often-quoted scene from *Le Bourgeois Gentilhomme.*. After a typically witty lovers' quarrel between Cléonte and Lucile, Corvielle, Cléonte's valet, is on the stage talking to his master and drawing out his real opinion of that most exasperating she:

CLÉONTE: Say everything bad of her that you can think of. Draw a portrait of her which will make her forever contemptible in my eyes. Bring out clearly, that I may be thoroughly disgusted with her, all the faults that you can find in her.

CORVIELLE: I see nothing in her above the average and you will find a hundred women more worthy of you. First of all, she has little eyes.

CLÉONTE: That's true, her eyes are little; but they are full of fire — the most brilliant, the most piercing in the world — the most touching that can be seen.

CORVIELLE: Her mouth is big.

CLÉONTE: Yes — but it has a grace that one does not see in other mouths; and, when you see that mouth it awakens all sorts of desires, it is the most attractive, the most seductive mouth in the world.

CORVIELLE: As for her figure — she isn't very tall...

CLÉONTE: No — but she is graceful — and beautifully made.

CORVIELLE: She is affected and full of airs in her speech and action.

CLÉONTE: It's true, but she is affected with so much grace; and her manners are so engaging; they have an indescribable charm that wins the heart.

CORVIELLE: As for her wit...

CLÉONTE: Ah, that she has, Corvielle! the most pointed, the most delicate wit!

CORVIELLE: Her conversation...

CLÉONTE: Her conversation is charming.

CORVIELLE: She is always serious.

CLÉONTE: Do you prefer a constant state of jollity — of full-throated mirth — do you know anything more irritating than a woman who laughs at everything?

CORVIELLE: But, after all, she's as capricious as any one in the world.

CLÉONTE: Yes, she is capricious, I agree with you there — But everything is becoming to a lovely woman — we suffer everything from the fair.

Molière's biographers have all been moved to tears over the double meaning latent in the French phrase: 'On souffre tout des belles,' seeing in it a picture of Molière's sorrows — he who not only stood everything, but suffered everything at the hands of the perfidious Armande. That Molière suffered much, there is no doubt at all, and that Armande was the cause, and some of his masterpieces the result of that suffering, must also be remembered. Important as Madeleine was in his life, turning him to the theatre, helping, guiding, comforting, and sustaining him through his years of trial, it is Armande who moved and inspired him during his years of dramatic creativeness. It was her charm and her illusiveness that animated and exasperated his genius. Without her it is conceivable that there would have been no Célimène — and without Célimène, certainly no Misanthrope. As a commentary on Armande's character, it must also be remembered that the whole force of *Le Misanthrope* lies in the fact that Célimène is essentially loyal to her lover, though she drives him to despair because she is unable or unwilling to handle the difficult humours of a man whom she does not understand and whom she is too proud to placate.

The production of Molière's great play — *Le Misanthrope* — and the rupture between husband and wife approximately coincide, but before this happens, the poor little Louis had died and the little girl already mentioned had been born and christened Esprit-Madeleine. Armande and Molière lived during these years in that house on the rue Saint-Thomas du Louvre which contained such a curious collection of Molière's past and present lovers, relatives and friends. It is not surprising that he should be subject to many domestic inconveniences in a dwelling which sheltered not only his wife, but one ex-mistress who was his wife's sister or mother, Madeleine Béjart, another who was his wife's professional, and, occasionally, personal rival, the talented and lovely Catherine de Brie, as well as a motley collection of actors and friends, including the Baron de Modène, who was possibly Armande's father, the Veuve Béjart, her mother or grandmother, and various members of the Béjart connection. Perhaps Armande, high-spirited and quick of tongue, retorted in kind to some of her husband's accusations of unfaithfulness. At any rate, Molière could stand the strain no longer. He retreated to bachelor quarters at Auteuil, where he could write in peace, and where his friends could find him of an evening and talk art, literature, and life into the small hours — while Armande remained in Paris with Madeleine and the rest of the denizens of the house on the rue Saint-Thomas du Louvre.

During the four or five years that they lived separately, Armande and Molière met daily at the theatre. Armande's professional career continued uninterruptedly. She played Alcmène in *L'Amphitryon* in 1668, and the ruthless Angélique in *George Dandin* the same year. In this farce, with its undercurrent of cruelty, Molière gives Armande the least engaging of his heroines to create. It is not perhaps as direct an attack on her as that supposed to be contained in the one rôle which bears her name, the Armande of *Les Femmes Savantes*, but it is a definitely unsympathetic part. It was followed almost at once, however, by the spirited and delightful Élise of *L'Avare*, so that

whatever Molière may have thought of Armande off the
stage, he continued to provide her with excellent parts on
it. In 1670, while they were still living apart, he wrote *Le
Bourgeois Gentilhomme*, in which, as we have seen, Armande is forever enshrined, and he also gave her the rôle
of Elmire in *Le Tartuffe*, when, after five years of waiting,
the King at last permitted its production. Robinet, the
versifying critic of the day, has a word to say of her in this
part:

> Mais pas moins encore je n'admire
> Son épouse la jeune Elmire,
> Car on sçaroit constamment
> Jouer plus naturellement.

(Nor did I admire less the young Elmire, his wife, for it
would be impossible for any one to act with greater
naturalness than she.)

With these excellent parts in her repertory, and with
additional small rôles in such ballet pantomimes as those
built at the King's order around *M. de Pourceaugnac* and
Les Amants Magnifiques, Armande's talents were in constant use, and her popularity on the stage ever increasing.
In 1671, an elaborate tragedy-comedy-ballet was staged
by Molière in the great Hall of the Machines at the Tuileries, in which Armande appeared in the title rôle of
Psyché. Here once again she had an opportunity of appearing in the sort of artificial and tinsel splendour dear
to her luxury-loving heart. If she could act Elmire with
simplicity and grace, she could also declaim the saccharine verses of *Psyché* and sing its incidental lyrics to the
delight of an admiring Court. Wafted on the cloud-ma-
chines of Vigarani and the poetry of Molière, Quinault,
and Corneille, who collaborated on this magnificent absurdity, Armande triumphed once again. After the command performances before the King, Molière decided to
remake his own theatre and continue the production for
the delectation of the town. By July, 1671, the Palais-

Royal was ready, and the play ran successfully throughout the summer.

In the mean while a reconciliation between Armande and Molière was in the air. It finally took place late in 1671 or early in 1672, after Armande had been playing *Psyché* for several months with the handsome young actor Baron as l'Amour. Like everything which surrounds Armande, her final reconciliation with her husband is made the cause for further scandal rather than an answer to it. The accusation is, of course, obvious. It was impossible to see the two young lovers on the stage without deciding that they carried on their parts after the play, and it has even been said that the unfortunate infant born September 15, 1672, and proudly baptised Pierre Jean-Baptiste, was Baron's and not Molière's son. There is no evidence to prove this accusation, any more than there is for the stories of Armande's other love-affairs. Like most conjectures of the kind, it is based on ingenious deductions and malicious gossip, and is of very little worth. All we know is that Molière returned to Paris during the winter of 1671-72, and this time established himself and his wife in a house of their own where Armande could satisfy her lavish taste in decoration, furniture, and appointments and where the *ménage* was once more united in apparent amity.

Shortly after the reconciliation between Armande and Molière, Madeleine died, leaving the bulk of her painstakingly amassed fortune to Armande and Armande's child, and carrying with her the secret, if there was one, of Armande's birth. Molière followed her funeral procession to the grave, rounding out the full cycle of their partnership. The passion of their youth had long since passed, but their comradeship in a chosen vocation had remained intact — the illustrious theatre inspired by Madeleine had been made a reality by Molière. He himself had only one short year to live, a year which saw the birth and death of his second son and namesake, and the growing burden of his own ill health. Molière was dying, and undoubtedly knew it even as he wrote that last supreme comedy in which he makes hilarious fun of the anguish he was only too really suffering. What a supreme gesture of mockery and defiance the creation and acting of *Le Malade Imaginaire* by so desperately ill a man! In this play Armande is once more entrusted with a charming part, in which she is shown to her best advantage. As Angélique she is called upon on the stage to deplore in jest a tragedy which was so soon to occur in grim reality.

The day of the fourth performance of *Le Malade Imaginaire* found Molière more ill than usual. Armande, seconded by Baron, who, in spite of scandalous rumours, was still an intimate friend of the family, begged Molière not to go to the theatre. Their pleading was in vain, and with a determination which was in this case suicidal, Molière went through his part of mock illness and mock death. Toward the end of the performance he was taken seriously ill and died shortly after he had been carried to his house. Alas, for Armande's story, she was not in the room at the supreme moment, but it is from Baron that we know these details, and there was dislike, if not extinguished love, between Baron and Armande. For Armande's case let it be said that from this time forward her conduct was exemplary. She made every possible effort to obtain a proper burial for her husband — a Christian burial denied to him as an actor. She went to the King and the Archbishop, fittingly arrayed in widow's weeds, and finally obtained such concessions as were possible. She distributed largess to the Paris mob, so that it would let the torchlit procession of her husband's funeral go unmolested. Finally, she supported as best she could the efforts of the actors of Molière's company to hold their own after the irreparable loss of their chief.

Armande obviously did not have Madeleine's head for business. She was altogether of a lighter and weaker stamp, though undoubtedly an equally good, perhaps a better, actress. At any rate, she knew enough to allow La Grange to manage the rudderless company, Armande providing money and the use of Molière's plays as a background for their effort. From this time on, Armande's life falls into a steady routine of work and more or less uneventful quiet, broken by one comedy lawsuit in which a woman of the town passed herself off as La Molière and got a public whipping for her pains, and another affair which involved a libel suit and from which Armande emerged with flying colours, having won her case and cleared her reputation.

Life as a widow, however, was proving somewhat difficult. She was never free from attacks and calumnies, so that four years after Molière's death it was very natural for her to marry again. Her second husband, Isaac-François Guérin, sieur d'Estriche, had joined Mademoiselle Molière's company when it was fused with that of the Marais. He was an excellent actor, an honorable and an upright man with whom Armande lived in peace for the rest of her life. One son, who lived till after Armande's death, blessed this marriage and divided Armande's inheritance with Esprit-Madeleine, Molière's only surviving child. Armande died on the thirtieth of November, 1700, six years after her retirement from her company, which by its amalgamation with the Hôtel de Bourgogne had become the only regular theatre in Paris — the original Comédie Française.

Armande was buried at Saint-Sulpice on the second of December, 1700, since when she has been very far from reposing in peace. Everything that in any way concerns Molière is inevitably of keenest interest to all lovers of the theatre and nothing could concern him more closely than the woman whom he married. Armande is an enigmatic and alluring figure, appearing at one moment in all the glamour of her stellar rôles, dressed with such originality and taste that all Paris flocked to see her, tossing her curly head and sparkling the lines that seemed the very expres-

sion of her own wit, while she leads the gallants on and off
the stage a merry dance. Or again, in another mood we
see her as heartless and sinister, driving a great poet to
despair, turning the gay, barnstorming youth of Madeleine's day into the stern poet of *Le Misanthrope*, pouring
bitterness into a heart held up to her in love and tender-
ness. At one moment she is the protected darling of
Madeleine and Molière, the fresh young beauty carried
royally through kingly pageants, and at another a grasp-
ing, selfish parasite who married Molière for the sake of
his theatre and his money and forthwith betrayed him.

Armande played as many rôles off as on the stage, but
those that Molière gave her were, with few exceptions,
charming, or at least spirited and witty, while his friends,
joining in this his enemies, have, until recent years, combined to condemn her. Whatever her personal shortcomings may have been, Armande must hold forever a unique
position among the women of the theatre. Coming shortly
after they were admitted to its precincts, she had the supreme privilege of inspiring and creating some of its most
delicious heroines, and her personality, spirited, vivacious,
and original, did much to fix a type long dominant in the
French theatre, and to justify a title, once given her in
derision — that of *La Fameuse Comédienne*.

CHAPTER VII

ENTER IANTHE, VEIL'D

THE FIRST ACTRESS IN ENGLAND

LIKE Eve in the Garden of Eden, the first English actress was a breaker of the law. She was not only a pioneer and innovator, as were Isabella Andreini and Madeleine Béjart, she had not merely to affront custom and prejudice as her Continental predecessors had done, but she made her appearance in defiance of positive legal prohibitions, and ran the risk of being arrested, fined, and imprisoned for her pains. Long denied any position on the English stage, she took it upon herself to make her first attempt during that dark period in the history of the English theatre when Puritan fanaticism ruled by force of arms, when the great theatres,

'Which so did take Eliza and our James,'

had been branded as dens of 'theft and whoredom, pride and prodigality, villainy and blasphemy,' and closed to the public. Between 1642 and 1660, the playhouses of London were effectually suppressed, the drama banished, and the actors — there were then no actresses — scattered abroad. Only such uplifting pastimes as bear-baiting, puppet shows, and drolls were tolerated, while the degrading influence of Elizabethan tragedy was steadfastly refused countenance.

In this atmosphere of theatrical desolation, Ianthe, the first English actress, made her initial bow. The scene of her advent was Rutland House in Aldergate Street, London, the time a mild September afternoon in the year of grace 1656. The company which assembled to witness her début had arrived discreetly, hiding elegant apparel under mantles of proper Puritan gloom. Once safely within doors, however, the protective cloaks were thrown aside. Silks and velvets were boldly displayed. The ladies flaunted borders of lace on the wide white collars that fashion affected; lace fluttered from the cuffs and neck-pieces of the equally resplendent gentlemen. Perfume and colour, a French phrase, an anecdote of the wars, or a bit of gossip from the Court of Louis XIV hinted at Continental travel and loyalty to the 'black boy over the water' which might safely be displayed in this selected company.

The gathering was aristocratic and outwardly calm, but a current of excitement stirred below the surface of elegant and light-hearted talk. At any moment the place might be invaded by soldiers armed with sticks and staves, bent on upholding the law. To be sure, D'Avenant, who was in charge, had obtained some sort of permission for his entertainment, but it might be difficult to prove on the spot that an 'opera, made a Representation by the Art of Perspective in Scenes,' was not a stage-play, and that *The Siege of Rhodes*, about to be presented for the first time on a miniature stage 'eleven foot in height and about fifteen in depth including the places of passage reserv'd for the Musick,' was really only a 'Moral representation' such as he had given before, and therefore harmless in the eyes of the Lord Protector's men.

The occasion had, moreover, an importance all its own, aside from the pleasurable exhilaration to be derived from taking part in an amusement banned by law. Sir William D'Avenant, just back from France, where he had been following Prince Charlie's fortunes and sharing some of his theatrical amusements as well, was about to inaugurate a new era in the English theatre. On this famous afternoon he introduced several innovations to his English audience; he produced the first opera England had known, he set it in scenes with wings and back-drop painted in perspective, and he introduced the first actress to the English stage.

Behind the curtains the performers waited nervously
for the audience to assemble. The musicians tuned their
fiddles, the actors conned their lines and hummed the
melodies which Dr. Charles Coleman had pricked down
for them. In the tiring-room, Mr. Edward Coleman,
dressed and ready, made his wife run through her lines in
a last-minute effort to get them in her head, while she,
more interested in her appearance than in her rôle, adjusted her flowing white garments, straightened her veil,
and watched Captain Cook stalk about the room in his
Solyman costume, murmuring his lines and working himself up into a proper mood for an effective entrance. The
candles were snuffed, the curtain of purple and cloth of
gold was drawn aside; the play had begun at last. The
buzz of comment and admiration which greeted the vision
of John Webb's masterly portrayal of the Island and
Harbour of Rhodes on an eleven-foot canvas back-drop
— a 'contracted trifle as that of the head of the Cæsars
carved upon a nut' — subsided and the actors began.
Upon the tiny stage which represented the camp of Solyman the Magnificent, a veiled figure appeared.

'This is Ianthe, the Sicilian flower!' proclaimed Solyman's general, and from behind that shrouding gauze
which still obscures the features of this earliest of English
actresses a woman's voice gave answer. For the first time
on record a serious heroic part was entrusted to a woman.
And although this Ianthe, singing her lines in recitative
and unable to 'get any of it without book in order to the
stage,' as she told Mr. Pepys some years later, undoubtedly gave a halting and inept performance, yet she paved
the way for the general and inevitable change which led to
the complete replacement of the boy players of Shakespeare's stage by the brilliant company of Restoration
actresses. This burgeoning of feminine beauty and talent
in the English theatre was spectacularly rapid and sweeping. In other countries the change came, as we have seen,
by imperceptible degrees, but in England the curtain of

legal prohibition drops in 1642 on a stage peopled by squeaking Cleopatras and rises eighteen years later on a rout of beautiful, witty, and accomplished actresses.

Before the curtain dropped, however, we have glimpses of Ianthe testing her way on unfamiliar grounds. She came, as so many good things do, from the less respectable walks of life. Like many of her most brilliant followers, she began her career in the tavern. There is an indication that a certain Moll Frith, known to the Town, appeared at the Fortune in 1610 in Middleton and Dekker's play, *The Roaring Girle, or Moll Cut-Purse*. The epilogue informs the audience that if they are dissatisfied with the performance they have witnessed:

> The Roaring Girle her selfe some few days hence
> Shall on this Stage give larger recompense.

If Moll really did appear, as this would indicate, it is probable that the occasion was more riotous than refined, and possibly some of the serious-minded in the audience felt as Richard Madox did when, in 1583, he 'went to the theatre to see a scurvie play set out al by one virgin which she proved a fyemarten without voice, so that we stayed not the matter.' Women freaks were exhibited by enterprising showmen and there were women acrobats, tight-rope walkers, dancers and singers in England as on the continent, but none of these could possibly be classed as actresses.

Coryat in the book of travels in which he describes the mountebanks of Venice, sets an even earlier date than Dekker's play for these first experimental attempts. His *Crudities* published in 1611, date from a journey to the Continent taken in 1608. 'In Venice,' he says, 'I was at some of their playhouses where I saw a comedy acted. The house is very beggarly and bare in comparison with our stately playhouses in England, neither can their acting compare with ours for apparel, shows and musick. Here I observed certain things that I never saw before, for

I saw women act, a thing I never saw before, though I have heard that it hath been sometimes used in London, and they performed it with as good grace, action, gesture, and whatsoever convenient for a play as ever I saw a masculine actor.' The identity of these actresses, of whose presence Coryat had heard rumours, is not known. They may have been the band of Italian players who had aroused such ire, or an earlier group of French actresses from the Continent. Possibly they represent some unrecorded attempt on the English stage itself. At any rate, it was unsuccessful, for when a French company came to London in 1629 and played at Blackfriars, the Red Bull, and the Fortune, the idea was still objectionable to English theatre-goers, and the French players were badly received. The delicate sensibilities of the groundlings were revolted by the scandalous innovation and the actresses were hooted and pippin-pelted off the stage.

Undoubtedly, however, travellers from the Continent brought back many glowing reports, such as that of Coryat, and little by little the foreign practice gained its supporters in the English audiences. Three years after the attack on the French actresses, one of the characters in *The Court Beggar*, given at the Cockpit in 1632, remarks that 'if you have a short speech or two, the boy's a pretty actor, and his mother can play her part — women actors now grow in request.' The Cavaliers of the Court of Charles I were beginning to affect a taste for Continental customs and to consider the boy actresses of the English stage somewhat crude and absurd in comparison with the French and Italian actresses. In a play called *The Ball*, given in 1639, Freshwater, speaking of the French stage says:

> Yet the women are the best actors, they play
> Their own parts, a thing much desir'd in England.

The courtiers, indeed, were accustomed to the sight of women in pageants and revelries, if not in regular 'stage plays.' The Masques organised in the reigns of James and Charles were gorgeous and vastly expensive affairs in which the ladies of the royal family itself occasionally deigned to appear. The true professional actress, however, was unknown in England, when the Puritan ascendancy closed the theatres in 1642.

This arbitrary act, which brought to an abrupt end a great period of dramatic efflorescence, had an important effect in bringing about the introduction of women to the English stage. At the time of the first edict, London could boast seven, possibly eight, theatres of varying size and importance, and their closing threw out of employment a large group of experienced actors and stopped the training of the boys who played women's parts. A certain amount of theatrical bootlegging was, of course, carried on in spite of the severity of the Fathers of the Commonwealth, but the plays were probably given by actors already trained in their parts. Performances continued surreptitiously at the smaller theatres, such as the Cockpit and Salisbury Court, until a second and more stringent edict in 1647 scattered the player bands and sent many of the leading actors to the wars.

Before striking their colours, however, the players gave vent to their grievances in 'The Actors Remonstrance, or, Complaint... for the Silencing of their Profession, and banishment of their severall Play-Houses,' a pamphlet circulated in 1643 which voices with no little wit the difficulties under which 'comedians, tragedians and actors of all sorts and sizes' were languishing. One of the main points that the unfortunate actors make is that 'our boyes, ere we shall have libertie to act againe, will be grown out of use like crackt organ pipes, and have faces as old as our flags.' A calamity which did, indeed, take place, for, in spite of Remonstrances and Petitions to Parliament, the Roundheads remained obdurate, and the theatres were officially inactive for eighteen years. By the time of the reopening, the boy actors trained under the old régime had disastrously outgrown their pink-cheeked youth, and such unfortunate accidents occurred as that which forced King Charles II to wait impatiently in his royal box while the player-queen shaved himself before appearing on the boards.

On the Continent, as we have already seen, actresses were flourishing long before this, and the banishment of the English actors and managers from their native land brought them into direct contact with these players. George Jolly, the English manager, toured Germany during the interregnum, and finding that his competitors were outdistancing him in the elaboration of their scenic display, especially in this matter of actresses, he very quickly added women to the company he recruited during his travels. Writing to the Council of Basle in 1654, he asked permission to play in the city, boasting that he could now delight all who love the theatre 'with his well-practiced company, not only by means of good instructive stories but also with repeated changes of expensive costume, and a theatre decorated in the Italian manner, with beautiful English music and skillful women.' The women were undoubtedly Germans or Italians, one of them being the wife of his chief actor, Schwartz, but Jolly's excursion into elaborate productions with music, scenery, and actresses makes him D'Avenant's predecessor by several years, as Leslie Hotson in his *Commonwealth and Restoration Stage* points out.

In England itself, however, it is D'Avenant who made the first experiment. While Jolly was still in Germany, D'Avenant was feeling his way toward the reopening of the theatres. Even before the *Siege of Rhodes* he had given his *First Day's Entertainment at Rutland House* on the 23d of May, 1656, in which 'Ned Coleman and his wife, another woman and other inconsiderable voices,' took part. Mrs. Coleman was therefore ready to play on that famous afternoon in the following September when D'Avenant finally presented his *Siege of Rhodes*, in his semi-private theatre at Rutland House. D'Avenant did not stop here, however. He was determined to introduce his 'opera' into one of the public theatres over which he had obtained control. In 1658–59, we find him giving another 'moral representation' concerning the *Cruelty of the Spaniards in Peru* and the second part of the *Siege of Rhodes* at the Cockpit in Drury Lane with a woman again in the cast. In spite of D'Avenant's judicious propaganda in his own behalf, these activities were looked upon askance by the authorities. In December, 1658, Richard Cromwell and the Council of State issued an order 'for taking into consideration the *Opera* shewed at the *Cockpit* in *Drury*-lane, and the persons to whom it stands referr'd are to send for the Poet and Actors and to inform themselves of the nature of the work, and examine by what authority the same is exposed to publick view; and they are also to take the best information they can concerning the acting of Stage-playes, and upon the whole to make report.'

But Parliament was too busy with other affairs to take action concerning D'Avenant and his opera. The period of suppression was almost over. With the arrival of Monk in February, 1660, and of Charles himself in May of that year, the restrictions on the players were immediately lightened. Groups of actors gathered here and there in the old playhouses and regaled the returning Cavaliers with revivals of pre-Commonwealth plays. It is noticeable, however, that one of the first groups of which we have record, organised by John Rhodes at the Cockpit or Phœnix in 1659–60, included besides Thomas Betterton, Robert Nokes, and other young actors, another six who 'commonly Acted Womens Parts,' among them Edward Kynaston, William Betterton, and James Nokes, who later became one of the leading comedians of the Restoration stage.

Edward Kynaston was one of the last as well as one of the most successful of boy actresses. Downes, whose

Roscius Anglicanus gives so many vivid contemporary
glimpses of plays and players seen by him from his point
of vantage at the prompter's desk in the early theatres of
the Restoration, says that this boy 'being then very
Young made a Compleat Female Stage Beauty, performing his parts so well — that it has since been Disputable
among the Judicious, whether any Woman that succeeded
him so Sensibly touched the Audience as he.' Pepys, who
saw him soon after the formation of the Rhodes company,
was equally enthusiastic. 'Captain Ferris took me and
Creed to the Cockpit play,' he writes on August 18, 1660,
'the first that I have had time to see since my coming
from the sea. *The Loyal Subject* where one Kinaston, a
boy, acted the Duke's sister, but made the loveliest lady
that ever I saw in my life.' And later, 'Tom and I and
my wife to the theatre and there saw the *Silent Woman*.
Among other things here Kinaston, the boy, had the good
turn to appear in three shapes; first as a poor woman in
ordinary clothes to please Morose; then in fine clothes as
a gallant, and then was clearly the prettiest woman in the
whole house; and lastly as a man, and then likewise did
appear the handsomest man in the whole house.'

Kynaston's beauty and success as an actor of women's
parts only hastened the disappearance of the boy actresses
from the stage. He was so fascinating to the ladies of
fashion that they took him riding in the park in their
coaches, dressed in his stage clothes — a spectacle most
shocking to the moralists, who now raised as vigorous a
cry against 'men in women's clothing' as they had pre-
viously made against 'female players' impersonating
their own sex. The times were changing, and what had
once been considered impossible was being slowly accepted as the only correct procedure. In October, 1660,
a petition declares that after considerable harassing, the
old actor band had consented to appear 'with woemen'
at the new theatre to be built by Killigrew. This and
other incidents indicate that women were already acting

in some of the groups of players gathered together immediately after the Restoration. A comedy called *The Tamer Tam'd*, produced in June, 1660, carries an epilogue 'spoken by the Tamer, a Woman,' who may have been a real woman and one of these unrecorded pioneers. The date usually given as that of the début of the first actress on the English stage by those who count Ianthe and her predecessors as of slight importance, is December 8, 1660. On that day Killigrew's company produced *Othello*, and the learned scholars believe that the following prologue, written by Thomas Jordan 'to introduce the first Woman who came to Act on the Stage in the Tragedy, call'd The Moor of Venice,' was spoken on this occasion.

> I come, unknown to any of the rest,
> To tell you news; I saw the lady drest:
> The woman plays to-day; mistake me not,
> No man in gown, nor page in petticoat:
> A woman to my knowledge; yet I can't,
> If I should die make affidavit on't.
> . . . . . . In this reforming age
> We have intents to civilize the stage.
> Our women are defective and so sized
> You'd think they were some of the guard disguis'd.
> For, to speak truth, men act, that are between
> Forty and fifty, wenches of fifteen;
> With bone so large, and nerve so incompliant,
> When you call DESDEMONA, enter GIANT.

No one knows who acted this first Desdemona, and there are many claimants to the distinguished title of first lady of the English stage. Mrs. Coleman, whom we have seen make her bow at Rutland House in the first part of the *Siege of Rhodes*, disappears almost immediately from theatrical history. It is evident that her interest in the stage was connubial rather than professional, and that she played that afternoon merely to amuse herself and because her husband insisted. Some years later, we hear of her at a party, at which Samuel Pepys was

fortunately present, protesting that she never had learned
the part and couldn't remember the music, but delighting
the company by 'her counterfeiting of Captain Cook's
part,' and doing it most excellently. Mrs. Coleman
probably acted on this one occasion only. The rôle of
Ianthe was entrusted on its next performance to Mary
Saunderson, better known as Mrs. Betterton, wife of the
leading actor of the Restoration stage. Mrs. Betterton is
so closely associated with the part that she is always referred to as Ianthe by Mr. Pepys in his frequent and always admiring comments on her acting. Mrs. Norris,
mother of the comedian Henry Norris, is another pioneer
cited by certain authorities as the first of England's
actresses, while Margaret Hughes and Anne Marshall
have each been named as the original Desdemona.

By 1660, Ianthe, whoever she may have been, had
gathered to herself a train of sister actresses. Women
were accepted as part of the two companies then forming
under the royal patents granted to Thomas Killigrew and
Sir William D'Avenant on August 21, 1660, though in
this document they are still classed as 'hirelings' and not
included among the sharing members. On January 3,
1661, Pepys records his first sight of women on the stage,
and by way of sealing the triumph of their entrance to a
profession so long denied them, the royal patent of 1662
officially acknowledges their position in the following
weighty clause:

'... And forasmuch as many plays formerly acted do
contain several prophane, obscene, and scurrilous passages, and the women's parts therein have been acted by
men in the habits of women, at which some have taken
offence; for the preventing of these abuses for the future
we do strictly charge, command and enjoin that from
henceforth no new play shall be acted by either of the
said companies, containing any passage offensive to piety
and good manners... And we do likewise permit and give
leave that all the women's parts to be acted in either of

the said two companies from this time to come may be performed by women, so long as these recreations, which by reason of the abuses aforesaid were scandalous and offensive, may by such reformation be esteemed not only harmless delights, but useful and instructive representations of human life, by such of our good subjects as shall resort to see the same.'

It is evident from this impressive document, that the introduction of actresses to the English stage was presented as a reformation and refinement of the theatre and went hand in hand with the censoring of plays and the regulation of the stage toward carrying out Charles II's noble effort to make the theatre 'serve as innocent and harmlesse divertisement' for his loyal subjects. In view of what we know of the manners and customs of Charles and his Court and of the theatre which catered to their pleasure, the uplifting sentiments of the royal patents are particularly diverting. Nor, from the point of view of behaviour, can the first actresses of the English stage be held up as examples for the rising generations. Their free and amoral ways, however, were but the reflection of the age in which they lived, while their dramatic gifts, their charm and brilliant beauty, the speed with which they incorporated themselves into the life of the theatre and their influence upon the drama of the day — these things were their own and have made them a group apart in the annals of the stage. It would be invidious to choose one among so many lovely ladies. Mrs. Betterton is among the first and is certainly the most important of them all, but the portrait of the first English actress would be incomplete without a glance at the shorter and more adventurous careers of some of her contemporaries. The first actresses tumbled on to the stage in Ianthe's wake in a glittering and light-hearted band, and in a few years they had made indisputably their own a world from which it is impossible to imagine them excluded.

CHAPTER VIII

MARY BETTERTON

AND THE RESTORATION ACTRESSES

THE Restoration theatre into which Ianthe and her sister actresses made their spectacular entrance came into official life with the royal patent, already mentioned, which was granted to D'Avenant and Killigrew in August, 1660. Charles II was scarcely back in power, he had not yet been crowned by his recently rebellious subjects, when he took steps to provide for his own and incidentally for their amusement by the ordering and regulation of the stage. This famous patent permitting the establishment of two theatres, and two theatres only, in London, inaugurated an age-long warfare in the theatrical world which lasted through innumerable changes and permutations well into the nineteenth century.

At first the arrangement seemed sensible and satisfactory enough. The enthusiasm for the stage before the Civil War had been so great that there was every reason to suppose that two theatres at the very least would flourish under the new régime. One of them the King took under his own patronage, putting Thomas Killigrew in charge. This company, known as the King's, or His Majesty's Servants, acted at first in Gibbon's tennis-court on Vere Street and later in the Theatre Royal, Drury Lane. Seven actresses were included in the original company, among them Margaret Hughes and Anne Marshall of Desdemona fame. D'Avenant, whose *Siege of Rhodes* had been the entering wedge of the new dispensation, was in charge of the second company, which was placed under the ægis of the Duke of York. It established itself at first in Lisle's tennis-court in Lincoln's Inn Fields, not far from Killigrew's original playhouse, and later, in 1671, after D'Avenant's death, it moved to the large Dorset Garden Theatre. D'Avenant's playhouse is often referred to by Pepys as the Opera, to distinguish it from the Theatre, as Killigrew's was called. In these two theatres and under these two men the first English actresses were trained for their profession and made their first essays in the dramatic arts.

The world in which they found themselves was acutely 'modern' in its tastes and proclivities. Across the chasm of Civil War, of exile, wandering, and discomfort, the returning Cavaliers looked back upon the old days as infinitely remote and barbarous. 'The old plays,' John Evelyn notes in his diary, 'begin to disgust this refined age, since his majesty is so long abroad.' One of the chief refinements demanded by Charles II and his courtiers was the introduction of women on the stage. They were familiar with the Continental custom; they had seen actresses in Holland, in France, and in Italy, and they had no intention of being deprived of that pretty and diverting vision. The influence of the Court on the Restoration theatre cannot be overestimated. It was a hothouse flower which burst into amazing and prolific bloom in the forcing-house of royal favour and aristocratic patronage. Unlike its Elizabethan and Jacobean predecessors, it received very little general public support. Where Shakespeare's London had thirteen playhouses opened at one time or another between 1576 and 1629, the two patent theatres of the Restoration ran to half-empty houses and were forced to unite in 1682 in order to exist at all.

The drama of the period was also a product of the environment. It had its appropriate setting in the rarefied atmosphere of court favour and court intrigue. The playwrights of the day, when they were not themselves of noble birth like George Villiers, Duke of Buckingham, Sir Charles Sedley, or Sir George Etherege, were experienced courtiers like John Dryden and men thoroughly familiar with the ways of the elegant and dissolute world which surrounded the Merrie Monarch and his satellites. The plays themselves aimed at an aristocratic freedom of expression, a complete absence of that pious hypocrisy which to Stuart sympathisers was associated with the dark days of the Commonwealth and the Roundheads' despised rule. The men who directed the fortunes of the two theatres were friends of the King and members of his immediate circle. Killigrew was the son of a knight and on terms of intimacy with Charles, while Sir William D'Avenant, who had become poet laureate on the death of Ben Jonson, was a courtier as well as a poet, playwright, and producer.

The King himself was a constant attendant at the play, and though his Lord Chamberlain was officially in charge of theatre affairs, His Majesty was the ultimate court of appeal and frequently decided playhouse disputes. The actresses, like the actors, were styled His Majesty's 'Comœdians,' and as such were duly provided with 'foure yards of bastard scarlet cloath and one quarter of a yard of velvett for their liueries.' One would like to know whether that pretty wench of a Nelly wore a 'cloake of scarlett with crimson velvett for the Cape of itt,' when she went about the King's business at the theatre or in Whitehall. What a sight it would have been to see her and her merry sisterhood picking their way down Drury Lane in such trappings! But whether they wore them or not, the actresses in the King's Company were duly and regularly supplied with these materials, and the fact, set down in the Lord Chamberlain's books together with innumerable other items concerning the affairs of the two theatres, indicates the close connection between Court and stage.

Theatrical affairs were in a state of chaos during the opening years of the Restoration, and it is to be feared that not a little of the confusion was due to the introduction of the gay and careless damsels from Lucknor

Lane and its environs into the ranks of the players. Discipline was unknown among them and no precedent had yet been established for the control of the actor bands. Men and women alike treated theatre property and theatre responsibilities with cheerful levity and were constantly involved in broils with each other and with their patrons. The old forms of theatre organisation, as represented by the self-governing companies of Shakespeare's day, no longer existed, and the two patentees, though in nominal control of the situation, actually found much difficulty in governing their companies and making their theatres pay.

The actresses were particularly difficult to control. They were forever dashing off on private business, handing over their parts to some more stolid sister who at the moment had no lover to divert her from her duties. They were fond of appearing in public in their stage costumes, which were far more elegant and beautiful than anything they themselves could afford. The Restoration actress played everything in 'modern dress,' and these clothes were often a gift to the theatre from a lady patroness of the arts. The temptation for a pretty actress to slip out to an evening rout in the Duchess of York's coronation robes, in which she had been playing her part all the afternoon, was practically irresistible, and scoldings were of little avail when it came to the poignant question of making an effective appearance.

Not only did the actresses wear the theatre wardrobe out of hours, but they also fought bitterly over the assignment of costumes from the manager's stock for their stage appearances. On one occasion two actresses cast for the Queens in Lee's popular tragedy of *The Rival Queens* came to blows on the stage over a matter of personal adornment. They both wished to wear a certain much-prized lace veil to enhance their royal beauties. The dispute was settled by the stage manager, who presented the treasured object to his favourite, whereupon the other lady, taking advantage of a scene in the play in which she is supposed to stab her enemy, did it to such good effect that she ran the blunt stage dagger an inch into her unfortunate victim's side. Undoubtedly much swooning and shrieking ensued. The pit and gallery took sides, pandemonium broke loose in the theatre, and the Court and Town gossiped for weeks over the latest scandal in the playhouse.

Such episodes were hardly soothing to the feelings of the harassed managers, and equally disastrous to the harmony of the company's affairs were the scenes that took place nightly over the 'sharing table' when the spoils of the day were divided among the shareholders. From time to time efforts were made to overcome some of these difficulties, and finally in 1675 an agreement was drawn up by the actors, actresses, and manager of the King's company which stipulated among other things:

'1[1] That noe man or Weoman shall dispose of their parts without the consent of the Company Subpœna 20 shillings

'2 That neither Man nor Weoman shall refuse any part the Company shall thinke them fitt for Subpœna a weekes wages

'3 That noe hired man or Weoman neglect rehearsall vpon forfeiture as formerly

'4 Whereas by Experience Wee find Our Cloathes Tarnished & Imberelled by frequent Weareing them out of the Playhouse It is thought fitt noe Weoman presume to goe out of the House with the Play House Cloathes or Properties upon Penalty of theire Weekes pay

'5 That neither Man or Weoman make vse of either Scenes or Cloathes without the Generall consent of the whole Company

'6 Upon Complaynt of People of quality of Mrs. Meggs Severall Maydes [the orange girls] offending them in the Pitt besides offending the Stage with theire Noise &

[1] From Allardyce Nicoll: *Restoration Drama, 1660–1700.*

treading vpon theire Cloathes & other affronts wee desire she may be obliged to strictly observe her Covenants...

'9 That neither Feathers nor Clothes nor Ribbons nor any thing relating to the Stage be taken vp without the Consent of the Company vpon penalty of paying for them themselves

'10 To prevent the Disorders of the shareing Table by an Inundation of People that presse vpon them in theire businesse Henry Hayles is appoynted to stand at the Dore & there to admitt them as they are called and by one to deliver up theire charge and soe dismiss them

'11 To avoyd the future inconveniency of strangers frequent Egresse & regresse when a play is done in ye House, it is thought fitt that some one or two be appoynted to stand at the Tyring house Dore till the House is discharged the persons appoynted are David Middleton and Brittaine

'12 That no persons Vnconcerned in the Businesse of the Play be admitted to stand betweene the Scenes...'

This last provision is an important one, indicating as it does one of the great 'plagues and inconveniences' of the early theatres. The gentlemen of the audience had the privilege, on payment of a small fee, of going behind the scenes, penetrating into the 'tyring room' where the women were dressing for their parts, and dawdling about in the wings and 'scene-room' while the actors were playing on the stage. The acting of the women must have suffered greatly from the presence of these 'unlicked Cubs of Condition' behind the scenes, for though during the first decade of the Restoration the public was not allowed on the stage itself, the 'pretty gentlemen' were fond of going behind the scenes to visit their latest flame or to pick up a bit of gossip from the players. Colley Cibber, who as an actor groaned under this affliction, and as a manager finally did away with it, describes vividly the effect of such a system on the efforts of actors and actresses to concentrate on their rôles. 'In many a laboured scene of the warmest humour,' he tells us, 'I have seen the best Actors disconcerted while these buzzing Muscatos have been fluttering around their eyes and ears. How was it possible an actor so embarrass'd should keep his Impatience from entering into that different Temper which his personated character might require him to be master of.'

The women were naturally more demoralised than the men by this state of affairs, for the wits and gallants who pursued them behind the scenes, who lolled in the boxes, or flirted with the orange girls in pit and gallery, looked upon the newly made actresses as little more than public women, an attitude which the ladies themselves were far from discouraging. The only difference these dashing sparks saw between the actresses on the stage and the professional vizard-masks in the audience was that with the former the glamour of the theatre added piquancy to adventure, and the pursuit of pleasure could be elegantly tricked out with the patronage of art.

There were, however, striking exceptions to the general run of light-hearted and light-headed ladies who adorned the more spectacular moments of the Restoration stage, women who devoted their whole existence to the theatre, who lived and breathed and had their being within its bounds, acted an inconceivable number of parts and brought to their profession a hardy devotion which made of them the true mainstays of the stage. Chief among these steady workers was Mrs. Corey, of the King's company, who played second to the more showy performances of the King's favourites and for more than thirty years appeared as the friend, confidante, attendant, sister, or mother to the varying procession of heroines in each new play. Mrs. Boutel was another competent and faithful servant of the stage. She created several of Wycherley's leading rôles, and could boast almost as many years of service as Mrs. Corey. Nor should we forget Mrs. Kneppe, to whom we owe a debt of gratitude for initiating Pepys into so many theatrical mysteries, and who played the Lady Fidgets and the Lady Flippants of Restoration comedy with such success. All these actresses, if not exactly sober and industrious workers, were capable comedians, able to give the necessary polish to their high-spirited heroines, able also to wring tears from the susceptible Restoration rakes who enjoyed 'sorrowful' tragedy almost if not quite as much as they did the elegantly indecent comedy of the day.

The leading actress of them all, however, was Mary Saunderson. Born just before the closing of the theatres, she grew up, during Cromwell's rule, in a theatreless world. She was only nineteen when she came under the influence of D'Avenant and began her stage career in his 'moral representations' and early operas. Perhaps the secret of her long and honourable career, her unsullied reputation, and her eminent position in the theatre of her time is that, like Isabella Andreini, she was fortunate enough to find in the man whom she loved and married not only a devoted and faithful husband, but a leader in her own profession. She was not snatched from it, as was her friend and companion, the beautiful Davenport, for the temporary solace of some hair-brained lordling, nor was she distracted from her art by the pursuit of adventure on her own account. She appears to have loved and admired her husband inordinately, and though of a quiet and somewhat melancholy disposition, to have been quite content with her lot. Betterton was a man who elicited the most ardent devotion from every one who knew him. He has been called the greatest actor of the English stage and he was without doubt the leading figure of his day. Colley Cibber, writing just after his death, said of him:

'I never heard a line of tragedy come from Mr. Betterton wherein my judgement, my ear and my imagination were not fully satisfied; which since his time I cannot equally say of any other actor whatsoever.... [In comedy]

he had a tempered spirit that gave life to wit, and a dry
reserve in his smile that threw ridicule into its brightest
colours.' 'Divinity hung round that man,' the young actor Booth exclaimed after he had played the Ghost to Betterton's Hamlet, and all his contemporaries joined in affectionate praise of his great qualities both on and off the
stage.

When Mary Saunderson first met him, he was already
taking his place as leading actor in the Duke's Company.
He was a handsome, rather florid young man with a low,
well-modulated voice, which already held the noisy pit
and gallery enthralled. She herself is reputed to have
had much beauty and even greater sweetness and grace,
though no portrait exists by which we may reconstruct
her actual appearance. She was living at this time with
Sir William and Lady D'Avenant in the house which ad-
joined the Lincoln's Inn Fields Theatre, for Sir William
had agreed to maintain the newly acquired women of the
company on the shares allotted to him for the purpose, as
well as to house four of them under his own roof. Mary
Saunderson was one of the four selected for that honour
and she therefore had an opportunity of meeting and
knowing Betterton in the pleasant atmosphere of the
D'Avenants' home, as well as in the theatre.

The Lincoln's Inn Fields 'Opera' was opened in June,
1661, with a gorgeously mounted production of the second
part of *The Siege of Rhodes*. The play was an enormous
success, and Mary Saunderson quite literally made a
name for herself in the part of Ianthe. 'All the parts were
justly and excellently performed,' Downes tells us, 'and
the play was acted twelve days together without inter-
ruption.' Pepys saw it on the fourth day and gives us a
glimpse of some of the dangers that attend playgoing in
a newly opened theatre as well as the inconvenience of
royal patronage:

'Went to Sir William D'Avenant's Opera,' he writes in
his entry for July 2, 1661, 'this being the fourth day that

it has begun, and the first that I have seen it. To-day was acted the second part of *The Siege of Rhodes*. We staid a very great while for the King and the Queen of Bohemia; and by the breaking of a board over our heads, we had a great deal of dust fell into the ladies' necks and the men's hair which made good sport. The King being come, the scene opened; which indeed is very fine and magnificent, and well acted, all but the Eunuche, who was so much out that he was hissed off the stage.' The play was indeed so successful, and D'Avenant's scenes, costumes, music, and actresses so charming that two days later, when Pepys went to Killigrew's rival theatre which was only a few blocks away, he says that it was 'strange to see this house, that used to be so thronged, now empty since the Opera began; and so will continue for a while, I believe.'

Successful as was the *Siege of Rhodes*, it could not hold the boards long, for the society that attended the Restoration theatres was on the whole a restricted one. The same people came to the playhouse again and again, and naturally demanded a change of bill to hold their interest. D'Avenant, therefore, while giving the *Siege of Rhodes*, was preparing other productions. He turned to the list of Shakespeare's plays that had been allotted to him, and after due consideration decided that *Hamlet* would be his next important effort. The parts were promptly assigned, Betterton as Hamlet. Mary Saunderson, fresh from her triumphs as Ianthe, was given Ophelia, the first Ophelia ever acted by a woman. In August, the play was produced, again with great success, for Betterton, who 'acted the Prince's part beyond imagination' as Pepys says, was one of the great Hamlets of stage history and played the part all his life with never-failing power. D'Avenant in producing Shakespeare felt himself very much within his rights. He liked to air the legend which made him the illegitimate son of the Bard, though his supposed relationship did not prevent him from indulging

in the quaint practice of 'reformeing' and making
Shakespeare fit for the stage, which was one of the favourite pastimes of the Restoration playwrights from Dryden
down.

It was in fact under D'Avenant's management and
with Mary Saunderson as Juliet that one of the most
startling of these 'reformeinges' was perpetrated — Hon.
Edward Howard's emendation of Shakespeare's *Romeo
and Juliet*. The curious playgoer could take his choice
between the tragedy, as 'wrote by Mr. Shakespeare,' or
Howard's version in which the star-crossed lovers were in
the end saved from death. The play was acted 'alternately tragical one day and tragi-comical another,' with
Betterton as Mercutio, Harris as Romeo, and Mary
Saunderson as Juliet in both casts.

Mary Saunderson's claim to fame rests largely on her
interpretation of Shakespeare; hers was the unique
privilege of being the first woman to create a number of
his greatest woman characters. *The Tempest*, *Measure
for Measure*, *Much Ado*, *Twelfth Night*, *King Lear*, and
Macbeth were among the plays allotted to D'Avenant,
and though there is no complete record of the casts of all
these plays, it is probable that Mary Saunderson played
the leading rôle in each. We know definitely that she was
the first feminine Ophelia, the first Juliet and Miranda,
the first Lady Macbeth, and the first Queen Katherine
to grace the English stage. She was so much admired by
her contemporaries in these rôles that she undoubtedly
did much to keep Shakespeare before the public when he
was looked upon as entirely too crude and uncouth for
the taste of a refined age. Pepys, who cared very little
for Shakespeare, always speaks of 'Ianthe' with affection
and respect. He admired her sweet voice and her 'in-
comperable acting,' and bore with Shakespeare for her
sake and for the sake of Betterton who was even more
famous for his Shakespearean rôles.

The players of D'Avenant's company had been acting

together some eighteen months in the theatre in Lincoln's Inn Fields when a quiet wedding took place in December, 1662, consecrating, so some authorities believe, a union already happily accomplished. Mary Saunderson, of St. Giles' Cripplegate, spinster, supposed to be about twenty-five years of age, was duly married to Thomas Betterton, leading actor of the Duke's company, two years her senior. Their life seems to have been uneventful, like those happy countries that have long known peace. All their interests were centred in the theatre in which they lived and where they worked in partnership for more than thirty years. Betterton was the most important theatric figure of his day; his wife, as Thomas Campbell says, 'was the greatest actress for many years after the Restoration.' Their joint careers mirror the whole history of the acting companies during the last quarter of the seventeenth century. They represent qualities not usually associated with the Restoration stage, stability, devotion, and fidelity.

Yet these virtues did not make them less loved and admired by their contemporaries. They held open house and had many friends. Etherege thought highly of them both, and gave Mrs. Betterton two of his heroines to create. She was so popular at Court that when Crowne's Masque of *Calisto, or, The Chaste Nymph*, was performed with much splendour and elaboration at Whitehall in the early months of 1675, she coached the Princesses Mary and Anne, daughters of the Duke of York (later James II), in their rôles. 'These Princesses,' so Doran tells us in his Annals of the stage, 'derived from Mrs. Betterton's lessons the accomplishment, for which they were both distinguished when Queens, of pronouncing speeches from the throne in a distinct and clear voice, with sweetness of intonation and grace of enunciation.' Anne did not forget her former teacher when she became Queen of England, allotting her a pension in her old age, a gracious gesture only marred by the fact that, unfortunately, it was never paid.

For twenty years after her marriage, Mary Betterton held her own as leading actress in the Duke's company. In 1663, she appeared in one of her most important Shakespearean rôles, Queen Katherine in *Henry the VIII*, revived with new 'scenes and dresses and performed 15 days together with general applause,' as Downes records. Queen Katherine was one of Mrs. Betterton's most successful creations and ranks with her Lady Macbeth and her Duchess of Malfi in Webster's tragedy of that name, as outstanding expressions of her theatric talent. Colley Cibber, who only saw her in her old age, is loud in his praises of the effect she produced in these tragic rôles:

'Though far advanced in years,' he tells us in his *Apology*, 'she was so great a Mistress of Nature that even Mrs. *Barry*, who acted the Lady *Macbeth* after her, could not in that Part, with all her Superior Strength and Melody of Voice, throw out those quick and careless Strokes of Terror from the Disorder of a guilty mind, which the other gave us with a Facility in her Manner that render'd them at once tremendous and delightful. Time could not impair her skill, tho' he brought her Person to decay. She was to the last the Admiration of all true Judges of Nature and Lovers of *Shakespeare*, in whose Plays she chiefly excell'd, and without a Rival. When she quitted the stage several good Actresses were the better for her Instruction. She was a Woman of an unblemish'd and sober life, a faithful companion to her husband and his fellow laborer for five and forty years.'

Though ranking as a tragedienne, Mrs. Betterton's career was not by any means exclusively devoted to Shakespeare. We have an actual record of sixty different rôles which she performed between 1661 and 1694, and this does not by any means cover her entire repertory. Many revivals were given of which no account has come down to us. Stock plays were constantly performed with a recasting of parts necessitating the learning of a new rôle by the hard-worked actresses. In those spirited times repertory meant a change of bill every four or five days. If a play ran twelve or fifteen days together, it was considered unusual, the mark of an outstanding success. It was therefore necessary for a leading actress like Mrs. Betterton to have innumerable parts word-perfect and to be able to memorise a new rôle in a few days' time. When we read the ponderous and long-winded tragedies of the day, we are filled with admiration for the actress who could memorise these turgid lines and carry them off with such effect as to move her audiences.

The comedies were equally exacting and followed each other with the same bewildering rapidity. Among Mrs. Betterton's chief comedy parts were Lady Leycock in her husband's *Amorous Widow*. Mrs. Jilt in Shadwell's *Epsom Wells* and Graciana in Etherege's *Love in a Tub*, which inaugurated the era of the comedy of manners. She created in all some twenty-five original rôles during her years of active service, ranging through the whole gamut of Restoration comedy and tragedy, farce and opera, from Bellinda in *The Man of Mode* to Jocasta in Dryden's *Œdipus*. The same actress, who played Lady Macbeth with such touching and terrifying effect, delighted her audiences in the ribald comedies of Aphra Behn, or sang her way triumphantly through D'Avenant's many operatic versions of Shakespearean and current tragedies.

Furthermore she could dance admirably, both in the stately measures suited to courtly pageantry, when, clothed in magnificent robes, her hair piled high in a powder-white edifice shining with brilliants and quivering with feathers and bows, her heavy make-up touched to life by the inevitable black patch, she stepped delicately to the music of the latest *courant* from France. Or again she could tread a more lively measure in the pastoral scenes of the Restoration's Arcadian moments, dancing and singing in the billowing skirts and laced bodices of a purely theatrical shepherdess 'to the admiration of all.' The one criticism levelled against her husband, whose acting was considered beyond praise, was that he could not dance. Mary Betterton, though not as outstanding a figure as an actress as Betterton was as an actor, had all the versatility and technical equipment which made her an invaluable member of the company.

In 1671, the Duke's players moved into their magnificent new playhouse in Dorset Garden. D'Avenant had died three years before and Betterton was now the head of the enterprise. He and his wife took up their residence in an apartment in the theatre itself, where they lived for many years watching over the fortunes of the playhouse, working, acting, and receiving their friends, all under the same roof. These were the great days of the Restoration theatre when poets and wits wrote for the stage and an unrivalled band of actors and actresses performed under Betterton's direction. The plays produced during the decade following the installation of the company in the Dorset Garden Theatre included some of the most famous tragedies and comedies of the age: Dryden's *The Spanish Fryar*, with Elizabeth Barry as the Queen of Aragon, Mary Betterton as Elvira, and Lee, Smith, Nokes, and Underhill in the cast, as well as Betterton himself; Otway's *Venice Preserv'd*, with Betterton and Barry as the first of Jaffiers and Belvideres; Etherege's *The Man of Mode*, or *Sir Fopling Flutter*, in which Mrs. Betterton played Bellinda to Mrs. Barry's Mrs. Loveit — to name only a few from the long list of masterpieces produced during these rich years.

Yet in spite of brilliant acting, important plays, and elaborate productions, theatrical affairs did not prosper as they should. Neither of the two patent houses could hold its own against decreasing audiences and falling receipts. In order to overcome some of the difficulties, the King ordered the actors to join forces, and a union of the two companies took place in 1682. Betterton naturally took the lead in the new organisation, but his wife was shouldered aside by the younger actresses in her own and the rival group. For a while she played only minor parts in the many revivals with which the United Company sought to recoup its shattered fortunes, but in 1690 she became active once again, playing some of her old rôles and even undertaking new parts. This renewed energy may have been due to the fact that early in 1690 Betterton lost all his savings through a speculative venture into which he had been led by his friend, Sir Francis Watson. Instead of being able to retire on their capital, both Mr. and Mrs. Betterton were forced to continue their professional career. Yet far from resenting the difficulties in which Watson had placed them, the Bettertons adopted his daughter and brought her up as their own. She was trained by Betterton for the stage and became a successful actress, finally marrying the actor Bowman and playing with Betterton and his company for many years.

The term of Mrs. Betterton's professional career was approaching. She had outlasted all the other actresses of the original group and outlived many of her famous contemporaries. Charles II, whose happy home-coming had made possible the rebirth of the theatre in England, was dead. D'Avenant, the innovator and experimenter under whose guiding hand she had made her bow, had been gone these many years. Many of the old players, men and women, had died or retired, but the remaining members of the old group rallied round her at her exit. She made her last appearance in Dryden's last play, *Love Triumphant*, produced at the Theatre Royal, Drury Lane, in 1693. Kynaston, the boy actress of her youth, was on the stage with her playing one of those kingly rôles suited to the dignity of his carriage and the sonorous beauty of his voice. Cave Underhill, another of the original acting company, had a small rôle, and Betterton himself played the lead as her son. The two chief women's parts were taken by the twin stars of the post-Restoration stage,

Elizabeth Barry and Ann Bracegirdle, whose rising brilliance had long outshone her own ageing charms.

Mrs. Betterton's retirement took place on the eve of an important event in her husband's career. After the union of the two companies, things went smoothly for a while, but very soon the actors grew restless under the harsh treatment of the patentees. Led by Betterton, the old actors seceded in a body, and took over Lisle's tennis-court in Lincoln's Inn Fields which had housed the Duke's company on its first venture so many years before. On April 29, 1695, the New Playhouse, as the refurbished tennis-court was called, opened with the first performance of Congreve's *Love for Love*. In all the brilliant company which assembled on that famous day — the noblemen who had contributed good money to the enterprise, the courtiers who admired and patronised Betterton, Congreve's friends and Bracegirdle's lovers — no one was more deeply interested, more anxious and agitated than Mary Betterton.

She herself took no official part in the proceedings, but we can imagine her watching every detail with anxious eyes. Going behind the scenes to help her husband prepare for the part of the dashing young Valentine which he carried off with such success in spite of his sixty years, she must have remembered with emotion that June day thirty-four years before when she and Betterton in their enchanted youth appeared for the first time on the stage which had stood in this very spot. Did she realise later in the evening, as she followed the play from a modest seat in the back of the stage box, that she was witnessing one of the most brilliant first-nights in history, the high-water mark of the Restoration Theatre? On the stage before her, Congreve's incomparable *Love for Love* ran its course, witty, coolly satiric, devastatingly elegant and suave, one of the most perfect products of the English genius. It was extraordinarily well acted, Downes tells us, with Betterton in the lead and Dogget as Ben the

Sailor. Mrs. Barry, unrivalled interpreter of the heroic tragedy of the period, the idol of Otway and the creator of his Monimia and Belvidera, played Mrs. Frail. Anne Bracegirdle, whose name is inextricably associated with the comedy of manners, bright star of Congreve and of Rowe, the original Millamant and Lavinia, was on this occasion an irresistible, an all-conquering Angelica. Mrs. Betterton, watching the audience as well as the play, saw by its instantaneous enthusiasm that her husband's new venture had begun auspiciously.

Betterton's enterprise, licensed by the King and seconded by a group which included almost all the best actors in London, received for a while sufficient support to keep it going in fairly comfortable circumstances. But the storm-clouds were gathering in and out of the theatre. The players, freed from the restricting government of the patentees, grew increasingly careless and inattentive. The performances became slipshod, the fickle public turned back to the larger house, and the New Playhouse began to get into difficulties. Outside the theatre an even more formidable danger threatened. The Puritan element in the community, long silenced by the noisy revelry which followed the restoration of the Stuarts, suddenly burst into stern rebuke. Its spokesman was Jeremy Collier, that learned divine, who, convinced that 'nothing has gone further in Debauching the Age than the Stage Poets and Play-Houses,' launched against them his famous diatribe known as *A Short View of the Immorality and Profaneness of the English Stage*, in which he revels for three hundred pages in the 'lewdness and downright blasphemy' of the plays of his time. The attack caused a great commotion. Arguments for and against raged in every drawing-room, theatre, and pulpit. The controversy must have rung familiarly in Mrs. Betterton's ears, reminding her of the days when the Roundheads were in power, and she, an enterprising and fearless young woman, was preparing the way for the first English actresses. Her life, which had spanned the whole of the Restoration and post-Restoration stage, drew to its close to the sound of the rolling thunders of the moralists.

In 1705, Betterton gave up his independent theatre and became a salaried actor in the new theatre in the Haymarket built for him and his company. He died in harness in April, 1710, and we hear of Mrs. Betterton only once again in the annals of the theatre when, on June 4, 1711, a performance of *Sir Fopling Flutter* was given by the Drury Lane Company, for the benefit of 'the widow of the late Famous Tragedian, Mr. Betterton.' Her will is dated March 10, 1712, and this first and oldest of the Restoration actresses must have died during the year, having long outlived all her contemporaries and seen the English actress forever firmly established on the English stage.

If Mrs. Betterton of the Duke's Company was the foremost of the first group of actresses, Nell Gwyn of His Majesties' Servants was and is by far the most famous. Her spectacular success as His Majesty's mistress rather outshines her achievements in the theatre, but she was undoubtedly a capable comedian and her dashing, high-spirited methods of acting set the pace for the long line of lively cabotines who have been, ever since, the delight of the English stage, even in its dullest moments. Nell began her service to the theatre in the far from exalted capacity of orange girl. Born in poverty and, as she herself is reported to have described it, 'brought up in a brothel to fill strong waters to the gentlemen,' it was a step upward in her career when Mrs. Meggs engaged her to peddle fruit and favors within the precincts of Killigrew's newly built Theatre Royal on Bridges Street, Drury Lane.

Nell did not stay long among Orange Moll's Severall Maydes, for she was already acting in 1665 at the age of fifteen. She never entirely forgot her orange-girl manners,

however, when she made her way from the pit to the
stage, or, for that matter, even after she had attained
her exalted rank in the royal seraglio. Pepys, coming
upon her one day in the 'woman's shift' where she was
dressing and was 'all unready,' speaks with amusement
of her methods of expression: 'But to see how Nell cursed
for having so few people in the pit, was pretty,' he exclaimed. Etherege wrote with less good-humour when,
linking her with Moll Knight in his lampoon, he makes
her say:

> Louder we swore than plundering dragoons,
> S'blood followed s'blood and zounds succeeded zounds!

Nell remained all her life a cheerful hoyden, and many
are the tales of her quick wit and uncensored tongue.
She could act, however, as well as swear, and her brief
theatrical career made an indelible impression on the
stage. For her Dryden wrote his gay and airy heroines.
She was the original Florimel in *Secret Love*, and her inimitable verve in such parts moved Pepys to exclaim
that 'I never can hope to see the like done again by man
or woman — so great a performance of a comical part
was never I believe in the world before as Nell do this.'
She was particularly captivating in 'breeches' parts and
in the piquant and highly personal prologues and epilogues which were written for her and which she recited
with admirable address. On one occasion she came out
in an immense cart-wheel of a hat — outbrimming the
broad brim of the rival theatre's headgear, and pronounced Dryden's famous satire on scribblers who think
they can write a play 'when they have got A broad-
brimmed hat and waist-belt toward a plot!' The result
was so devastating that Downes says the whole theatre
was convulsed, and as for the King — ''twas beyond odso
and odsfish, for he wanted little of being suffocated with
laughter.'

Curiously enough, this dashing comedienne made her

début in a serious part, that of Cyderia in Dryden's
Indian Emperour in 1665. Pepys 'was most infinitely
displeased' with her in this rôle. When he saw it again
two years later he adds: 'It is a great and serious part
which she does most basely.... It is a miracle to me to
think how ill she do any serious part, just like a fool or
a changeling: and in a mad part do beyond imitation
almost.' Indeed, her appearance in a tragedy was so
contrary to the expectation of her audience, which was
accustomed to seeing its favorite appear again and again
in the same type of part, that her infringement of custom
had to be explained. Dryden wrote a comic epilogue to
his perfectly serious tragedy of *Tyrannick Love* in order
to give Nell a chance of setting herself right with her dis-
appointed admirers. She is supposed to have died at the
end of the play and is left lying on the ground. A porter
comes out and is about to carry her off the stage when she
jumps to her feet and flies at him with the words:

> Hold, are you mad? you damn'd confounded dog
> I am to rise and speak the Epilogue!
>
> I come, kind gentlemen, strange news to tell ye,
> I am the ghost of poor departed Nelly.
> Sweet ladies, be not frightened, I'll be civil:
> I'm what I was, a little harmless devil....
>
> To tell you true I walk because I die
> Out of my calling in a tragedy. —
> O poet, damn'd dull poet, who could prove
> So senseless to make Nelly die for Love!
> Nay, what's yet worse, to kill me in the prime
> Of Easter-Term, in Tart and Cheesecake-time!
> I'll fit the fop, for I'll not one word say
> T' excuse his godly, out-of-fashion play.
>
> As for my Epitaph, when I am gone
> I'll trust no poet, but will write my own:
> Here Nelly lies, who, though she lived a slattern
> Yet died a Princess, acting in St. Cathar'n.

This sort of 'mad, fantastic foolery' was Nell's particular forte, and tradition, with its usual inaccuracy, has it that her delivery of this very epilogue so fascinated the King, who was in the Royal Box that night, that he went behind the scenes and carried her off there and then. Mr. Pepys, however, recording for future generations the gossip of the 'tyring room,' had heard from his actress friend, Mrs. Kneppe, more than a year before, of Nelly's success with the King.

Her professional career did not stop when she became a member of the Whitehall band. In 1667, she created her famous rôle of Florimel, and in that and the following three years, she took the leading part in no fewer than eleven plays new and old. In 1670, the opening performance of Dryden's *Conquest of Granada*, in which she was cast as Almahilde, had to be postponed on account of the birth of her son, later created Duke of St. Albans by his indulgent father, Charles II. This was her last year in the theatre. She was appointed Lady of the Bedchamber to the long-suffering Queen in 1675, and it seems doubtful whether even Charles would have permitted her to return to the stage while she held a position of honour near the person of the Queen. Nell remained in high favour with the capricious King, even though he never ceased adding new ornaments to his collection. At his death he recommended her to the tender mercies of his brother. 'Don't let poor Nelly starve!' he whispered from that bed on which he took such an unconscionable time a-dying. James II carried out his wishes and Nelly lived in comfort for the few years remaining to her. She died in 1687, leaving one son, a respectable estate, and a reputation for wit, high spirits, and 'good nature' which have made her the heroine of many a tale from that day to our own.

The leading serious actress of the King's company during the years when Nelly was delighting its audiences with her gay and naughty ways, and Mrs. Betterton was leading the forces in the rival house, was Anne Marshall, one of the candidates for the honour of first woman on the English stage. She was in Killigrew's original company and she may have been the Desdemona of Jordan's prologue. We know at any rate that she acted Celia in Beaumont and Fletcher's *The Humorous Lieutenant* at the opening of the Theatre Royal, Drury Lane, in May, 1663. The following year she created her first important rôle, that of the Indian Queen in Dryden and Howard's tragedy of that name. Pepys tells us that on February 1, 1664, he went 'to the King's Theatre'... and there saw... 'the *Indian Queen* acted, which indeed is a most pleasant show, and beyond my expectation; the play good but spoiled by the ryme which breaks the sense. But above my expectation most, the eldest Marshall did do her part most excellently well as I ever heard a woman in my life; but her voice is not so sweet as Ianthe's: but however, we come home mightily content.'

Part of Pepys' satisfaction may have been due to the 'rich scenes' with which the play had been embellished and the costumes of the Queen herself. Aphra Behn, in her *History of Oroonoko*, tells the story of this 'forreigne-habitt' which was one of the treasures of the Theatre Royal wardrobe. When she was travelling in Surinam in South America, she met a band of native Indians. 'We traded with 'em for feathers,' she writes, 'which they order into all Shapes, making themselves little short Habits of 'em and glorious Wreaths for their Heads, Necks, Arms and Legs, whose Tinctures are inconceivable: I had a set of these presented to me, and I gave 'em to the King's Theatre; It was the dress of the Indian Queen, infinitely admir'd by persons of quality; and was inimitable.' Smith's mezzotint of *The Indian Queen*, which is usually given as a portrait of Mrs. Bracegirdle, bears a marked resemblance to this description. The 'glorious wreath' on the lady's head and the 'little short habits' of the diminutive black page-boys may be Mrs.

The Indian Queen

'THE INDIAN QUEEN'
From the mezzotint by W. Vincent, published by J. Smith

NELL GWYN

From the engraving by Thomas Wright after the portrait by
Sir Peter Lely

Behn's gift, or they may merely be a variation of the usual feathers of high tragedy. Possibly the lady in the picture is Anne Marshall, as there is no record that Mrs. Bracegirdle ever played the part, while, as Pepys tell us, Mrs. Marshall certainly did. On the other hand, Mrs. Bracegirdle appeared many years later as an Indian Queen in Mrs. Behn's own posthumous play *The Widdow Ranter* and this may be the rôle the mezzotint represents.

At any rate, the eldest Marshall took all the leading rôles at the King's Theatre from 1663 to 1677. She and her sister Rebecca were supposed to be the daughters of Stephen Marshall, the reverend divine who had preached sermons to the Long Parliament. As usual the gossip to this effect is retailed to us by Pepys, who describes a quarrel between Beck Marshall and Nell Gwyn, Nell retorting to Beck's accusation that Nell was Lord Buckhurst's mistress, by remarking that she herself was but one man's mistress, while Beck was 'a mistress to three or four, though a Presbyter's praying daughter.' Anne, Beck's older sister, figures less frequently in the *chronique scandaleuse* of the day than do most of her contemporaries. She must have been thoroughly occupied with her profession, for besides playing in all the revivals of Beaumont and Fletcher, Shakespeare, and Jonson, given by the King's company, she created a number of those excessively grandiose heroines which so delighted Restoration audiences. Rhymed heroic tragedy was the enthusiasm of the moment, and Orrery, Lee, and Dryden were providing the Theatre Royal with a succession of scenes of Love and Honour, not to say Blood and Bombast, in which Anne Marshall excelled.

Among her important rôles were Almeria in Dryden's *Indian Emperour*, the play in which Nell Gwyn made her début. It was specially written in order to make use of the scenes and costumes of *The Indian Queen*, but, as Dryden explained in the handbill distributed to the audience on the opening night, since only two characters from the previous tragedy had survived the holocaust which closed the former piece, the new play had very little to do with the old. Berenice in *Tyrannick Love* and Nourmahal in *Aureng-Zebe* were two other famous Dryden heroines created by Anne Marshall. She was also the first Roxana in Lee's *Rival Queens* as well as the Gloriana of his equally popular and successful tragedy of that name. She left the stage before the union of the two companies in 1682, bequeathing her particular line of heroines to Elizabeth Barry who at that time excelled in the heroic style.

Margaret Hughes' career, like that of Nell Gwyn and many another Restoration actress, was more spectacular outside the theatre than in it. With Anne Marshall she claims the distinction of having been the first Desdemona, her right to the title resting on the fact that her name appears in the first complete cast of *Othello* given by Downes in 1669. To be sure, the date of the performance which he records is nine years after the original production, but in those days a part belonged by rights to the first actor or actress who appeared in it to the satisfaction of the public and was only relinquished on retirement or under extraordinary circumstances. Desdemona was in this sense Peg Hughes' property, just as Ianthe belonged to Mrs. Betterton and Florimel to Nell Gwyn. Not long after the performance of *Othello* recorded by Downes, Margaret Hughes retired from the stage, wafted to a magnificent country house in Hammersmith, there to reign as accredited mistress of Prince Rupert, cousin of Charles II. In 1673, her daughter, Ruperta, was born. The child quickly won its way to its princely father's heart and was not forgotten on his deathbed. The Verney manuscripts tell us that Prince Rupert 'sent his garter to the king desiring Lord Burford (Nell Gwyn's son) might have it with his daughter by Peg Hughes, to which last two he has left all his jewels and personal estate and arrears due him from his Majesty.' Peg, as gossip tells us, had one fatal vice, a vice almost universal in her day and generation, she could not resist the gaming-table, and before long she had sold her jewels to Nell Gwyn, gambled away all the wealth left her by her lover, and was forced back into the theatre by dire necessity.

The Restoration stage was nothing if not extreme. Leaping suddenly from a womanless stage, it had in a few years an unlimited supply of more or less talented actresses. Where men had acted women's parts, women in men's clothes were soon the fashion. Mrs. Long of D'Avenant's company did much to start the vogue for breeches parts even before Nelly came on the stage. She was one of the first 'principal boys' so popular with English audiences through the eighteenth and nineteenth centuries. Downes gives an account of a play by Shirley in which the character of 'Dulcino the Grateful Servant, being acted by Mrs. Long, the first time she appeared in Man's Habit, prov'd as Beneficial to the Company as several succeeding new plays.' The box-office argument was naturally irresistible, and we find almost all the actresses of the day trying the effect of a shapely leg on the meagre audience that for all the brilliancy and dash of Restoration acting were the constant bane of managers and players. Small audiences meant small, and often unpaid, salaries and slender pickings at the sharing table over which the company quarrelled after the play, and if Nell Gwyn or the 'Matchless Bracegirdle' dressed as a man would fill the stage and pit with admiring throngs — why, so much the better. To add spice to the occasion, the poet would write into the prologue lines that drew as much attention as possible to the unconventionality of the situation. In D'Urfey's prologue to the *Marriage Hater Matched*, Mrs. Bracegirdle is made to express keen embarrassment at finding herself on the stage in breeches. Her companion reassures her by sundry references to her unimpeachable reputation, and finally with a 'Lord, I'm so ashamed,' she turns to the audience and plunges into her speech.

The vogue once started grew so intense that by 1664 whole plays were given by women only, and these plays were as indecent as any that ribald age produced. In October, 1664, only three years after he had seen women on the stage for the first time, Pepys records a performance of Killigrew's *The Parson's Wedding*, which even in that liberal day had an unsavory reputation, acted by women only, and later the King's Company gave *Philaster*, *The Maiden Queen*, and some of Dryden's coarsest comedies with actresses taking all the parts. Anne Marshall spoke the prologues and epilogues to the two first-mentioned plays in which she described the plight of the performers who now had to produce their plays with a beardless Prince where of old there had been only bearded Princesses.

Not satisfied with putting indecent lines in the mouths of women, dressed, for the greater delectation of masculine eyes, in breeches and tight-fitting coats, the purveyors of popular amusement, toward the close of the century, hit upon the happy scheme of introducing little girls of six or eight to lisp a scabrous prologue or sing a particularly ribald song, wherein the contrast between an apparent childish innocence and the most filthy innuendo gave the necessary fillip to attention. Such incidents as these gave material for Collier's fulminations against the stage and led to a situation described by the *Spectator*, when 'some Ladies wholly absent themselves from the Playhouse; and others never miss the first day of a new play, lest it should prove too luscious to admit of their going with any countenance on the second.'

Every one had a word to say as to who was to blame for these shocking conditions. As early as 1666, John Evelyn laid it squarely at the feet of the ladies. 'This night,' he notes in his journal for September 18 of that year, 'was acted my Lord Broghill's tragedy call'd *Mustapha* before their Majesties at Court, at which I was present, very seldom going to the public theatres for many reasons, now as they are abused to an atheistical liberty, fowle and undecent women now (and never till now) permitted to appear and to act, who inflaming severall young noblemen and gallants, became their misses, and to some their wives; witness the Earle of Oxford, Sir R. Howard, P. Rupert, the Earle of Dorset, and another greater person than any of these, who fell into their snares, to the reproach of their noble families, and ruine of both body and soule.'

Jeremy Collier, on the other hand, belaboured the playwrights, while they in turn, through the mouth of John Dryden, in his epilogue to *The Pilgrim*, pointed the finger of scorn at his good friends of the Court.

> Perhaps the parson stretch'd a point too far
> When with our theatre he waged a war
> He tells you that this very moral age
> Received the first infection from the Stage.
> But sure, a banished court with lewdness fraught
> The seeds of open vice returning brought....
> The sin was of our natural growth, 'tis true
> The scandal of the sin was wholly new.
> Misses there were, but modestly concealed
> Whitehall the naked Venus first revealed.

Dryden's defence of the stage is even more justly a defence of its first actresses. Recruited from tavern and brothel, reared in an atmosphere of intrigue and debauchery, courted by dissolute fops and admired by a society which counted the King's mistresses among its most brilliant leaders, it is hardly surprising that many of these gay ladies were, in Downes' inimitable phrase, 'erept the stage by force of love.' It is only astonishing to find in their number a single one with the unblemished reputation and high artistic standing of Mary Betterton, the talent and ability of Anne Marshall, the briefer but no less brilliant successes of Nell Gwyn and Peg Hughes.

At first barely tolerated in the theatre and classed as

mere 'hirelings,' they had, by the close of the century, become respected members of the profession. When Mrs. Barry and Mrs. Bracegirdle were made sharers with Betterton in the organisation of the Lincoln's Inn Fields Company in 1695 and were named on equal terms with the actors in the licence granted to the new group, the position of women on the stage was definitely established. Ianthe had won her final economic equality, and we see her at the head of the procession of English actresses, clothed in the splendour of Dryden's poetry, the strength of Wycherley's comedy, the glitter of Congreve's wit, looking at this distance like Millamant herself as she sweeps on to the stage in that most perfect picture of the Way of this particular World: 'Here she comes i' faith full Sail, with her Fan spread and Streamers out, and a shoal of Fools for Tenders.'

CHAPTER IX
APHRA BEHN
ENGLAND'S FIRST PROFESSIONAL WOMAN PLAYWRIGHT

FOLLOWING hard upon the dancing footsteps of the first actress to invade the English stage, the first woman playwright made her appearance and won an equally prompt and brilliant success. Ianthe and Astræa flourished side by side in that dashing, gay, and feckless age that followed the return of Charles II to the throne of his fathers. We have seen the merry ladies of the Restoration stage take the town by storm. They were soon reenforced by the advent of playwrights of their own sex, among whom Aphra Behn, 'the Admired, the Adored, the Lovely, Witty Astræa,' stands first and foremost.

The name of Aphra Behn is little known outside the small circle of students of English dramatic literature and even there it is associated more with scandal than with admiration. Pope's mocking couplet —

> The stage how loosely does Astræa tread
> Who fairly puts all characters to bed —

has been accepted as sufficient epitaph with which to damn both her personal character and her literary achievement. The usual opinion is that Aphra Behn wrote the most scandalous comedies of a scandalous age and that she lived with an equal disregard of decorum and decency. Truth, however, has a disconcerting way of overlooking the simple conclusions of prejudice, and the Aphra Behn who emerges from the battle of the pedants and the dust of her own garnered works proves to be a woman of unusual spirit and remarkable gifts, neither better nor worse than her time, but one who was honoured with the dangerous distinction of eminence in her own day and has been the object of much ignorant criticism in later generations.

For Aphra Behn was not only the first woman to succeed as a professional playwright, she was also in many ways the first modern — the first exponent of the revolutionary idea that men and women are created with an equal aptitude for life, liberty, and the pursuit of happiness. Finding herself 'forced to write for bread and not ashamed to own it,' Aphra Behn boldly entered the lists with the other playwrights of her day and carried off a not unworthy trophy. If she did not have the originality of Etherege, the force of Wycherley, and the incomparable refinement and polish of Congreve, her work will bear comparison with many writers of her period. She was one of the most popular and prolific of Restoration dramatists, and the charm of her personality, the vigour of her pen, and the honeyed sweetness of her verse are a delight to this day.

She was not, of course, the first woman to attempt play-writing. The penning of tragedies and the translation of the classics had occupied the idle hours of a number of cultured English women from the Renaissance onward. Queen Elizabeth herself is reputed to have translated parts of the plays of Seneca, and the unfortunate Lady Jane Grey also indulged in this vein of learning. Some of these noble ladies were given to original work as well. We find Lady Elizabeth Carew writing a play on the subject of *Miriam the Fair Queen of Jewry*, which was published in 1613, while Mary Cavendish, the Thrice Noble, Illustrious, and Excellent Princess, the Lady Marchioness of Newcastle, published two separate folios in 1662 and 1668 containing in all some twenty original plays, which, though never acted, have from time to time received the disrespectful attention of the critics. The scholarly Langbaine, however, is warm in his defence of the Lady Mary. 'I know,' he writes, 'there are some who have a mean opinion of her plays, but if we consider that both the language and plots of them are her own, I think she might with justice be preferred to others of her sex which have built their fame on other people's foundations.'

The only important contribution to the English stage from the pen of a woman before Aphra Behn's day was that made by another poetess whose name was often linked with hers in the flowery verses that glorified Astræa. The Matchless Orinda preceded Astræa on the stage, as she preceded her in the hearts of the elegant versifiers of the Restoration, but her contribution was, again, only a translation and not an original creation. Orinda, whose real name was Catherine Phillips, held a unique position in Restoration circles. A quiet, modest woman, the wife of a Welsh gentleman of small means, she enjoyed a brief apotheosis as Queen of Poetry in the early years of this period. She organised and inspired a Society of Friendship whose pure ideals she celebrated with so clear and true a note that Keats found her poetry admirable more than a century and a half later. Though she lived in the country, far from the Court with its French enthusiasms, Mrs. Phillips was sensitive to the new impulses that were flowing into English literature. The trend toward a disciplined poetic form was reflected in her verse, and during her quiet years in Wales she translated Corneille's *Pompée* into English rhymed couplets.

A business trip to Dublin brought Orinda into contact with the lettered nobles and wits just returned from the Continent and made it possible for her play to win precedence over all others by being produced in the fine new theatre in Smock Alley as early as February, 1662. Her *Pompey* is the first sign-post along the way in which English tragedy was to go during the following fourteen years. From this time forward, in spite of Pepys' disapproval, all noble heroes and chaste heroines were forced to sing their star-crossed passions in rhymed couplets until exhaustion and the Duke of Buckingham's mockery in *The Rehearsal* joined to break the fashion. *Pompey* was produced in London in 1663 and received royal approbation. In 1664, the Matchless Orinda died of the plague leaving her translation of *Horace* unfinished. It was completed by Sir John Denham and acted many times at the Theatre Royal and in Whitehall. Mrs. Phillips' contribution to the stage was to fix a poetic form. She was a poet, not a playwright. Aphra Behn's approach was strictly professional. Having evolved the novel idea of depending on her pen rather than on her person for maintenance, her natural genius led her to the stage, where her wit, her courage, and her unflagging energy won her a substantial success.

In undertaking the career of playwright, Aphra Behn challenged every prejudice and prerogative of a thoroughly masculine society. The honourable occupations open to a woman in 1660 were strictly limited to that of daughter, wife, and mother. We have an excellent picture of the average woman of the Restoration in the glimpses we get of Mrs. Pepys, 'poor wretch,' through her husband's faithful diary. He was unusually, if intermittently, kind and concerned, provided his wife with dancing and singing lessons, and even tried to teach her the rudiments of learning. On the whole, however, the ladies were kept in their place and were not expected to show any signs of independent activity. Outside marriage and the family only one profession existed — a profession spectacularly exploited during the Restoration, but one on which Aphra Behn did not care to place an exclusive reliance.

The theatre, as we have already seen, had at this time only just opened its doors to women, and the reputation of the majority of the newly made actresses was not above suspicion. Aphra Behn had to look elsewhere for an occupation that would give her the social standing she desired and the money she needed. For one so gifted a literary career would to-day be unquestioned. In Aphra's day it meant a degree of originality and courage which served to indicate the calibre of her pioneer spirit, and to explain in no small measure why her plays could be passed off as 'writ by a man' when she thought it expedient to do so. Like a man, too, she took her fun where she found it, and lived her life with the same freedom and gusto with which she wrote her plays. 'She was a woman of sense,' as her first biographer sagely remarks, 'and by consequence a lover of pleasure, as indeed all, both man and woman, are.'

Ayfara Amis was born in Wye, near Canterbury, and christened there on the tenth of July, 1640. Of her father and mother, John and Amy Amis (or Amies), we know little except that they had the originality to select so unusual a name for their daughter. Ayfara was a pagan actress turned Christian hermit and saint, and father and mother Amis builded better than they knew when they made her protectress of the little girl who was to become England's first woman playwright. Ayfara Amis became in time Afara, Apharra, or, as it is written on her tombstone to-day, Aphra, Behn, and in the course of her poetic career acquired the melodious *nom de guerre* of Astræa, probably derived from D'Urfé's long-winded romance *Astrée* which was so much in vogue in the early seventeenth century.

Aphra's father is supposed to have been a distant relative of Francis, Lord Willoughby, who held an important position in connection with the British colonies in the West Indies. While Aphra was still young — a pretty child 'whose wit and understanding far outstrip'd its Years,' John Amis was sent to Surinam to be, according to Aphra's hyperbolic account, 'Lieutenant General of Many Isles beside the Continent of Surinam.' The whole matter of this voyage to South America has been challenged by recent scholarship, but there seems to be sufficient evidence to believe that it actually occurred. Whatever her father's appointment may have been, he died on the high seas on his way to his post, leaving his widow and children to complete the voyage alone. The family, on its arrival, was provided with a house and remained some years in Surinam, where Aphra lived the exciting, adventurous, and care-free life she has so admirably recorded in her novel *Oroonoko*. Her experiences in this distant and lonely outpost of civilisation are in piquant contrast with the life she was later to lead as a reigning wit and beauty in Restoration London.

Here in the wilds she revelled in the colourful tropic scene. She hunted 'tyger cubs' and took long trips into the interior. Her physical courage and energy is as remarkable in an age of delicate, swooning heroines as her moral courage in later and more complex situations. On one occasion a group of the most enterprising colonists, led by Aphra, had made an eight-day trip into the heart of the unexplored country, among Indians known to be unfriendly and who later proved themselves ferocious enemies of the Dutch colonists. The travellers came upon a settlement of these Indians, and Aphra insisted upon approaching them alone and unarmed in the hope of making friends with them. She and her brother and her waiting-woman went into the village and were immediately surrounded by yelling, naked savages. 'We thought their cries had been for those that should kill us,' she tells us, 'but it seems it was of wonder and amazement. They were all naked; and we dress'd so as is most convenient for the hot Countries, very glittering and rich; so that we appear'd extremely fine; my own hair was cut short and I had a Taffety Cap, with black Feathers on my head. My brother was in a Stuff Suit with Silver Loops and Buttons and abundance of Green Ribbon. This was all infinitely surprising to 'em' — and not a little to us with our dull notions of suitable travelling costumes. The pretty Aphra must indeed have looked like something from another world with her clear pink-and-white complexion, her large, rather prominent brown eyes, and her mop of short brown curls. The Indians touched her tentatively, demanded from her interpreter, who came up later, whether she had 'wits,' and finally took her hand in friendship — a friendship very valuable to the British settlers as long as they remained in the colony.

From her experiences in Surinam and her friendship with the slave Cæsar, the exiled Indian Prince Oroonoko, Aphra derived the material for her famous novel. This book was published in 1688, and all critics agree that it is a landmark in the history of English fiction. Coming at a time when the ten, twelve, and fifteen volume novels of Scudéry and La Calprenède were still in fashion, when the romantic maunderings of endless pairs of lovers through equally endless and inane adventures, in which 'all the knights were valiant and all the ladies passionate and chaste,' still formed the only pabulum for novel readers, Aphra's direct and vivid style, her simple narrative and colourful descriptions, were a revelation. *Oroonoko* opened a new field in fiction, and had an incalculable effect on later literary developments.

Aphra Behn was the first writer to sing the praises of the noble savage and the joys of the return to nature. Bernardin de Saint-Pierre, Chateaubriand, even Rousseau, can be counted among those who followed her. Aphra at least had seen the savage and knew whereof she spoke. *Oroonoko* has also been classed as the first emancipation novel, though it was written without the propaganda zeal that characterises *Uncle Tom's Cabin*. As a novel it earned a prompt and deserved fame and in the tragedy which Thomas Southerne derived from it and produced in 1696, Oroonoko and his beloved Imoinda lived for many years upon the English stage.

Aphra and her family returned to England shortly after the Restoration, and for a while she seems to have enjoyed the gaieties of town and court life and the company of the brilliant band of cavaliers and courtiers gathered there. It is at this time that she married and, shortly after, lost the shadowy Mr. Behn, who left her, as far as is known, nothing tangible but his name and possibly some Dutch affiliations, for he is supposed to have been a wealthy merchant of that country. Evidently his money did not outlast his life, for in 1666 Aphra Behn found herself dependent upon her own efforts to support herself and her mother. In this predicament she undertook a secret government mission to Holland. Her letters from Antwerp, addressed to Tom Killigrew in his capacity as courtier and personal friend of the King, and to James Halsall, who was also a power at Court and His Majesty's cup-bearer, are still in existence and give a vivid account of the difficulties, risks, and sordid money troubles that attended her efforts to serve her king and country in the humble capacity of confidential agent or spy. The episode has been clothed with romantic details by Aphra's biographers. Furnished with Dutch lovers, amorous assignations, practical jokes, and wild adventure, it appears more like one of her own farcical comedies than any form of reality. The truth, as shown in her letters and petitions, is more interesting if less picturesque.

Aphra spent six months in Antwerp in close communication with one William Scott, a spy in the service of England, whose information, coupled with her own discoveries, she retailed in her letters to the authorities at home. During this period she was unable to obtain from the Government any of the money due to her or Scott for their services and expenses. Her letters were ignored, her appeals unanswered, she spent every penny of the forty pounds she had brought with her and which represented all the money she had in the world. Finally, in desperation she succeeded in raising a personal loan of one hundred and fifty pounds with which she paid off her debts and went back to London.

For two years after her return she importuned in vain for her money. In the end her creditors became impatient and threw her into prison. We do not know who finally saved her from her desperate predicament. It may possibly have been that the good-natured Killigrew bestirred himself in response to her pathetic appeals and rescued the future playwright from jail. It is a pleasant supposition and one supported by Aphra's enthusiastic friendship for Killigrew. At any rate, she was shortly free and out of debt, but thoroughly disillusioned with the possibilities of government service as a means of livelihood. 'The rest of her Life,' her first biographer succinctly remarks, 'was entirely dedicated to Pleasure and Poetry,' an optimistic résumé of an exceedingly active and arduous career, which included the production of eighteen plays — tragedies, tragi-comedies, comedies and farces — as well as the publication of thirteen novels, innumerable poems, translations, dedications, verses and songs.

Aphra was twenty-eight when she finally freed herself from debtors' prison. Her first play was produced some two years later. Thoughtful biographers have provided her with one or more protectors to care for her during these years and supplement her later earnings. The question of Astræa's love-affairs is one of the many contested details of this charming lady's career. Her enemies, during her lifetime and afterwards, endowed her with all the vices and indiscretions of her insouciant heroines and harlots. Her friends have been willing to allow her the virtues of these ladies and a life not differing greatly from the free and untrammelled existence of many of her colleagues. It is impossible to read her comedies, novels, and poems without being convinced that Aphra Behn had a fairly wide experience in the peripatetics of love. In spite of the marked artificiality of all her productions, the stereotyped intrigue, the elegantly trivial verse, there is a certain vein of richness in her style, a wealth of

invention, a relish for detail, that indicate something
more than book-learning as a source of material for her
plots. We need not believe the slander with which she
was vilified in her own day to carry away the conviction
that gallant adventure was familiar to her both in and out
of the theatre.

The only lover of whom anything definite is known,
however, and that little enough, is a certain John Hoyle,
lawyer, wit, and rake, to whom Astræa is supposed to
have addressed the eight love-letters published after her
death. It is probable that he is the black-eyed, saturnine
Lysidas of the *Pastoral Cabal*, the J. H. to whom several
poems are addressed, the Amyntas of various Arcadian
love-lyrics. To judge by her letters, this affair of poor
Aphra's was anything but the airy, indifferent triflings
of a Lady Fancy. Astræa, proud, high-spirited, and
sensitive, was not able to maintain the true Restoration
attitude of brittle indifference in her personal relations.
She was afflicted with a warm heart not entirely under
the control of a clear and incisive brain. She fell into a
trap a genuine comedy-of-manners heroine would have
scorned, and we see her in these letters caring not at all
wisely and entirely too well for her unfaithful swain.
The glimpses we have of her, fleeting as they are, bear
witness to the truth of the description written by her
first biographer, one of the Fair Sex, who says of her that
'she was of a generous and open temper, something passionate, very serviceable to her Friends in all that was in
her Power, and one who would sooner forgive an Injury
than do one. She had Wit, Honour, Good Humour and
Judgment. She was Mistress of all the pleasing Arts of
Conversation but us'd 'em not to any but those who
loved Plain-dealing.'

In a period that is marred by some of the ugliest
literary quarrels in history, where the skein of animosities
is so tangled that it cannot be unravelled, Aphra Behn
had the unique distinction of remaining loyal to her

friends and aloof from quarrelling cliques. She counted the leading poets of the day among her intimates. Dryden, Otway, Waller, Killigrew, and Betterton were of the number, and she was hailed with an excess of hyperbolic adulation by the poetasters who sat at her feet and sang her praises.

> Oh, wonder of thy Sex, Where can we see
> Beauty and Knowledge joined except in thee?

they warbled, and many a perfervid lyric effusion in celebration of her wit, her charms, her beauty and kindness bear witness to her popularity.

Aphra Behn's career as a dramatist began in December, 1670, when D'Avenant produced her first play, *The Forc'd Marriage, or, The Jealous Bridegroom*, at the little Lincoln's Inn Fields theatre. She could not have made her bow under better auspices, with Betterton as Alcippus and Ianthe as the unfortunate Erminia. What good acting could do for a weak tragi-comedy was undoubtedly done, for the play ran six nights, an excellent record for the period and one which spelled success for the young playwright.

Mrs. Behn's intimate knowledge of the theatre of her day is evident throughout her work. Even as early as this she must have been at home behind the scenes and influential in the casting and production of her play. It was owing to her good offices with Betterton that the poet Otway, then a young man just up from Oxford, was given the part of the King, with the results which John Downes, who held the book and prompted the players on that memorable opening night, has recorded: 'Mr. Otway,' he says, 'being not used to the stage, the full house put him in such a sweat and tremendous agony, being dash'd, spoilt him for an actor.' Perhaps fortunately, for had he succeeded in 'turning actor' as he intended, *The Orphan* and *Venice Preserv'd*, those two tragic masterpieces of the Restoration stage, might never have been written.

Though *The Forc'd Marriage* is far from being one of
Mrs. Behn's best plays, it has the peculiar interest of
illustrating a tendency in the much-maligned Aphra's
work which her reputation as a purveyor of undiluted
pornography would hardly lead one to expect. It is
amusing to find in her work the seeds of that drama with
a purpose which was finally to swamp the English stage.
In this play, as in *The Lucky Chance*, *The Town Fopp*, and
The False Count, marriage forced upon unwilling daughters by deceit or interest is very pointedly attacked.
There is a certain undeniable sincerity in Mrs. Behn's
indignation, though too much weight cannot be attached
to a situation which, while providing the playwright with
every opportunity of indulging in the popular pastime of
cuckolding the villainous old husband, yet gives the
heroine the justification of a previous vow and an enforced matrimonial bondage as a moral mantle for her
adulteries. The fact that Mrs. Behn should so carefully
provide her married heroines with this sort of protection,
as she inevitably brings in a priest to sanctify the amours
of the unmarried ones when they are Ladies of Quality,
proves that her stage had its taboos as well as ours.

In her own day, Mrs. Behn always maintained hotly
that her comedies were highly moral and decent, bordering on the dull:

> My Plot, I fear, will take but with a few,
> A rich young Heiress to her first Love true!
> 'Tis damn'd unnatural, and past enduring,
> Against the fundamental Laws of Whoring.

Mrs. Behn's heroines are prone to be 'true,' even if it
involves infidelity to a husband to whom they have been
unwillingly united. Her heroes, it will be admitted, have
more latitude, but even the wildest of them submit to
matrimony before they lead off the not exactly modest,
but certainly chaste, virgin of the piece.

Mrs. Behn's earliest plays are of a romantic serio-dramatic trend. *The Amorous Prince*, produced in the spring following her first appearance as a playwright, is of this school. The prologue describes it as

> A damn'd intrigue of an unpracticed muse,
> Not serious, nor yet comick, what is't then?
> The imperfect issue of a lukewarm brain.

Which, to a modern reader, is not inapt as a description of this type of stilted romantic tale. *The Young King, or The Mistake*, founded on an episode in La Calprenède's *Cléopâtre*, produced several years later, is of the same general description. It is supposed to be Mrs. Behn's first play, refused by the managers, and later rewritten and produced at the Duke's Theatre. In these three plays, as also in her one tragedy, *Abdelazer, or, The Moore's Revenge*, we see Aphra under the influence of her reading of the popular novels and tragedies of the day and in the mood, sentimental and grandiose, which was as distinctly a part of the Restoration atmosphere as the dissolute comedy for which it has become a synonym. *The Amorous Prince* is written in blank and rhymed verse as are also *The Forc'd Marriage*, *The Young King*, and *Abdelazer*. The first is touched with the romantic element we associate with *Twelfth Night* and moves with a decorousness that Aphra did not long maintain. There are Shakespearean reminiscences, too, in the scene where Cloris, 'in male attire,' woos her inconstant lover in words that echo Viola's —

> Of her it was I learn'd to speak and sigh,
> And look, as oft you say, I do on you.

But Mrs. Behn's individual talent was beginning to show itself. She is a master hand at 'the conduct of a plot,' and in these early plays her skill develops rapidly. With *The Dutch Lover*, produced in February, 1672, her mastery of the comedy of intrigue is plainly evident. This play was not a success, though in many ways far more entertaining than her earlier efforts. It was produced hastily by her friends of the Duke's Company who had just moved into their fine new quarters at Dorset Garden and were evidently unprepared in their parts. Aphra complains that the 'intolerable negligence' of the cast was such that no one could follow the 'busie plot' or hear what was happening on the stage, with the inevitable result that the play was damned.

Temporarily discouraged by this setback, Mrs. Behn retired from the theatre, devoting the next two years to preparing for her second and triumphant reappearance on the boards. The winter 1676–77 saw no fewer than four plays from her pen; her tragedy, *Abdelazer*, her first comedy set in London, *The Town Fopp, or, Sir Timothy Tawdrey*, *The Debauchee*, attributed to her by Langbaine, and *The Rover, or, The Banish't Cavaliers*, her most successful and popular comedy. With the advent of *The Rover* in March, 1677, Mrs. Behn's position as a playwright was permanently assured. Astræa became the talk of the day and her Willmore the delight of Court and Town alike. The play was produced at the Dorset Garden Theatre with a brilliant cast including the Bettertons, Mrs. Barry, Smith, and those two incomparable comedians, Lee and Underhill, as the comic butts of the piece. In *The Rover* we have Mrs. Behn in her best vein of romantic intrigue, spiced with wit and sauced with buffoonery and displaying in the leading characters a high-spirited, rollicking adventurousness that has its own special charm. There is something of Dryden's merry hoydens in the gypsy Hellena, acted on this first production by Elizabeth Barry who shortly after became one of the reigning favourites of the stage. Smith was a handsome and capable actor. The romantic Mountford, who, later, took the part of the Rover, was so fascinating that even Queen Mary, who disapproved of the play, is reputed to have said that 'it was dangerous to see him act, he made vice so alluring.'

The character of Willmore the Rover proved irresistible to the gallants and ladies of the day. They saw in him the dashing, handsome adventurer, the beau ideal of Charles II's wandering cavaliers. He is the gallant soldier not yet turned town fop and court wit, but who has already crystallised the Restoration attitude toward sex. He sees in it a function as deserving the attention of a man of parts as the ordering of a meal or the conduct of an equipage. His code in intrigue is as impeccable as his bearing at the card table, and he would as soon disappoint a pretty woman as fail to pay a gambling debt. Mrs. Behn presented him with so much gusto that she successfully passed off her play on its first production as the work of a man. Her authorship, however, was soon acknowledged and with it her indebtedness to Killigrew's *Thomasso, or, The Wanderer*, from which she derived its general plan and many salient details.

Aphra's borrowings, here and elsewhere, were copious, but in this she followed a habit so prevalent at the time and so sanctified by custom that it does not materially affect the value of her work. Her enemies, however, not satisfied with accusing her of plagiarism, further affirmed that she was assisted in the actual writing of her plays by one or another of her scribbling friends or lovers. Ravenscroft and Hoyle have both been credited with writing scenes for her, but as the insinuation is largely based on the scurrilous *Tom Brown's Letters from the Dead to the Living*, it can fairly be attributed to the malice of those who resented her achievement. For with *The Rover* and *The Town Fopp*, both produced during the same winter, Aphra Behn was firmly established among the leading comedy writers of her day. The critic-gallants and envious wits might sneer as much as they pleased, they might, as did one 'long, lithering, phlegmatick, white, ill favour'd wretched Fop,' shout aloud in the pit, 'that they were to expect a woful play, God damn him, for it was a woman's,' their raillery was unavailing. Her plays were warmly welcomed, her name on billboard or book-cover spelled success to playhouse or printer, and her standing as a popular playwright was completely assured.

In *The Town Fopp, or, Sir Timothy Tawdrey*, Mrs. Behn makes her first excursion into the type of comedy chiefly associated with the Restoration. The scene of her play is London, and the characters are akin to those first introduced to the stage by George Etherege and epitomised in his Sir Foppling Flutter who had taken the town by storm only the year before. The comedy of manners had just burst upon a delighted society, which saw in it, not what Charles Lamb so engagingly describes as a world apart, a Utopia of Gallantry where no cold moral reigns, but a vivid and speaking likeness of the times. Wycherley, writing with a more cruel irony, a more biting scorn than the debonair Etherege, had already produced *The Country Wife*, and his last play, *The Plain Dealer*, appeared on the boards of the rival house in the same month, December, 1676, that saw the production of Mrs. Behn's *Town Fopp*, under Betterton at Dorset Garden. Congreve, greatest of them all, who carried the comedy of manners to its final perfection in the last decade of the century, had not yet appeared even in the drawing-rooms and ordinaries which he was soon to immortalise.

Mrs. Behn never achieved the ironic detachment, the crisp, elegant, indifference of the masters of the genre, but she aims many a pointed shaft at the follies of her day and her dialogue is fresh and vigorous. In Sir Timothy Tawdrey she draws one of the typical butts and laughing-stocks of the true wits of the age. He is the false variety, the sham gallant, the base imitation of an ideal of sophistication, who is 'fain to speak in the vulgar modish style of this damn'd Leud Town, and Railly Matrimony and the rest,' to the scorn and disgust of the real gentlemen of the play. There is a strong element of romantic intrigue still evident, however, and realistic scenes in a

MRS. APHRA BEHN
By Sir Peter Lely

Mrs ELLYN GUYN Miſtreſs of KING CHARLES II.^d

EPILOGUE to SIR PATIENT FANCY.

"That we have nobler Souls than you we prove,
By how much more we're sensible of Love.

Pub.^d del.   Publiſhed by Fielding & Walker Decem.^r 2 1779.   Cook.^e Sc.

LADY KNOWELL IN 'SIR PATIENT FANCY'

London brothel are incongruously mixed with blank verse despairs and heroic love-makings.

Sir Patient Fancy, given the following year, is a more uniform production and the best of her comedies of the 'manners' type. It is modelled largely on Molière, as are so many of the Restoration plays, but the plot is more intricate and the action more farcical. The play was produced with an unusually strong cast, including the two comedians Tony Leigh and James Nokes, for whom it provided such an excellent vehicle that it was a favourite in their repertory as long as they lived. A Mrs. Gwin played the part of Lady Knowell, though this was probably not the sprightly Nelly as a later engraving would have us believe. Nell Gwyn was by this time well established in her honorific position as mistress to the King and had left the stage for good, but her friendship with Mrs. Behn was sufficiently well known to give credence to the idea that she had acted in her play.

Mrs. Behn followed *Sir Patient* with a return to her favourite type of theatre — the comedy of romantic intrigue. The scene of *The Feign'd Curtizans, or, A Nights Intrigue*, is laid in Rome and the plot, entirely of Aphra's own devising, is one of those involved affairs that so much delighted her contemporaries. These complicated plots were evidently the cross-word puzzles of a day deprived of that form of intellectual stimulation, for it requires a lively attention and no little skill to unravel their intricacies. They are a direct descendant of the *commedia dell'arte* scenario, furbished up for the taste of the day, and Isabella Andreini would have found herself at home in them. *The Feign'd Curtizans* contains every ingredient the formula demands — several pairs of lovers, innumerable disguisings, girls dressed as men, sword-play, masques, music, mummery, love-making and slapstick, all combined in a quick-paced entertainment of which the text can give only the faintest echo.

Mrs. Behn dedicated this merry potpourri to Nell

Gwyn, 'infinitely fair, witty, and deserving,' in such ful-
some terms that it has often been quoted as a model of
dedicatory flattery in an age which could boast an astonishing lavishness in that particular form of log-rolling.
Read with others of its kind, it loses its preëminence,
though it proves that Aphra was as ready as Dryden or
any other writer of her day with the expected phrases of
flattery and adulation. Yet she could laugh at the custom, even while she practised it, and begins one of her
addresses to the reader with 'Dear, Sweet, Honey,
Sugar-Candied Reader — (Which I think is more than
any one has called you).' When it came to the serious
business of obtaining patronage, however, she could wield
grandiose compliments with the best of them, just as she
could storm at the fops in the playhouse pit, and mock
the affectations of poets, wits, and gallants in the railing
prologues and epilogues which were then in fashion.

The years between 1678 and 1685 were years of acute
political unrest. Plots against the King, the revolt of
Monmouth, the disruptive struggles between Whigs and
Tories, kept the country in a state of unrest bordering on
revolution. The political battles of the day were fought
in the playhouse as well as in the streets and taverns, and
where the plays themselves were not satiric or frankly
partisan, the prologues and epilogues were sure to be
barbed with political allusion. Aphra, ever an ardent
royalist, entered the arena with an adaptation of Tat-
ham's *The Rump*, which she called *The Roundheads, or,
The Good Old Cause*, and in which she mercilessly ridiculed
the conventicling hypocrites 'Whose cloak of Zeal Covers
the Knave that cants of Commonweal.' *The City-Heiress,
or, Sir Timothy Treat-all*, is also steeped in political satire,
and both plays, produced at Dorset Garden in the
winter of 1681–82, were received with enthusiasm by
largely Tory audiences. But the Whigs had their parti-
sans as well, and political first-nights were noisy affairs,
with victory to the most strident.

The Luckey Chance, or, An Alderman's Bargain, one of Aphra's most spirited, not to say wanton, comedies, was almost swamped by the clique whose disapproval was political rather than moral. Indeed, Aphra's sympathies threatened at one time to land her in prison. There is a warrant extant for her arrest for having by her writing 'committed Severall Misdemeanors and made abusive reflections upon Persons of Quality and also written... Scandalous speeches.' The abusive reflections were contained in an epilogue which she wrote for an anonymous tragedy, where she referred slightingly to the recently exiled Duke of Monmouth. That hopeful youth, natural son of Charles II and Lucy Walter, had just headed a rebellion against his indulgent father who in spite of his son's treachery would tolerate no satiric references to that erstwhile favourite. The path of politics on the stage, as in the world, was strewn with difficulties, and after this misadventure Aphra, though abating nothing of her loyalty to the Stuarts, turned her attention to the safer pastime of attacking Whigs and Puritans and amusing the 'distracted age' with farce.

The Emperor of the Moon was the last play of her own which Mrs. Behn saw on the stage. It is a rollicking adaptation of *commedia dell'arte* scenes and characters, welded into what critics have described as one of the best pantomimic farces ever seen. It was produced in March, 1687, with Tony Leigh as Scaramouch and Tom Jevon, 'young, slim, and most graceful of dancers, the king of all Harlequins past, present, and to come' in the two main rôles. Mrs. Behn had introduced Harlequin and Scaramouch into the second part of *The Rover*, where they spoke extempore in Italian and performed their familiar *lazzi*, but in *The Emperor of the Moon* they are more in evidence. The play held the boards for over a hundred years and was the precursor of many of its kind. Aphra wrote two other plays which were not produced till after her death. The scene of *The Widdow Ranter, or,*

The History of Bacon in Virginia, is laid in America, and shows Mrs. Behn's familiarity with a certain type of colonial whom she presents in no flattering terms. *The Younger Brother, or, The Amorous Jilt*, is in her usual vein of merry and romantic comedy. It deserved a better fate than the prompt damning it received at the hand of a prejudiced audience. Her other plays remained in repertory for many years and were long popular on the English stage.

Mrs. Behn's seventeen years of active association with the theatre came to an end with *The Emperor of the Moon*. In the prologue to this farce with which she closed her career, she traces with more spirit than poetry the successive stages through which the theatre, and particularly her own contribution to it, had passed during that time:

> Long, and at vast Expence, th' industrious Stage
> Has strove to please a dull ungrateful Age:
> With Heroes and with Gods we first began,
> And thunder'd to you in heroick Strain:
> Some dying Love-sick Queen each Night you injoy'd,
> And with Magnificence at last were cloy'd....
>   In humble Comedy we next appear.
> No Fop or Cuckold, but slap-dash we had him here;
> We show'd you all, but you malicious grown,
> Friends vices to expose, and hide your own,
> Cry, damn it — This is such, or such a one.
> Yet nettled, Plague, what does the Scribbler mean
> With his damn'd Characters and Plot obscene?
> No Woman without Vizard in the Nation
> Can see it twice and keep her Reputation...
>   Our next Recourse was dwindling down to Farce...
> Well this will be but nine days wonder too,
> There's nothing lasting but the Puppet show!

Her last words to the stage are conveyed in the Epilogue:

> And who would drudge for such a wretched Age
> That wants the Bravery to support one Stage?

Aphra, at any rate, was weary of the drudgery, ill, disillusioned, and unhappy. The last two years of her life were darkened by suffering and anxiety. 'I am very ill,' she wrote early in 1688, 'and have been dying this twelvemonth.' Yet in spite of pain and depression, her literary output in these last years was large. She had already published two books of poems and various Pindarics on royal events, such as the death of Charles II and the accession of James II. Now she turned her attention to the publication of her novels, writing a number during these years and bringing out those she had written before. *Oroonoko* appeared in 1688, while *The Fair Jilt*, *Agnes de Castro*, and six or seven other novels belong to the same period. She translated Fontenelle's version of Van Dale's *De Oraculis*, calling it *The History of Oracles and the Cheats of the Pagan Priests*, versified Æsop's *Fables* for an elaborate edition published in 1687, translated Fontenelle's *Theory of the System of Several New Inhabited Worlds*, and finally put into English verse the sixth book of Cowley's *Sex Libri Plantarum* and wrote an *Essay on Translated Prose* as a summary of her experiences and experiments in this line.

Several long poems also were published during these years, and Astræa's last effort was a Pindaric to Dr. Burnet who had inquired after her health during what proved to be her last illness. Through the conventional lines of this poem we see a reflection of the melancholy which overwhelmed the courageous Aphra in the last months of her life. Political as well as personal events had combined to darken her horizon. Always a staunch partisan of the Stuart régime, she lived to see its eclipse and the dawning of a new era. The world that she had known, in which she had won for herself an envied and happy position, had crumbled about her:

> The Brieze that wafts the Crowding Nations o're,
>   Leaves me unpity'd far behind
>   On the Forsaken Barren Shore,
> To Sigh with Echo, and the Murmuring Wind....

> Though I the Wondrous change deplore
> That Makes me Useless and Forlorn,
> Yet I the great Design adore,
> Though Ruin'd in the Universal Turn.

Poor Astræa had not long to live Useless and Forlorn. A month later, on April 16, 1689, at the age of forty-nine, she died. On a black marble slab marking her grave in the East Cloister of Westminster Abbey were inscribed these lines, written by 'a very ingenious gentleman, tho' no Poet':

> Here lies a Proof that Wit can never be
> Defence enough against Mortality.

Aphra Behn's wit has, indeed, barely succeeded in saving her writings from neglect and her fame from obloquy. Only in recent years has criticism shaken off the purely moralistic attitude and approached her writings with an open mind. Her latest biographers and editors have done much to rescue her from the Chamber of Horrors in which the Victorians had confined her, and set her once more in her proper place on the Restoration stage. That stage has disappeared from actuality, and with it Aphra Behn's plays which were so closely adapted to the needs and tastes of the theatre of the moment that they could not long survive its destruction. To-day we prefer a different order of bedroom farce. Mrs. Behn would undoubtedly be as horrified by some of the things she might see on our stage and in our moving pictures as Macaulay was by everything he read of hers. Nor should she be judged alone and without reference to the general tenor of her age. As Dryden pointed out, it was not only the Restoration stage that was licentious. The example of the Court and the life of the town was frankly pleasure-seeking and disillusioned. The playwrights were preoccupied with the æsthetics of gallantry rather than the ethics of love. Aphra, for all her looseness of tread, was far from being the worst offender, as even her sharpest critics have been forced to acknowledge, but the fact that she was a woman and yet failed in the pretty prerogative of her sex, and, 'instead of raising man to woman's moral standards, sank woman to the level of man's coarseness,' could not be forgiven.

The accusation of immorality was not the invention of Jeremy Collier or the special province of nineteenth-century criticism. It was one which Restoration writers hurled at each other with enthusiasm, and it formed the basis of repeated attacks on Aphra during her lifetime. She returned the charge with spirit, proclaiming that

> Her humble Muse soars not in the High-road
> Of Wit transverst, or Baudy-à-la-Mode.

And her assertion was endorsed by many of her contemporaries who looked upon her as the final arbiter in matters of poetic taste and elegant distinction. In the preface to *The Luckey Chance* she takes up the cudgels in her own defence with even greater energy. 'This one thing I venture to say,' she writes, 'though against my Nature, because it has a Vanity in it: That had the Plays I have writ come forth under any Man's Name and never known to have been mine, I appeal to all unbyast Judges of Sense if they had not said that Person had made as many good Comedies as any one Man that has writ in our Age, but a Devil on't the Woman damns the Poet.... All I ask is the privilege for my masculine Part, the Poet in me, to tread in those successful Paths my Predecessors have long thriv'd in, to take those Measures that both the Ancient and Modern Writers have set me, and by which they have pleas'd the World so well. If I must not, because of my Sex, have this Freedom, I lay down my Quill, and you shall hear no more of me.... I value Fame as much as if I had been born a Hero; and if you rob me of that I can retire from the ungrateful World and scorn its Fickle Favours.'

The obvious truth is that in the matter of license of scene and speech, as in so many aspects of Aphra's career, she made the most of the gifts she had, following the custom of the day, and reaping the reward of the moment, rather than branching out into any new forms of art. For all her protests, she could write a bawdy scene with the best of them, and as comedy was her forte and immediate success her object, it is hardly surprising that her plays, entirely devoted to amorous intrigue, should abound in scenes as nicely calculated to delight the courtiers of Charles II as they have proved successful in horrifying more staid and sober generations.

Aphra Behn's plays taken as a whole are to-day chiefly interesting in that they present an illuminating cross-section of Restoration drama. She touched on almost every phase of dramatic expression, from the extremes of Love and Honour grandeurs to the wildest kind of theatrical horseplay. If she has not survived, as Dryden, Otway, Etherege, Wycherley, and Congreve have survived, it is because she was prone to mix her mediums. Highly sensitive to the tendency and point of view of her day, she reflected too many contradictory attitudes to produce a clear-cut result. Her poetic vein was not sufficiently sustained to carry her into the finer flights of tragedy, where her sincerity and passion might have found its natural outlet.

Her comedy, where it follows Etherege in a reflection of the manners and customs of those around her, slips again and again into a fine frenzy of feeling that shivers the brittle artificiality of this type of play. A scene such as that in *The City Heiress*, in which Lady Gaillard, having been seduced in the usual airy manner by the typical gallant Wilding, returns to the stage with a sudden burst of Love and Honour emotions — 'Undone, undone! Unhand me, false, forsworn!' is distressingly out of keeping with the tenor of the play. We feel like echoing Wilding's own protest when his mistress indulges in this sort of rant: 'Do you bring me into your chamber to preach virtue to me — what other business can I have but Love and Rapture and...' Indeed, no one has any business in a thoroughgoing Restoration comedy unless he can be consistently gay and careless about sex. When Aphra allows sentiment to intervene, she spoils the picture. Her happiest creations are, in consequence, the pure comedies of intrigue, where the complexity of plot, the farcical treatment of underplot, and the complete artificiality of the situations evolved, preclude the possibility of taking the multitudinous couplings as anything but a merry jest. Willmore in *The Rover* is an excellent and completely successful exponent of the creed. He announces it roundly in his first exchange of amenities with the feigned gypsy Hellena:

WILL: Prithee, dear Creature, give me Credit for a Heart, for faith, I'm a very honest Fellow... Thy Lodging, Sweetheart, thy Lodging, or I'm a dead man.

HELL: Why must we be guilty of Fornication or Murder if we so much as converse with you Men? And is there no difference between leave to love me, and leave to lie with me?

WILL: Faith, Child, they were made to go together.

And again in conversation with his friend Belville who asks his help in adventure:

BELV: Will you not assist me?

WILL: I know not what thou mean'st, but I'll make one at any Mischief where a Woman's concern'd — but she'll be grateful to us for the favour, will she not?

BELV: How mean you?

WILL: How should I mean? Thou know'st there's but one way for a Woman to oblige me.

BELV: Don't Prophane — the Maid is nicely virtuous.

WILL: Why, pox, then she's fit for nothing but a Husband!

Here in a sentence is the Restoration creed, the Restoration comedy attitude, the formula for almost every

Restoration play, and no one knew better than Aphra
Behn how to weave a complex adventure about this
central theme. Her originality was less marked than her
ingenuity, but the results were equally entertaining to her
audiences. Perhaps her most distinguishing gift as a
playwright was her power of vigorous and racy dialogue.
She had a rich flow of verbal expression, a wealth and
appositeness of phrase, that makes it possible to read her
plays with pleasure to-day when theme and method have
lost their interest. The cadence of Restoration prose lost
nothing in her hands, though the speed and carelessness
of her composition can often be detected. There is an
exuberant vitality in her writing that shows a talent
worthy, perhaps, of better uses than that to which it was
dedicated.

Her poetry, too, indicates her latent power, even
though it falls short of any transcendent achievement.
In a day when every one wrote verse, Astræa's songs
stand out as the product of a true poetic vein, neither
exalted nor sustained, but genuinely lyric. Some of her
songs are truly lovely in the patterned, artificial style of
her choice. She had a delicate sense of the melody of
words, an easy, flowing fancy, and, though her verse
plays endlessly on the one theme of love and amorous
dalliance, it yet achieves at times a true grace and a
flowery perfection. Her poems, as well as her novels,
were extraordinarily popular both in her own day and
later.

She carried to the last extreme the sensuous, pastoral-
passionate descriptions, so dear to the 'refined age' in
which she lived. The same pen that could write the
crude scenes of *The Luckey Chance* or of *Sir Patient Fancy*
could pen the airy and sentimental trifles that fill *The
Lovers Watch* and *Lycidus*. Her variations on her theme
produced not a few lovely harmonies, which can well
bear the test of time. In the midst of much artifice and
conceit, we can hear again and again a true lyric note:

'Tis not your saying that you love,
Can ease me of my Smart;
Your Actions must your Words approve,
Or else you break my Heart.

In vain you bid my Passion cease,
And ease my troubled Breast;
Your Love alone must give me Peace
Restore my wonted Rest.

But if I fail your Heart to move,
And 'tis not yours to give;
I cannot, wonnot cease to love,
But I will cease to live.

Or this song in the vein of her *Voyage to the Isle of Love*:

Love in Fantastique Triumph satt,
While Bleeding Hearts a round him flow'd
For whom Fresh pains he did Create,
And strange Tyranick power he show'd;
From thy Bright Eyes he took his fire,
Which round about, in sport he hurl'd;
But 'twas from mine he took desire,
Enough to undo the Amorous World.

From me he took his sighs and tears,
From thee his Pride and Crueltie;
From me his Languishments and Feares,
And every Killing Dart from thee;
Thus thou and I, the God have arme'd,
And sett him up a Deity;
But my poor Heart alone is harm'd
Whilst thine the Victor is, and free.

It is difficult to detect the real Aphra under the Watteau mask of the singing Shepherdess, but now and again, as in the following stanza, her vivid, understanding smile is momentarily unveiled:

All calm and innocent I sate,
Content with my indifferent fate,

(A Medium, I confess, I hate.)
For when the mind so cool is grown
As neither Love nor Hate to own,
The Life but dully lingers on.
Thus in the midst of careless thought,
A paper to my hand was brought....

The verse was smooth, the thought was fine,
The fancy new, the wit divine.
But fill'd with praises of my face and Eyes,
My verse, and all those usual flatteries
To me as common as the Air;
Nor cou'd my vanity procure my care.
All which as things of course are writ
And less to shew esteem than wit.
But here was some strange something more
Than ever flatter'd me before;
My heart was by my Eyes misled;
I blusht and trembled as I read.

Here is the gay, the witty Astræa herself, never dull
nor indifferent to the passing show, writing her high-flown
tragedies, her romantic comedies, her naughty, ribald
farces, while she received a world of poets, fops, and
courtiers in her drawing-room; pricking the bubble of
flattery even while she welcomes it; calling a spade by
its most Anglo-Saxon name, or tossing off garlands of
luscious verse; laughing at the very affectations in which
she herself indulges, while with a vigorous and undaunted
courage she fights for recognition and reward as a poet
and playwright. There is a gallant courage in her career,
as in the high carriage of her head that cannot fail to
provoke admiration. She was a woman not supremely
gifted but supremely daring, one whose genius lay in an
acceptance of the world as she found it rather than in any
impulse toward its reformation or improvement. Thoroughly of her own day, she failed, perhaps, to transcend
it, and, as has been the fate of many a better man, the
evil that she did has lived after her. But whatever her

shortcomings, literary and human, Aphra Behn remains a striking figure in the annals of stage history. The first woman to attempt a professional career as a playwright, she has had, among women, few rivals and no superior in what Molière termed the difficult undertaking of making gentlefolk laugh. 'I take it Comedy was never meant for a converting or conforming ordinance,' she wrote in one of her prefaces, 'and I think a play is the best divertissement that wise men have. This being my opinion, I studied only to make mine as entertaining as I could.' In this modest ambition Aphra Behn was, in her own time, strikingly successful, and in spite of changing literary and moral tastes, remains to-day an admirable and engaging human being.

CHAPTER X

CAROLINA NEUBER

GERMANY'S PIONEER ACTRESS-MANAGER

SEVEN hundred years after the death of Hrotsvitha of Gandersheim, that first of women playwrights and patron saint of the theatre's arts, a Saxon girl, born within a hundred and fifty miles of Hrotsvitha's convent, ran away from her father's house and plunged into a career which was to change the face of the German theatre. If Herr Weissenborn had been less stern, or Frederika Carolina less pretty, if Frau Weissenborn had not succumbed at an early age to the too great trouble of living, or if Frederika Carolina had stopped with one, and not indulged in two, elopements from the arid prison which was her home, the story of the modern German stage would not begin in Leipzig in the year 1727. The theatre in Germany was so far behind that of the other European countries, it is perhaps fortunate Carolina's struggle for liberty landed her on the stage and that she there continued a fight for freedom so dramatically inaugurated in her father's house.

Frederika Carolina Neuber, *née* Weissenborn, known to the stage as *die Neuberin*, holds a unique position in the history of the European theatre. She did not have the genius of Hrotsvitha, the theatric gifts of Isabella, the golden opportunities of those companions of genius Madeleine and Armande Béjart, but she was as remarkable as any of them in that she was the first actor, man or woman, who made any serious attempt to reform the German stage. She had the intelligence, the imagination, and the courage to break away from the stale tradition of the theatre as she found it and to open it to influences that gave it new life. Her reforms were, indeed, so much needed and so radical that they brought about a development in the German theatre, which swept it, even in her own lifetime, far beyond her reach. Carolina's career is tragi-comic throughout, from her first frustrated elopement to her final pathetic end, but wherever we touch it, a dauntless energy is visible, a courage and determination which made possible the sudden shifting of the German theatre from its steady decline to an upward and onward course which placed it before long in line with the other theatres of Europe. Carolina Neuber gave it its initial impetus, and though not the first, she was certainly the foremost, of German actress-managers.

When the little Frederika Carolina was born in Reichenbach on the seventh of March in the year 1697, the very last thing that would have entered her mother's mind, when she recovered sufficiently to dwell on the possibilities of her daughter's future career, was the thought that the infant might some day become an actress. The theatrical profession in Germany at that time was not a career to be contemplated with enthusiasm by a worthy member of the bourgeois class. To be sure, one or two acting companies had earned a certain standing in the community, but the theatre as a whole was still in the dark ages of its development. From Hrotsvitha's time to the opening of the eighteenth century, it had followed in general lines the path trodden by the theatres of Italy, France, and England. Like them, Germany had had its period of religious drama, its classic revival, even its moment of native genius when Hans Sachs poured out his innumerable shrovetide plays and seemed about to inaugurate a living school of German comedy. The *commedia dell'arte* troupes had been welcomed on the one hand, the travelling English comedians on the other, but none of these sparks had kindled a lasting flame.

'Some of the chief products of humanity,' John Addington Symonds remarks in his study of the Renaissance, 'seem to require the coöperation of whole peoples working

sympathetically to a common end. Foremost among
these are architecture and the drama.' This happy state
of concentration and united effort had never come
about in Germany and the theatre had suffered acutely
in consequence. Germany was not a state, but a collection
of principalities and powers, distracted by wars, con-
quests, and rivalries, torn apart by religious factions,
pillaged by every brigand-dynast who could lay claim to
any part of its heterogeneous mass. Its course was
charted by such sign-posts of destruction as the Thirty
Years' War, the War of the League of Augsburg, and the
War of the Spanish Succession. It had no capital city,
no focus of intellectual and artistic life. Under the circumstances, it is hardly surprising that the theatre failed
to find itself.

In all this early history of the theatre in Germany,
women took very much the same part as they had in
other countries. We hear of them occasionally in mystery
plays, as in that tale of Till Eulenspiegel who made a
play at the Easter Fair wherein the one-eyed concubine
of the parish priest appeared, to the great scandal of all
beholders. They played occasionally in the later mystery
and morality plays and appeared in the pageants and
royal entries where their singing and dancing were
essential. Where the influence of the English actors prevailed, however, or where plays were given by students
at the universities, boys were cast in the women's parts.
There were boy actors only in the company assembled
by the Landgrave Maurice when he inaugurated the
first German Court theatre at Cassell in the early years
of the seventeenth century. Where Italian actors pre-
dominated, the way was prepared for actresses, and by
the time Carolina Neuber appeared on the scene, women
were accepted without question as part of the misera-
bly poor companies which managed to eke out a living
by travelling from town to town and from court to
court throughout Germany, performing those torrid

and inchoate pieces generally described as *Haupt-und-Staatsaktions* which were the best the country had yet produced in the way of native theatric fare.

These plays were devoted almost exclusively to tales of war, murder, martyrdom, and bloodshed. They depicted the trials and anguishes of pasteboard heroes and heroines with all the elaboration of machinery and display which the theatres could command. Tricks and wonders, fire-spouting dragons, devils in hell, storms, battles, whirlwinds, and prodigies were their chief ornaments. Their subject-matter, snatched bodily from history and myth and thrown on the stage with a sublime disregard of probability, ranged from *The Golden Apple Brought from Istria to Hyperborea* through *The Twelve Terrible Labours of Hercules* and *Queen Octavia's Love, Fall and Unhappy End* to that mighty show concerning the Asiatic Banise [1] — *The Bloody yet Brave Pegu; or, The Sun of the Realm brilliantly rising on the Asiatic Horizon in the praiseworthy person of the Asiatic Banise*, which was the most popular of all. These 'chief plays' were preceded and followed by farces and cowneries of the lowest type and were in themselves little more than dumb-shows and noise.

The life of the roving players of that day was arid and precarious in the extreme. They were outcasts from decent society, looked upon with contempt and even suspicion by the ordinary citizen. The cautious housekeeper locked up his plate when the actors came to town, and the pot-bellied burgomaster, eager enough to see the play and gossip with the players, men and women, when no one was looking, treated the company when it came cap in hand begging him for permission to play in the market-place or in the Rathhouse of his tiny domain, with the insolence accorded the gypsies and mountebanks with whom play-actors were inextricably associated in his mind.

[1] From Karl Mantzius: *A History of Theatrical Art*, vol. v.

It is obvious that the women of these companies had little chance of being anything but what the good burgomaster and his like hoped and feared that they were, rather bedraggled representatives of the world, the flesh, and the Devil. The few thalers the company managed to collect on its wanderings hardly sufficed to keep it alive. Playing was necessarily mixed with acrobatic and gymnastic displays, with all those tricks and tumbles which attract the groundling. Acting as an art was nonexistent, as a profession unsavory. Such a career would hardly have been one to which a loving mother, gazing for the first time on her newborn babe, would voluntarily condemn it, especially when the child was a flaxen-haired girl baby whose future charms were already foreshadowed in the flawless perfection of her complexion and the blue of her corn-flower eyes.

The fate to which Frau Weissenborn condemned her daughter by dying shortly after the baby was born and leaving her to the tender mercies of her father, who, so the neighbours believed, had driven his wife to her grave, proved in the end as harsh as the worst of players' lives, and Carolina revolted from it as soon as she could. She was a high-spirited and adventurous girl, impatient of restraint. Hers was not the temperament to submit tamely to paternal discipline. She found no pleasure in walking with downcast eyes and demure steps to and from the village church, in cooking and cleaning house, in serving her irascible parent and waiting patiently for him to choose a husband for her as old and domineering as himself.

Herr Weissenborn, barrister and judicial inspector of his district, gloried in his position and considered himself entitled to the most perfect obedience. He was of the same school of thought as two other German parents who, at about the same time, were achieving an unenviable immortality in the rôle of domestic tyrants. If we may judge Carolina's early life by what we know of the brutal and sanctimonious bullying to which Frederick the Great was subjected during his childhood — an infant martyrdom which began at the very moment that Carolina was making her break for liberty; or if we compare the Councillor Weissenborn of Zwickau to the far more famous Councillor Goethe of Frankfort whom he somewhat resembles, we can gain some idea of the stifling atmosphere of ill-natured scoldings and petty restrictions in which Frederika Carolina grew up. Her maturity, far from being retarded by the process of repression to which she was subjected, was greatly accelerated. At fourteen she had blossomed into a full-blown beauty whose charms proved irresistible to the young law-clerk, Gottfried Zorn, who was serving his legal apprenticeship under her father's stern rule.

The young people promptly fell in love with each other and carried on their affair in secret for some months. One day Herr Weissenborn had a quarrel with Zorn's mother; he used violent language, as was his wont, slapped her in the face, and ordered her son out of the house. There was nothing for the lovers to do but elope, which they did with all speed. Weissenborn started at once on their track. He advertised for the runaways as one would for escaped slaves, describing his daughter as 'not yet full grown, slender and fair.' He adds that the clothes she is wearing are quite ordinary, as she ran away from home late at night in the house dress she happened to have on at the moment. The young people were soon caught and brought back to Zwickau, where they were thrown into prison for seven months. The record of their trial remains as an arraignment of a brutal father, who, so the neighbours testified, beat his daughter with a dog-whip, deprived her of her clothes, and generally made her life miserable. Carolina herself maintained that he had connived at her affair with Zorn until it no longer suited his plans, and that she feared for her life if she returned to his house. When the prisoners were finally released, Zorn immediately disappeared, and Carolina, in spite of her fear, had no choice but to return to her home. There she remained for five years, suffering once more the brutalities of her unnatural parent, writing poetry in secret, and watching for an opportunity to make her escape once again.

The second attempt proved more successful. On this occasion she provided herself for good measure with two companions, one of whom, Johann Neuber, she married the following year. Together the three fugitives found refuge in the company of an actor named Spiegelberg, who had at one time been a member of the famous Velten company and now headed his own troupe of High German Comedians of World-Wide Fame. With her odd assortment of cavaliers, Carolina presented herself to 'Principal' Spiegelberg when he was playing the little town of Weissenfels in 1717 and had no difficulty in obtaining a hearing. The fact that she knew nothing about the theatre was compensated for by her physical charms and her natural good sense. In later years, Carolina Neuber tended toward a cheery rotundity, but in her youth she could boast an almost perfect figure. Tall and graceful, deep-bosomed, blonde and fresh, flaxen-haired as a Saxon beauty should be, with a pleasant, open expression, and a mouth touched even in repose by a half-formed smile, Carolina at nineteen could have won attention by her looks alone. But she was, in addition, far better educated and endowed with more intelligence than the average actress of her days. She stepped at once upon the stage, taking Johann Neuber with her, and began a career which was to lead her to the heights of professional achievement. The second young man, by the way, having provided the necessary margin of safety for elopement number two, disappears at this point from the scene, leaving the Neubers undisturbed in their lifelong partnership on and off the stage.

For ten years Carolina and her husband served their apprenticeship in various migratory troupes, learning in the hard field of experience just what kind of performances pleased the boorish and heavy-witted audiences on whose good pleasure it was their fate to attend. The whole condition of the German stage at this time became familiar to Carolina. She knew the poverty of its material, the lamentable lack of poetry, beauty, or order in the plays which formed the repertories of the travelling troupes. Above all, she became familiar with Hanswurst, that many times transformed Harlequin, Punch, or Pickleherring, who haunted the German stage and would let no performance go through without him. Like an incorrigible jumping-jack, he popped up between the acts of the most serious dramas. He played the fore- and after-pieces. He insinuated himself into the most unlikely situations, and finally he rioted through the tragedies where he did not belong, as impudently as through the farces which he had debased to his image. Oddly enough, he had been introduced into the written language by Martin Luther, who says that the name was generally applied to 'coarse, boorish persons who pretend to be wise, and yet speak and act in an unreasonable and clumsy way.' His chief portrayer on the stage was a certain Stranitzky, originally of the Velten troupe, who in 1708 crystallised the heterogeneous comic characteristics of this 'beery' clown and turned him loose on the German stage.

By the time Carolina had won a position of some small prominence in the theatre, Hanswurst was rampant. He epitomised everything that, as a woman of taste and sense, she objected to in the theatre as she found it. Like an evil conscience he haunted every play in which she appeared. All her efforts to develop her talent and improve her acting technique were frustrated by his incongruous presence and obscene fun-making. He was as disconcerting to the actors who appeared with him as he was distracting and objectionable to the more intelligent members of the public who attended the plays. After ten years of his company, Carolina was thoroughly disgusted with her inevitable companion-clown. She was equally discouraged by the general shiftlessness of production and by the lack of any literary or artistic value in the pieces she performed. Her years of training had developed her talents to the point where she was ready to embark on a new adventure. She needed only an inspiration and a cause to set her on her path, and these were suddenly thrust upon her by no less a person than Johann Christoph Gottsched, Master of Arts at the University of Leipzig and self-appointed redeemer of the German stage.

Gottsched was the dominant figure in the literary world of Germany in the first half of the eighteenth century. Born in Prussia in 1700, his fine physique and masterful disposition marked him at an early age as a preordained victim of Frederick William II's passion for soldier-making. He himself, however, had already chosen another path. He had no interest whatsoever in becoming a small cog in the Prussian war machine, and just as he was about to be swept into its clutches he made his escape to the neighbouring kingdom of Saxony and took refuge in Leipzig. There his native talents as a drill sergeant blossomed in a new field. He turned into a sort of literary Frederick William, organising, regimenting, drilling, and bullying the German language and German literature until it became a tool fit for the masterly uses of his successors. Just as Frederick William II prepared an army and a treasury with which Frederick the Great put Prussia on the map politically, so Gottsched prepared a weapon with which Lessing, Herder, Schiller, and Goethe could win for German literature an immortal fame. And even as Frederick William II was bitterly hated by his infinitely more distinguished son, so Gottsched was cordially despised by the men who succeeded him.

His pedantic and dictatorial approach to the mysteries of art, his complete lack of subtlety and intuition, his narrow-minded reliance on rule and measure, his fanatical adherence to the French school of pseudo-classicism, made him the object of bitter and scornful attacks by those who unconsciously benefited by his reforms. Lessing said that 'Hanswurst had more sense in his little finger than Gottsched in his whole body,' while Goethe, who went to see him in his old age, airily remarks that 'he is a fatuous old fool' and lets it go at that. Nevertheless, he rendered an incalculable service to German letters, and he was for many years the supreme arbiter of literary matters.

Gottsched went to Leipzig in 1725, and began at once his campaign of education. He pointed out to his students and to every one who would read his pamphlets that, while England could boast not only the great periods of Elizabethan and Miltonic poetry, but a vast body of post-Restoration literature and criticism as well, and Spain, Italy, and France had long since won their literary laurels, Germany as yet had contributed nothing of importance to world literature. He adjured his followers to study foreign models and improve their taste and language. Above all, he sang the praises of French culture, which shone in his eyes as the perfect example of refinement. He was not alone in his admiration for the literature and criticism of that country. France dominated the taste of Europe in the eighteenth century as Italy had in the sixteenth and seventeenth, and represented the height of civilisation as opposed to what Goethe called the 'hyperborean barbarity' of the little German states. Frederick the Great, only twelve years Gottsched's junior, worshipped French culture to such a degree that he would not allow German to be spoken in his presence. Gottsched's patriotism took the opposite form, and he devoted his life to the purification and refinement of his native tongue. He wrote innumerable treatises on grammar, rhetoric, the technique of versification, and the arts of composition. He believed that literature should be built according to rules — the French rules, of course — and that it should have as its object the moral and spiritual improvement of society.

The theatre was to be one of the chief weapons with which he hoped to mould public taste and bring about much-needed reforms. No branch of literary art was in worse case, and none more useful as a vehicle for propaganda. In 1724, he wrote a critique of a performance given by a travelling company which had come to Leipzig to play during one of the annual fairs. This pamphlet, called 'The Reasonable Censors,' is probably the first theatrical criticism in German and marks the moment when Gottsched first saw his future collaborator, Carolina Neuber. Watching her performance, and realising what a woman of her ability might achieve, Gottsched's ideas began to crystallise. He went to Hoffmann, then leader of the company, with suggestions for a reformation of the stage. Hoffmann received the idea coldly — he was sufficiently harassed as it was. The company, which he had just inherited from his wife, was disorganised. His stepchildren were quarrelling with him, and even Hanswurst with all his charms was not bringing in the necessary returns. The very thought of innovations terrified the struggling producer. He refused to listen to Gottsched's suggestions, and shortly after gave up the struggle altogether. The disbanded company re-formed under the direction of Johann and Carolina Neuber and a new epoch opened for the German theatre.

The moment Carolina found herself master of a company and in control of its destinies, she went at once to Gottsched and formed with him an offensive and defensive alliance for the betterment of the German stage. This was the first time in its history that the professional theatre had joined hands with the profession of literature. Talking eagerly to the pedantic but already influential young Master of Arts about plays and players, about the horrors of *Haupt- und-Staatsaktions* and the crimes of Hanswurst, about the beauties of the classic drama and the stupidities of the boorish public, Carolina felt herself part of the movement that was to transform Leipzig into the 'little Paris' of Goethe's day.

Supported by Gottsched's interest, she hoped to stage magnificent plays, give free rein to her taste for elaborate scenic effects, and create new rôles where her talents as an actress would have proper latitude. But where was she to find material for her ambitious dreams? How raise the standard of the drama when there was nothing to do it with? Her mentor had the answer ready. Translations of the classic French tragedies and comedies were to be used until native poets, stirred to emulation, should write native plays worthy of the approval of cultured native audiences. Gottsched's ideas and methods have been the source of much scornful criticism since his day, but as a matter of fact they were the obvious and inevitable outcome of the needs and the tastes of the moment and served the healthy purpose of stirring Germany from its isolation and provincialism to a consciousness of its true place in the literary firmament.

Carolina Neuber accepted Gottsched's programme with enthusiasm, and was soon at work training her company in the unprecedented efforts required for the staging of classic plays. Up to this time theatrical performances in Germany had been slipshod affairs. The actors had taken little trouble to memorise the formless prose of the old plays. They knew the type characters of their repertory and they improvised freely, but with the new dramas in verse, this was impossible. Parts had to be committed to memory and rehearsals attended. Carolina introduced some semblance of discipline into her troupe, insisting that they commit their lines to memory, speak them accurately, and give due emphasis to rhythm and measure. For the first time in the history of the

German theatre, stage business was worked out in detail. Carolina was as much interested in the movement and grouping of her actors as in their individual performance. She had the true director's sense for mass effects and was the first woman to earn a reputation for the way she handled her crowds.

The new plays were produced with as much splendour as the Neuber budget could afford. The enterprising directress had a particular fondness for scenic effects, and in her desire to make the new plays popular she spared no efforts to embellish her very modest stage. The classic plays were given, as was the custom throughout Europe, in what we would to-day call 'modern dress.' Cinna was played in periwig and ruffled shirt. Carolina decked herself in gorgeous full-skirted brocades and satins to play Iphigenia or Bérénice. Sometimes she was fortunate enough to be given the cast-off clothing of a noble patroness; sometimes through devious channels and the intervention of dark men in caftans and ceremonial curls, she obtained second-hand clothing and jewelry at comparatively small expense. The settings of the plays were more or less standardised: a drop-curtain with a palace painted in perspective, a garden scene with cut-out trees, a nondescript street scene which met every requirement and served alike for Athens or Amsterdam, were all that was needed. The travelling companies could not be too particular, and as there was no attempt at historic accuracy in costume or words, the background was less important than the clothes which displayed to best effect an actress's natural charms.

Carolina's original ideas of discipline and order extended even outside the theatre. She had seen enough of the free-and-easy ways of actor-folk and intended that her company should be distinguished for good behaviour as well as good acting. The young unmarried actresses lived in her house or under her maternal chaperonage. When they were not at the theatre rehearsing or acting,

they gathered in her sitting-room to sew on their costumes which were ever in need of a new ribbon, a new
ruffle, or the latest furbelow described in the *Mercure
Galant*, to talk and gossip and receive their friends under
her watchful eye. The young actors boarded with her
too. They ate at her table and helped her with details,
such as the making-out of playbills and the painting of
scenery. They were encouraged to work and were kept
away from the taverns and gambling-houses, while the
gospel of the New Theatre was preached to the assembled
troupe whenever the occasion arose. The company
boasted three or four excellent actors, among them
Gottfried Heinrich Koch, who, besides acting accepta-
bly in the classic French style, translated plays, wrote
poetry, and designed scenery; Johann Friedrich Schöne-
mann, who played comic parts and married Anna Rachel
Weigler, the ingénue of the troupe, and 'Little' or
'Handsome' Suppig, leading man of the company, who
was Carolina Neuber's lifelong friend and, according to
inevitable and quite unauthenticated gossip, her lover
as well.

Carolina Neuber was herself the mainstay of the
company. She was about thirty years old when she embarked on her adventurous efforts to reform the German
stage, a handsome, vigorous woman with a fine figure and
a commanding personality. She was of an impulsive,
even a passionate, disposition, throwing herself into her
rôles as into her causes and quarrels with an abandon
which was often effective but not always wise. Gottsched
said of her that she was 'not behind any French or
English woman in the art of acting,' a vague statement
dictated by his enthusiasm for an ally rather than by any
critical standard or experience. Lessing, on the other
hand, while not as admiring, gives a clearer impression of
her individual talents and interests. 'It would be unjust
to deny that this excellent actress has a thorough knowledge of her art,' he says. 'She has a masculine intelli-

gence and only on one point does she betray the weakness of her sex: she is too fond of trifling on the stage. All the plays of her invention abound in tricks and disguises, in finery, elegant clothes, and festivities. Everything glittering and marvellous delights her, but perhaps she understands her Leipzig audiences, and these things which I consider faults are merely her method of attracting the public.'

She was, in other words, in spite of her enthusiasm for the French neo-classic school, essentially a woman of the theatre, the theatre of her own day and time. Like Isabella Andreini, she played every type of rôle that a transition period provided. Not only was she the first German interpreter of such parts as Bérénice, Chimène and Phèdre, but she also played Armande Béjart's rôles, the Luciles and Célimènes of Molière, and the dainty, artificial heroines of Destouches and Marivaux. She appeared in every variety of comedy and in the pastorals and farces, musical interludes, and satiric skits with which her repertory was enlivened. Like Isabella, again, she played improvised as well as written plays — pieces such as that quoted by Mantzius, called *The Leather Seller of Bergamo*, in which 'Catheringen' appears successively as Pandolfo, Fräulein Hohlnätgen, a learned philosopher, Fräulein Hausgrath, a bandit, and finally as a poor woman with many children, in the true *commedia dell'arte* style. Like her English sisters, she was fond of appearing in male attire, and one of her favourite impersonations was that of the German university student in cap and knee-breeches, a penniless, care-free, dashing type of youth whose gaiety and high spirits Carolina interpreted with unfailing gusto. It was her versatility as well as her extraordinary enthusiasm and energy which made it possible for her to undertake so discouraging a task as that of reforming and revivifying the German stage.

Armed with an abundant faith, as well as a number of freshly translated plays, backed by a good company and

CAROLINA NEUBER AS ELIZABETH IN 'ESSEX'

Ich Strohfack stehe hier in Kupfer abgestochen,
Courage fehlt mir darauf will ich nicht pochen,
Doch was der Herren Gunst vergnüget Sinn und Hertz,
Ich bleib ihr Serviteur in Lustigkeit und schertz.

AN EIGHTEENTH-CENTURY HANSWURST

encouraged by her alliance with the literary dictator of
Leipzig, Carolina started out on her adventures. For
eight years she toured the principalities and dukedoms
of Germany, carrying the banner of the New Art and
preaching the gospel according to Gottsched. She gave
translations of Racine, Corneille, Molière, Destouches,
and the rest, to audiences which still preferred a coarser
fare. She overwhelmed them with a fearsome tragedy,
The Dying Cato, concocted by Gottsched from several
sources. She played the classic five-act tragedies with
commendable persistence and devotion. Her repertory
contained many excellent plays, all of foreign origin, of
course, for there were no German plays as good as the
French and English tragedies, but the effort to graft this
alien shoot on the hardy and resistant German stem was
infinitely discouraging. In the larger cities an audience
could be attracted for one or two nights; a few wealthy
patrons were discovered; but on the whole the response
was cold. Carolina, for all her devotion to the cause of
art, was a practical business woman. She had to support
not only herself, but her entire company, and she found
it quite impossible to do so on an undiluted classic fare.
And so Hanswurst is still found in her repertory, and the
old tricks and disguisings, the old mummery and magic
antics, were used to draw a public which remained
stonily indifferent to the sufferings of Phèdre or the
heroism of Rodrigue.

Yet, in spite of difficulties and drawbacks, the years
that immediately followed Carolina's association with
Gottsched were years of success. Her fame steadily
increased and her company was acknowledged the best
in Germany. By 1734, she had obtained several patents
and privileges and could describe herself in the high-flown
phraseology of the day as Directress of the Royal Polish
and Electoral Saxon Comedians as well as Principal of
the High-Princely Brunswick-Lünenburg-Wolfenbüttel
German Court Comedians. She played in Hamburg and

Leipzig during the great fairs, and travelled about to the smaller cities and the ducal courts when the season in the towns was less lucrative. The company was dependent during these travels on the favours of the rich, and the success of her entertainments often turned on Carolina's ability to ingratiate herself with the officers of the household in the local courts where she wished to play.

Sometimes her plans would be facilitated by the kindly attentions of a local dignitary. 'The musicians of the Ducal Court have consented to furnish the music for our play,' she wrote in triumph on one occasion; 'the Adjutant in Charge has ordered a troupe of soldiers to assist us, all carefully chosen of the same height, caps and shoes neat and clean. The men were as well turned out as though they had been appointed to serve some great gentleman.' Supers such as these must have been of great assistance in staging the older dramas of battle and sudden death which insisted upon appearing even in the purified repertory of the Neuber company.

Carolina further consolidated the patronage she secured from various dukes and lordlings by composing a number of odes and elegies in praise of this or that local prince, celebrating in pompous phrases an accession, a birthday, a wedding, or a funeral. When Princess Elizabeth of Brunswick-Lünenburg was sent off to Berlin to be married to Frederick the Great, then Crown Prince of Prussia, Carolina wrote her an ode, which for all its noble sentiments must have been poor comfort to that unhappy Princess. In addition to these occasional poems, Carolina concocted a number of short plays or *Vorspiel*, as they are called, which served as curtain-raisers before the main play of the day. In these skits she managed, very cleverly, to preach her reforms under the guise of allegorical dialogues. *The Origins of the Theatre, The Old and the New Styles, Those who Defend Wisdom against unWisdom*, are a few of the titles indicative of the tenor of the little play.

On one occasion she got herself into serious trouble by allowing her zeal for the cause and her exasperation with the slowness of public response to carry her too far. It was at the close of an unsuccessful season in Hamburg, and Carolina, forgetting for a moment that comedians in her age were the very humble servants of those who honoured them with their patronage, decided to tell her masters what she thought of them. She wrote a *Vorspiel* entitled *Conditions of the Drama During the Four Seasons*. This seemed harmless enough, but the play-bill in which she announced the performance contained slighting references to 'those who have not been able to see us, those who have not ventured to see us, or those who have not been willing to see us.' Such independence from a player, especially a woman player, was not to be toler-ated. The burgomaster, in the name of an insulted citizenry, closed the theatre, and Carolina had to depart with her unspoken comments burning in her heart.

The episode, though it failed to curb her impulsiveness, taught her a certain circumspection. In the preface to a *Vorspiel* given a few years later in Leipzig, at a time when the Neubers were fighting a rival player named Müller for control of the chief theatre of that important city, we see the doughty Carolina attempting to trim her sails, verbally, at least, and to present a meek and submissive front to her public. We can, however, read between the lines of this humble address, as we could in Hrotsvitha's own forewords so many years before, and see Carolina's vigorous personality masking behind the customary formula. Carolina the German does not dare speak with the frankness of Aphra Behn the English woman, but it is evident that she was moved by much the same spirit.

'Dear reader,' she says, 'here is something for you to read. To be sure, it is not written by a great, scholarly man. Oh, no! It is by a mere woman whose name you scarcely know and for whose station in life you have to look among the most humble of people, for she is nothing but a comedian. She cannot be responsible for anything but her own art, though she does know enough to understand another artist when he talks about his work. If you should ask her why she writes at all, her answer will be the customary feminine 'Because.' If any one asks you who helped her, you had better answer, 'I don't know' — for it may very well be that she did it all herself.

'The work is written in rhyme and those who understand such things will know whether the verses are good or bad. It has never been the author's aim to be known through her writings, but as an actress she has endeavoured to represent other people's passions in a conscientious, careful, sincere, and natural manner. Now, when she is obliged to play her own rôle before the whole world, she is by no means ashamed to have reproduced, in print, in these pages, her first personal appearance.

'If she has failed, she will not attempt to excuse her mistakes, since that will make them no better; she will merely beg forgiveness and try to do better next time. For the rest, she submits gladly to the judgment of those who think straight, who speak at the right moment and who know how to keep quiet when necessary. The others may think what they like, speak if they can and keep silent when they have to.'

In 1737, just ten years after she had started her campaign, Carolina felt herself strong enough to make a final attack on her old enemy Hanswurst. She had done a great deal to decrease his power, eliminating him from her genuine tragedies and relegating him to his own plays and to the skits and turns with which she opened and closed her programmes. Now she proposed to banish him completely from the theatre. Once more installed in her beloved Leipzig, from which Müller had temporarily dislodged her, and still in high favour with her 'sagacious' friend Gottsched, she brought out book, bell, and candle and prepared her final exorcism.

The deed was accomplished in a solemn *Vorspiel* from Carolina's own pen in which she herself, in the person of Thalia, wearing Minerva's helmet on her powdered wig and wielding Wisdom's spear in her strong right hand, attacked Hanswurst in an antique *pas de charge*. Thalia was attended by a goodly array of nymphs and Muses in looped skirts, low-necked, tight-fitting bodices, and high-heeled slippers. Hanswurst, quickly overcome and slaughtered by this silken army, was mourned by the Devil, a night watchman, Venus herself, and a crowd of petty rhymsters and ragged ballad-mongers, who carried him off stage while the Muses sang a song of triumph. Hanswurst, though dead, was not done for. As his friends removed him from the scene, he managed to make one last defiant and indecent gesture toward the audience, which, no doubt, applauded merrily, listening with small interest to a solemn funeral oration pronounced by no less a person than Apollo himself. 'Hanswurst is dead! Hanswurst is dead! There is no more Hanswurst!' warbled Carolina and her attendant Muses as the curtain was drawn on this historic scene, but, alas, Hanswurst had more lives than the proverbial cat, and before long he had insinuated himself once again into the empty corners of Carolina's repertory.

For Carolina continued to need that which she herself could not supply — sound and actable German plays which would interest her audiences and fill her theatres. After ten years of work, her main reliance was still necessarily on translations from the French, but these plays had never attracted the general public. From burgomaster to clerk, from prince to tradesman, German taste was more in sympathy with Harlequin than with Racine, and the result was that when Carolina wished to fill her theatre, she, like Aphra Behn before her, and many another since, was forced to 'dwindle down to farce.' Even in those circles where she might have hoped for more support, the courts and palaces of her ducal patrons, she was expected to give pretty pieces, ballets, pantomimes, and pastorals, the dainty, sentimental trifles which the French Court had made popular and which all Europe copied. In spite of these discouragements, Carolina continued stoutly to play her Polyeuctes and Mithridates, her Phèdres and Bérénices in the face of diminishing returns, but her exchequer could not stand the strain indefinitely, and when she finally quarrelled with Gottsched, the end of her career was at hand.

Gottsched began the trouble by demanding that the Neuber company perform Voltaire's *Alzire* in a translation made by his wife. Carolina had already used a very much better version, prepared for her by Peter Stüven, and she and her company had no desire to commit to memory a new set of verses for the mere pleasure of flattering Gottsched. An argument ensued which ended in a permanent break. To avenge herself, Carolina had the misguided idea of making fun of her ex-friend and former champion on the very stage where they had once worked together so harmoniously.

Her attacks took the form of a burlesque of Gottsched's ideas concerning costume, ideas with which Carolina had never agreed. She had joined him enthusiastically in the matter of regular plays, versified texts, French classic dramas, and the attempted elimination of Hanswurst, but when he insisted that classic plays should be acted in things resembling night-shifts, that Cæsar and Agamemnon, instead of being dressed in a slight variation of the latest fashion from Paris — high red heels, beruffled shirt, peruque, patch, snuff-box, and all — should wear strange garments unknown to civilised man and parade about in sandals, the suggestions had fallen on deaf ears. Now, in her annoyance with her former mentor, she decided to prove the absurdity of his scheme. She therefore staged the third act of his *Dying Cato* with costumes as prescribed by the author, even going so far as to make her actors wear pink tights under their flowing robes in order to create the illusion that their legs and feet were bare. The effect was pronounced ludicrous and even indecent by all the critics present and no one had anything but scorn and laughter for Gottsched's excellent suggestions which were at least fifty years in advance of the times.

A more serious attack on her old friend and present enemy took the form of a *Vorspiel* called *The Most Precious Treasure* in which she presented The Fault-finder, who was of course Gottsched, 'dressed as Night in a cloak spangled with stars, bat's wings on his shoulders, a dark lantern in his hand, and a crown of tinsel around his head.' The piece was a huge success and added a last load of bitterness to the disagreements between the two. Gottsched turned his own pen against the Neubers, and the fight spread to a general scrimmage in which Carolina was not the only one to suffer. From this time on Gottsched's power was broken and the dictator of German literature was ousted from his throne.

The results of the quarrel were in the end fatal for the Neuber troupe. Carolina made several attempts to re-gain her lost prestige. She went to Russia in the hope of finding a patroness in the Empress Anna, but when that sovereign died and a new set of favourites came into power, Carolina had to give up the venture. Thoroughly discouraged by this and several similar disappointments, she disbanded her company; but she could not bear to remain idle long and by 1744, she had once more called her actors and actresses together. They responded eagerly, and with her reorganised company she again toured the country, playing with renewed success in Frankfurt, Hamburg, Dresden, Kiel, and her other old haunts. Her companions were loyal and enthusiastic and Carolina could still command affectionate admiration and respect from her followers.

In spite of her split with Gottsched, Leipzig still remained her favourite abiding-place. Whenever she

appeared there her theatre was invaded by students from
the university, who were willing enough to give their
support to the pedantic professor's antagonist. The
young people of the town enjoyed Carolina's sallies and
admired her pretty actresses. Among the most assiduous
of these youths was a student of theology named Gott-
hold Ephraim Lessing, then about nineteen years old,
whose susceptible heart had been set on fire by the
charms of Fräulein Lorenz, the ingénue of the troupe.
He became a devoted friend of the directress as well,
haunted her modest salon and talked art, literature, and
the needs of the German theatre with her. His association with the Neuber company proved the turning-point
in his career. To the acute distress of his worthy parents,
his interest was permanently deflected from the Church.
For a while he dabbled in medicine, but in the end the
theatre claimed him. He began by translating foreign
dramas for the Neuber company and went on to the
writing of plays on his own account. In 1748, Carolina
performed his first comedy, *The Young Scholar*, written
some years before, and its success did much to fix him in
his new career. Though she may not have realised it at
the time, her dream of fostering a genuine German
theatre had finally materialised. Germany's first distinguished playwright and critic had made his bow under
her auspices.

This was her last period of comparative happiness and
success. Troubles, chiefly financial, accumulated at
every step. She could never learn to curb her extrava-
gances when it came to mounting a play or purchasing
costumes, and little by little she lost her hold on her
company. Again the troupe disbanded and its members
went their several ways. For a while Carolina appeared
in a Vienna theatre as a hired actress, but her style was
already out-moded and she had no success. She wandered
about Germany with Neuber, acting, teaching, and picking up a precarious living until a kind friend in Dresden

offered the impoverished couple a room in his house.
There the faithful and serviceable Johann Neuber died
after forty years of comradeship, leaving Carolina completely alone.

A year later, she was again homeless, driven out of this
last refuge by the accidents of war. Sixty-three years old,
ill, and almost destitute, she knocked at the door of a
peasant's house just outside the town of Laubergast
near Dresden. The man at first refused to take her in,
knowing her to be one of that dangerous breed of play-
actors, but in the end his kindness of heart conquered and
he received her in his house. There she died on November
30, 1760, maintaining to the end a dignity and kindliness
that won the hearts of the simple folk around her. Her
unwilling host had learned to love and respect her, and in
spite of the prohibition of the Church, managed to bury
her in a remote corner of the local graveyard. He had to
do it at night, lifting her coffin over the wall and digging
the grave himself, for the priest would give no sanction
or blessing to the burial of an actress. Sixteen years
later, a memorial was erected on the highway at Laubergast to Germany's first important actress-manager, the
innovator and reformer Frederika Carolina Neuber, who
had, as the inscription on the monument proclaims,
'introduced good taste on to the German stage.'

Carolina Neuber had done far more than this. She
had raised the standard of German acting by demanding
precision, care, and accuracy from her performers. She
had brought new methods of direction and new ideals of
production to the theatre, maintaining that a conscientious director must 'stand fast by her artistic purpose as
long as the means exist.' She had carried the dramatic
masterpieces of France over the length and breadth of
the German states, and finally she had proved that
actors and actresses were more than mere strolling
bohemians and could be the friends of, and co-workers
with, the writers and intellectuals of the day.

Her formal gestures, her declamatory style soon became absurd to a public which had at last, largely through her efforts, been aroused to a consciousness of the possibilities of dramatic art, but the German theatre owed her an incalculable debt of gratitude for having by her energetic, pioneering work swept it, in fifteen years, through those phases of development to which other countries had devoted fifty or a hundred. When Carolina took charge of her company in 1727, the German theatre was approximately in the condition of the French in 1600. Hanswurst was first cousin to Gautier-Garguille and his tribe. It would have been no mean task even for a man to purify, order, and discipline a stage so backward and corrupt and to prepare it to receive the impetus and inspiration of a new era. For a woman, particularly for a woman in eighteenth-century Germany, it bordered on the impossible. Yet Carolina Neuber accomplished the miracle, and for this feat she stands alone both in the annals of the German stage and of women's pioneering efforts in the arts of the theatre.

CHAPTER XI

LA MONTANSIER

A DIRECTRESS UNDER MARIE ANTOINETTE AND THE REVOLUTION

THE tiny theatre in the town of Versailles was crowded beyond capacity one late summer afternoon in the year 1776. Never before had so many dukes and marquises, so many counts and princes, so many beruffled gentlemen of the Court, and so many flounced and powdered ladies of high degree found their way down the narrow corridor of the little auditorium on the rue Satory, nor had its modest benches and boxes ever before been honoured by so resplendent a company. The stage-box on the left of the miniature proscenium had been draped in damask of blue and gold, hastily snatched from the property room for the occasion; wax candles, at vast expense, replaced the tallow dips in the pendent chandeliers, and behind the scenes hearts beat high in excited anticipation. Only a few hours before, word had come from the château that certain ladies of the Queen's immediate circle wished to see the play. The information was unofficial, merely a hint, but a hint sufficient for those who knew a young Queen's passion for the theatre, her love of incognito, and her special taste for rustic scenes.

The play to be performed was Favart's *Les Mois-sonneurs* — the very thing to lure abroad a princess enamoured of pastoral simplicities. When a little before five o'clock the royal box was invaded by a bevy of young women, all dressed in simplest white muslin gowns, organdy fichus pinned demurely across their breasts, sparkling eyes and laughing faces only half-hidden by wide straw hats, no one even pretended not to recognise among them the youthful Marie Antoinette escaping for

a moment from the chill indifference of her husband's
company and the watchful eyes of the dragons of court
etiquette.

The second act opened with a scene laid in the grange
of a country estate. The generous seigneur of the play
was seated at table, surrounded by his loyal peasants
and servitors. Before him stood a steaming tureen —
a huge bowl of cabbage soup which filled the theatre with
its plebeian but appetising odour. From the stage-box
came a delighted exclamation. 'Ah! How good it smells!
How delicious! I would gladly have a portion myself!'
A Queen, even incognito, could not be allowed to hunger.
No sooner had the curtain been drawn on the stage than
there came a knock at the door of the royal box. 'The
Directress presents her respectful greetings to Her
Majesty and would Her Majesty do her the very great
honour of tasting the player's humble *soupe-aux-choux.*'

Marie Antoinette turned and smiled. Curtsying low
before her was a plump, black-eyed woman dressed gid-
dily, but in the height of fashion. Under an enormous
pile of wig, decked with flowers and feathers, an eager,
intelligent face looked up at the Queen. The woman's
complexion was dazzling, an even white, which threw
into relief the thick arch of her inky eyebrows, the rich
curves of a sensuous mouth, and the mocking angle of a
slightly tip-tilted nose. Her voice was clear and assured,
touched with the warm accent of the South, a voice to be
remembered. On the threshold of the Queen's box,
Marguerite Brunet, known to history and the police as
La Demoiselle de Montansier, sank into the folds of her
silken skirt. In her hands — they were particularly
capable and sensitive hands, her one great beauty — she
held outstretched a bowl of cabbage soup.

So Mademoiselle Montansier, the first business manager and directress of the European theatre, makes her
appearance on the scene. Her gesture, at once theatrical
and canny, is typical of her career. She never failed to

take advantage of every accident that might serve her
purpose. The first woman to undertake stage management on a large scale, she owed her success to her quick
grasp of opportunity, the boldness of her imagination,
and the unscrupulous energy with which she pursued her
ends. Her astonishing career covers the most feverish
period in French history. Born seven years after Louis
XV came to the throne, she saw the disintegration of the
French monarchy under his successor, she weathered the
Revolution, the Terror, the First Republic. She knew
Napoleon; indeed, legend has it that she might have
married him. She witnessed his spectacular rise and his
fall, and finally died when her first friends of the Bourbon
dynasty were once again on the storm-tossed throne.
Through all these changing governments she carried on
her profession, producing plays, training actors, building
theatres, and inaugurating theatrical enterprises, while
she trimmed her political sails to the turbulent winds and
managed to keep alive to the ripe old age of ninety.

Before La Montansier's advent, a series of more or less
able actresses had served the French theatre with their
various talents. Madeleine and Armande Béjart had
shown the way, as we have seen, and a band of talented
actresses had followed their lead. For thirty years
Mademoiselle Duclos had stormed through post-Racinian
tragedy in all the glory of an enthusiastically bombastic
style. Adrienne Lecouvreur had come and gone, leaving
a memory of touching beauty, of simplicity and grace.
Voltaire's two great interpreters, Mademoiselle Dumesnil
and Mademoiselle Clairon, had contributed enormously
to the prestige of the French stage, and the latter had
inaugurated important reforms in costuming and technique. These and other distinguished actresses had taken
part in the deliberations and even in the direction of the
Comédie Française and had occasionally organised companies of their own in the provinces, but acting had been
their first and foremost interest. It remained for La

Montansier to establish management as a profession for women in France, and to prove that acting was not the only branch of theatrical art in which a woman could achieve success.

Marguerite Brunet was born at Bayonne and baptised there on the nineteenth of December, 1730, not long before Louis XV, who had married Marie Leczinska, daughter of the dethroned King of Poland, was to involve France in a war over his father-in-law's succession. The humble pin-maker of Bayonne, Jacques Brunet, and his worthy spouse Marie Capdeville, had little interest in these high affairs, except as the loves and wars of Versailles increased the intolerable load of taxation under which they struggled to achieve a bare living. Little did they dream that their daughter would one day consort with the grandchildren of the royal pair and walk familiarly in that fabulous world of pleasure and extravagance which Versailles epitomised.

Marguerite was only five years old when her mother died, and the little girl was promptly put into a convent, where she succeeded in acquiring a minimum of education. Her spelling, her grammar, and her ungodly ways do little credit to the teachings of the Ursuline Sisters, but Margot was probably a handful even at that early age. The next thing we hear of her is that she was taken to America by an uncle in the hope of being made heiress to a wealthy relative resident in those parts. The attempt was evidently a failure. The relative died, or the trip is apocryphal, as are so many of the legends clinging about La Montansier's name. At any rate, the first authentic information we have of her is that she was living in Paris in 1748 at number 12, rue Saint-Roch, nominally under the tutelage of her aunt, a certain Madame Montansier, dealer in second-hand clothes, but actually pursuing with success a profession to which her poverty, combined with her youth, her love of adventure, and her lively disposition, had inevitably conducted her. She was

known to the pleasure-loving gallants of the capital as
La Belle Béarnaise, and at the tender age of eighteen she
had already acquired a reputation for originality, wit,
and seductive charm which compensated for her lack of
classic beauty.

Marguerite was not long in acquiring a worthy and
solid protector, a certain Monsieur Husson, counsellor at
law, who took her to Martinique and set her up in a hat
shop in San Domingo. But she had already seen Paris
and had no intention of wasting her sweetness in the
colonies. The ladies of Martinique did not wear hats,
and the gentlemen, when compared to the Parisian
dandies, were no better than boors. In 1754, Marguerite,
who now called herself Mademoiselle Montansier, finding
the name more distinguished than her own, was back in
Paris, living on the third floor of a house at the corner
of the rue Saint-Honoré and the rue Neuve-du-Luxem-
bourg, and entertaining and being entertained by the
flower of the French capital — the gentlemen, that is —
who came to her apartment to partake of excellent sup-
pers, to gamble, flirt, drink, quarrel, and make love under
her hospitable roof. We have many details of her life as a
fille galante, for the chief of the Paris police, mindful of his
duties to his sovereign, provided Louis XV with a detailed
account of the less reputable doings of his subjects. From
this source we know that La Montansier returned from
Martinique with a small retinue, went about the narrow,
ill-paved streets of Paris in a hired coach attended by
two huge Negroes dressed in blue livery. A lackey and
two serving-women made up her household, and she lived
with all the appearance of a luxury for which she managed
to pay not a sou. We know that she had a series of titled
lovers, the marquis de Duras, Monsieur de Saujon, who
introduced her to the duc d'Orléans, with whom she had
supper on several occasions, the comte d'Esparbès, the
marquis de Ximenès, the young duc de la Trémoille, and
many more.

After ten years of this sort of life, Marguerite decided that it was time to settle down to a more stable profession. Her latest lover, a young noble named Saint-Contest some seven or eight years her junior, was ready to set her up in any business she desired. Marguerite had always loved the stage. During her years in Paris she had haunted the theatre. She had witnessed the début of Molé and of the charming Doligny. She had watched Voltaire's growing fame, had argued about his reforms in play-writing, acting, and *mise-en-scène*, she had seen the banishment of spectators from the stage of the Comédie Française and witnessed the agitating moment when Clairon appeared for the first time without the traditional exaggerated pannier which, like the ostrich plumes on the hero's head, was the accepted style of tragic costuming. She had been present when Voltaire's *Tancrède*, superbly played by Lekain and Clairon, had swept the classic unities from the stage and fired Paris to a frenzy of enthusiasm. She went to the Opéra and admired the innovations which Mademoiselle Sallé had introduced with so much difficulty, she saw the Italian players and enjoyed the farces and comedies at L'Ambigu Comique and the Théâtre Nicolet.

Slowly the idea took possession of her that, though she could not act — one or two abortive attempts had proved the point — she could and would manage and direct. At her instigation, Monsieur de Saint-Contest secured a theatre for her at Nantes, where her career began modestly enough. Here she made her first attempts at management and may have acted a little with her own company, but the provinces could not satisfy her for long. In 1768, Saint-Contest obtained permission for her to go to Versailles, the heart and centre of monarchic France, and there she rented the little theatre in the rue Satory, where she was destined, some eight years later, to meet and welcome her Queen.

Once established in Versailles, Mademoiselle Montansier went vigorously to work to consolidate and improve her position. To succeed at Court under Louis XV, patronage and influence were essential. Every move, even in the most legitimate business, was a matter of privilege, to be secured by bribery, intrigue, and corruption. In all this La Montansier was in her element. She cultivated her worldly friends, her ex-lovers, her dukes, marquises, and counts. She curried favour with the duc de Duras and the other Gentlemen of the Bedchamber whose prerogative it was to direct all theatrical enterprises. She paid court to the King's mistress, the all-powerful du Barry, and obtained her favour and assistance. At the same time she justified her demands by devoting herself to improving her theatre, producing such excellent and entertaining plays that little by little the courtiers began to find their way to her tiny playhouse.

Even at this early date, hampered by an inadequate equipment and a total lack of funds, La Montansier proved her capabilities as a directress by producing new plays and introducing new players, actors, actresses, and singers destined to long and honourable careers on the stage. Fleury was the most distinguished of her early theatrical finds, and he became in time a leading light in the Comédie. An excellent actor, very handsome and a great favourite with the ladies, he was already at the age of eighteen something of a spark. The *Mémoires* which bear his name contain some lively anecdotes of these early days at Versailles as well as a vivid description of his first directress in action:

'La Montansier was a charming woman,' he tells us; 'meridional in every sense of the term, in accent, gesture, and feeling. She was not young when I knew her, but endowed with something better than youth. Provocative rather than pretty, possessing a natural rather than a cultivated wit, she permitted herself every liberty of speech, and was in consequence often very amusing. In her relations with her artists this famous directress was always kind — she was also just, as far as her quick temper would permit, but she had no sense of order. I cannot imagine when she took time to rest. She gave her days to her work and her amusements — her nights she spent gambling, a taste which amounted with her to a passion.' A vice, it might be added, which she shared with most of her contemporaries from Marie Antoinette to Fleury himself!

Her apartment in Versailles was the rallying-ground of the dissipated young men of the day, as it had been in Paris, but while she gambled, intrigued, and plotted for the amusement of her guests, she worked steadily for her own advancement and the forwarding of a scheme dear to her heart — the building of a theatre which should be adequate to house her increasingly distinguished audience and which should provide a stage and appurtenances suitable for the plays and operas she planned to produce. The devious paths by which she finally obtained her object are too intricate to relate. She was on the brink of success when Louis XV died and she had to commence all over again with a new set of courtiers and favourites.

Only the most energetic determination could have carried her through the obstacles which barred the way and brought her finally to that glorious moment when Mademoiselle de Montansier — the particle slipped in on such elegant occasions — opened her new theatre on the rue des Réservoirs, with Louis XVI and Marie Antoinette in the royal box and all the Court in attendance. This did not take place till 1777, a year or more after the episode of the cabbage soup, and two years after she had been granted the exclusive privilege of giving plays in Versailles, Marly, Fontainebleau, or wherever the Court might be established.

The opening night of the new Salle on the rue des Réservoirs was a gala occasion. The theatre, which is still in use to-day, had been built by Boullet, builder and machinist of the Opéra, from designs by Heurtier, archi-

tect to the King. The decorations, in the most elaborate
and flamboyant taste of the period, had been executed by
Bocquet, also of the Opéra staff, so that no detail of gilt
and colour, no cupid, garland, nymph, or goddess, was
wanting to its splendour. The play, Piron's *Métromanie*,
was preceded by an allegorical piece in verse written by
a young poet of the Court, Joseph Aude, who was later to
become famous as the creator of Cadet Rousselle. In this
fore-piece Apollo, in a golden cuirass and jaunty kilt, surrounded by the Muses appropriately apparelled in enormous looped and draped overskirts, their white bosoms
gleaming, their wigs sculptured to incredible forms, dedicated this new temple to the arts, nor did he forget the
manager of the glorious enterprise:

> Muses, vous n'oublierez jamais
> Celle qui vous élève un temple...

The house applauded enthusiastically — Marie Antoinette was delighted with her new toy. When a covered gallery, running along the reservoirs from the palace
to the playhouse, made it possible for her to reach the
theatre without going out of doors, the Queen attended
every performance. La Montansier, witty, gay, a great
raconteuse, and an experienced courtier, amused the
Queen and was given the privilege of the 'petit lever,'
where she retailed such gossip as might entertain her
sovereign and curried favour with a light-headed and
warm-hearted Queen. 'The theatre, that convenient and
endlessly diverting resource of superficial minds, was the
main subject of conversation at Court,' Madame Campan, Marie Antoinette's first Lady of the Bedchamber,
tells us in her *Mémoires*. 'It was talked about habitually
in the Queen's *boudoir*.'

Marie Antoinette not only went to the theatre and
demanded constant amusement, diversion, and novelty
from her directress of entertainments, she played at
acting as well and was not unwilling to receive instruction

from so experienced a teacher as Mademoiselle Montansier. This intimacy of a much-observed and criticised sovereign with a woman whose character, conduct, and openly scandalous life were notorious, was one of the many imprudences which led Marie Antoinette to her destruction. It is not necessary to believe the filthy implications of the libellists to realise that La Montansier, with all her dashing capabilities as a business woman and manager, was not a fit companion for the Queen.

Mademoiselle Montansier's privilege, as directress of theatrical enterprises 'à la suite de la cour,' was far from being a sinecure. The twelve years during which she held it were crowded with enterprising and novel undertakings. Not content with running the theatre at Versailles, at Fontainebleau, and Marly, she obtained a privilege for the North, and built and ran theatres in Le Havre, Caen, and Rouen. During the summers she took her company on tours, playing in Normandy and in the Loire, at Orléans, Tours, Angers, and Bordeaux. Finally she evolved a magnificent scheme, which shows that she was not behind modern captains of industry in her conception of the possibilities of trusts. She wrote a Memorial addressed to the baron de Breteuil, drawing attention to the fact that the Paris Opéra was costing the King a subvention of 150,000 livres a year. She undertook to pay this subvention herself in exchange for the privilege of controlling all the theatres in France. She aimed at nothing less than a national theatrical monopoly, and she worked out a scheme which would coördinate all the different provincial theatres without interfering with their liberty and independence. Her petition was not granted as more serious matters were then occupying the powers about the throne, but her plan still exists to bear witness to her enterprising imagination as well as to her soaring ambition.

In the mean while the theatre at Versailles continued its successful career. The Queen was an exigent mistress

LA PETITE LOGE
By Moreau

THE FOYER OF THE THÉÂTRE MONTANSIER IN THE PALAIS
ROYAL ABOUT 1796
From an engraving by Bovinet after Binet

and demanded variety, as well as quality and quantity,
from her players. 'There were often two performances
in the same day,' Mademoiselle Campan records.
'Grand opera, French or Italian comedy at the usual
hour, and then, at eleven o'clock at night, we would go
back to the theatre to see parodies and skits in which the
leading actors of the Opéra took the most absurd parts
and wore the most extraordinary and bizarre costumes.'

From the beginning of her career at Versailles, Mademoiselle Montansier essayed every form of theatrical
enterprise. She put on Ducis's softly sentimental version of *Hamlet*, very popular at the time, and produced a
whole repertory of tragedies old and new. When de
Belloy's *Pierre le Cruel* failed on its first production in
Paris, she transferred it to her theatre and brought it out
with striking success. Little by little the theatre on the
rue des Réservoirs began to earn a reputation, not only
for the excellence of its productions, but for the originality of its material as well. Its directress discovered
and brought out a number of plays which were afterwards taken over by the Théâtre Français, among them
l'Héloïse anglaise by her young friend, Joseph Aude, a
drama which caused much excitement because of its
supposedly subversive material. It showed a child in
revolt against parental authority, and the conservative-
minded condemned it, while the younger generation of
the moment were loud in its praises. Revolt was in the
air and found its way even into the loyal fastness of the
Queen's favourite theatre.

On the whole, however, Mademoiselle Montansier's
performances were such as would please a court that was
dancing its way in silks and laces into the very jaws of
destruction. Not for her such plays as Beaumarchais'
Le Mariage de Figaro, which was making the rounds of
château and hôtel in manuscript and eliciting the enthusiastic admiration of the very nobles whose death-
knell it sounded. Mademoiselle Montansier was at the

moment in hot dispute with Beaumarchais on the subject
of authors' rights. As a directress she opposed his efforts
to secure proper payment for writers from the provincial
theatres where their works were pirated. Perhaps her
personal disagreement with him accounted for the fact
that her friend, the comte d'Artois, brother of the King,
turned to the actors of the Comédie Française rather
than to hers when he wished an unofficial performance of
the ill-omened *Mariage de Figaro* to be given. It was
finally produced in Paris in 1784, but La Montansier had
no share in this the first play of the oncoming Revolution.

She produced almost exclusively the pastoral, Ital-
ianate, highly artificial comedies whose titles alone are
enough to suggest their style: *La Coquette corrigée,
La feinte amour, Les folies amoureuses.* The plays of
Marivaux, Regnard, Dancourt, and Destouches were in
her repertory, which was further enlivened by excursions
into pure farce. She engaged Volange to play his famous
rôle of Janot at Versailles so that the Queen might see his
rough-and-tumble farce which was making such a stir in
Paris. It became as much the rage at Court as it was in
the capital, and Marie Antoinette presented busts of the
actor to her intimate friends as marks of particular favour.

In addition to her own productions, the astute directress imported special attractions from Paris — opera
singers, dancers, actors, and musicians. She brought over
an entire troupe of Italian singers from the Haymarket
in London to give grand opera at Versailles — the best
opera company that France had yet heard. They made
such a success that the theatre receipts were doubled and
Mademoiselle Montansier more than made up her year's
losses by this clever piece of business. One of her greatest
triumphs was the production of Dubuisson's *Le Roi
Théodore à Venise* with music by Paisiello, a gay and tuneful operetta, with Mademoiselle Lillié, that 'sweet nightingale,' in the leading rôle. The Queen was enchanted,

the Court in raptures, all Paris rushed to Versailles to see it.

'The execution of the grand finale of the second act was perfection,' a critic in the *Mercure de France* for March 3, 1787, tells us, 'not only on account of the precision and excellence of the *ensemble*, but also and more especially because of the way the whole scene has been conceived, the continuous movement of the actors, carried out without confusion and without distracting attention from the scene.' Mademoiselle Montansier was one of the first directors to understand and make use of crowd effects.

If her professional occupations were arduous and distracting, her private life was no less hectic. Besides her necessary attendance on the Queen, her endless pursuit of the Gentlemen of the Bedchamber for political influence and advancement, her duties as manager, playreader, directress and mistress-in-chief of a complicated organisation, she continued to hold her receptions in her apartments on the second floor of her theatre in the rue des Réservoirs and to carry on the strange and harrowing romance that ran like an undercurrent through her busy, distracted life.

When Mademoiselle Montansier went to Nantes to begin her career in the theatre, she met and fell in love with a handsome young actor named Honoré Bourdon, known on the stage as Nœuville or Neuville. She evidently really loved this man, who was a second-rate actor and something of a brute and a bully. He caused her endless anguish and anxiety by the violence of his temper, which often led him into disgraceful rows. On one occasion he was arrested for beating up a creditor who came to him for money; on another he nearly killed La Montansier herself. The imprudent woman had gone to the door of his apartment, which was in the theatre near her own, one night when he was entertaining a rival beauty. Neuville, at her knock, opened the door a few inches, thrust out his arm, and stabbed her savagely several times before she could get away. The affair caused a terrible uproar, but apparently the lady forgave both infidelity and assault, for when he fell into even more serious trouble a few months later, she rushed at once to his assistance.

This second stabbing affray took place in Rouen, where Neuville had been put in charge of Mademoiselle Montansier's theatre. Things were not going well, and he was extremely unpopular. One day a barber's assistant was shaving the irascible actor, when suddenly a quarrel broke out between the two men. In the scrimmage that followed, each wounded the other and then each accused the other of beginning the attack. Public opinion was against Neuville, and he fled the country. He was condemned to be broken on the wheel in effigy, to perpetual banishment, and the payment of a heavy fine, but thanks to Mademoiselle Montansier's untiring efforts a pardon was finally obtained, and after three years of exile Neuville returned once again to the fold.

La Montansier herself was often in difficulties, but they, being of a legal-pecuniary nature, were less sanguinary. Her whole career was strewn with lawsuits, with attacks and counter-attacks, processes, distrainers, and arrests. Her business system consisted in the excellent scheme of paying as few of her own debts as possible, while she harried those who owed her money by every method at her command. Occasionally she was caught in her own toils. Her quick tongue also got her into trouble, and once, even during the days of royal favour, she was thrown into prison on a *lettre de cachet* for some rash remark which was repeated to the King. The anecdote, recorded in the *Chronique Scandaleuse*, is typical of the stories current concerning La Montansier: 'When the King ordered her to prison, her first remark on seeing herself actually shut up between four walls was characteristic: "Will I then really have no company here, and does the King absolutely insist that I sleep alone?"' The

King, so the reporter tells us, was the first to laugh over this brazen sally; the Ministers laughed, too, but they thought it best to keep the lady in prison for a while. When she finally obtained her release, she was reinstated in her place as directress of court theatres and everything continued as before.

Outside the theatre, however, the horizon was darkening. Bankruptcy menaced the country, famine, fear, and discontent were abroad. In 1789, the King was forced to call the nation to his assistance, and in a whirl of excitement, hope, oratory, and polemics the States-General gathered at Versailles for the first time in a hundred and seventy-five years. The astute directress of royal amusements watched the trend of the times and made provision for the future. The once popular and adored Queen was no longer the source of all good things. She had become the scapegoat of the monarchy. On her head the people, still clinging to their ancient loyalties, heaped the onus of all the Bourbon sins, of all the graft and greed and cruelty of a social system tottering to its fall. The tide had turned against her, against Versailles and all it represented.

As early as 1785, La Montansier had had in mind a descent on the capital. She was at the gates of Paris, and she longed to direct a theatre in that seething and theatre-loving capital. It was impossible, of course, for her to do so, as the Théâtre Français had a monopoly of drama and the Académie de Musique of opera and ballet. Three other playhouses had managed to obtain limited concessions, and the theatres of the fairs played in spite of lawsuits and prohibitions, but La Montansier knew the difficulties of braving rights of the Comédie, and she therefore began negotiation for the little Théâtre des Beaujolais for the ostensible purpose of founding a school for child actors and actresses. In 1788, she succeeded in buying the eleven arcades in the Palais-Royal which contained this theatre as well as the apartment in which

she was destined to spend the rest of her long life. The
sum she paid for this property, 570,000 livres, was enormous, but La Montansier was a wise business woman and
knew what she was doing. She had found a place for herself in the very heart of Paris, which was the heart of
France itself. She could not possibly have foreseen the
events of the next five years — no one did; but she had
sensed the importance and growing power of the city and
she established herself in the strategic centre of events.

The cafés and gardens of the Palais-Royal were the
seed-bed of the Revolution. Clustered around the tables
reading the endless stream of inflammatory pamphlets,
and exchanging the latest news and rumours, the talkers
and 'patriots' who brought about the great change
swarmed in its gardens and arcades. Was La Montansier
in her apartment on that twelfth of July, 1789, when
Camille Desmoulins, rushing from the Café de Foy,
'sibylline in face, his hair streaming, in each hand a
pistol,' leaped upon a table under her windows and
shouted the battle-cry of the people — 'Death or
Deliverance — To arms! To arms!' — and led the mob
into that first act of revolt — the storming of the Bastille
on the fourteenth? She was probably not in Paris at the
moment, though she already owned the buildings and was
planning her occupancy.

We know, from a Memorial drawn up many years
later that she was in Versailles in September when the
Regiment of Flanders was fêted by the officers of the
Guard, to the great scandal of the people, she averred
that she had refused to allow the Guard to use her
theatre for their banquet. She was also there when, in
October, the mob of women from Paris marched on the
château and demanded bread of the King and Queen.
'I offered them my theatre as a refuge,' she tells us, 'and
they spent the night there. They were given food and
also some amusement — for there were violins as well.'
Let us hope that La Montansier's efforts in behalf of

that starving army of furies were not only patriotic, but tinged also with a last loyalty to her royal patrons. The food and music she gave the 'brave citizens of Paris' may have been designed to soothe the savage breast, as well as to comfort and succour the mob. On the following day, the women carried the Baker, the Baker's wife, and the Baker's boy off to the capital, and La Montansier followed shortly after, establishing herself in her little theatre by right of her royal patent, but with a wary eye on the Republican tastes and prejudices which raged around her in her new abiding-place.

Her theatre was very small, having been built for marionettes, so that at first she was unable to mount her plays and operas in the manner she desired. In 1791, however, she was able to achieve an almost miraculous transformation of her scene. The theatre, greatly enlarged and embellished, was made to seat thirteen hundred people, and given a stage, which, though small, was built for adults and not for dolls and children. Here, with the new liberty granted to all theatres by decree of the National Assembly in January, 1791, La Montansier and Neuville embarked on a series of productions including every type of theatre. They mounted opera in French, put on again *Le Roi Théodore* which had been such a success at Versailles, and staged any and all of the classic repertory now for the first time thrown open to all who wished to use it.

Their company, which was excellent, was reënforced by actors from the Théâtre Français, their singers were so very good that the Academy of Music became increasingly jealous and inimical. Grammont and the Sainval sisters played for them. Mademoiselle Mars, destined to become one of the most famous of French actresses, made her début under their direction. The Théâtre Montansier was a great success, but its directress was in constant danger. The storms that swept Paris and all France with war, revolution and sudden death, swept

in and out of the theatres as well, and no one was safe
or at peace for more than an hour at a time.

With her former royal patroness a virtual prisoner at
the Tuileries and, after August, 1792, an actual prisoner
in the Temple, La Montansier was the target of endless
accusations, personal libels, and political intrigues. She
was accused of hiding arms in the basement of her
theatre, of forwarding royalist plots, of every imaginable
form of *incivisme*, past, present, and to come. One
method of protecting herself, a method entirely in keeping with her tastes and habits, was to hold open house for
all the leaders of the day. No sooner had she established
herself in her quarters over the Café de Chartres than she
began to receive in her salon and in the foyer of her
theatre all her friends and acquaintances of every shade
of political opinion or no opinion at all.

During the first years of the Revolution, politics and
the theatre were curiously entangled. The actors and
playwrights were propagandists and pamphleteers, the
politicians and demagogues were actors, ranting through
the most bloody of melodramas. The theatres everywhere were battle-grounds of opinion. In Mademoiselle
Montansier's salon the two worlds mixed amicably
enough, discussions of impending uprisings in the Paris
clubs alternating with criticism of the latest play. On
one side of the room Talma might be heard complaining
of his treatment at the hands of his comrades of the
Théâtre Français, who in the teeth of public opinion
had closed the run of *Charles IX* because the Paris mob
had made it a rallying-ground of republicanism. On the
other, Hébert might be found, plotting an uprising in the
Cordelier or planning a new denunciation to be delivered
from the Tribune on the morrow. The lovely Contat,
creator of Suzanne in the *Mariage de Figaro* and leader
of the conservative element in the Comédie, was a friend
of Mademoiselle Montansier and often came to her
salon. Laya and La Harpe were there, and Saint-Just,

carrying under his arm the manuscript of his latest play.
Beaumarchais himself, forgetful of his disagreements
with his hostess, might come in, eager to discuss the
rights of authors and the rights of man with Fabre
d'Églantine, Dubuisson, or Chenier. Marat, Danton, and
le père Duchesne were her guests as well as the duc
d'Orléans; Volange, the comedian, and Vergniaud, killer
of kings; Collot d'Herbois and Tallien, Saint-Georges and
the duc de Lauzun — the most astonishing collection of
conflicting opinions and brooding enmities, united for a
moment under La Montansier's judicious eye, and all
alike seeking relaxation from intensities in the pleasant
company of pretty *cabotines* and the amiable ladies of
the opera and ballet.

Without joining any party, La Montansier received
them all. But love intrigues are sometimes more dangerous than politics, as she was to find to her cost. One day
she received a curt note from a certain pale and passionate gentleman whose suit for the favours of one of her
young actresses she had inadvertently obstructed. 'Citi-
zeness,' the ominous missive ran, 'it is said that the wit
of France has taken refuge in your theatre; see to it that
it is not used to mock me. And, further, if I respect your
pleasures — respect mine! I have few enough in the
midst of my grave responsibilities.... Robespierre.'

The Incorruptible had spoken! La Montansier realised
that it was time for her to make some spectacular demonstration of her patriotism. With the allied armies and
the *émigrés* massed on the frontier, France was seriously
threatened, and in July, 1792, had been declared 'in
danger.' Closing her theatre and rallying her staff
around her — actors, dancers, singers, musicians, and
mechanics, to the number of eighty strong — La Montansier presented herself at the bar of the Legislative
Assembly and asked that her company of volunteers be
sent to the front. The gesture was accepted with shouts
of enthusiasm and a rising vote of thanks and commen-

dation to the directress. The actor-warriors were des-
patched to barracks and then actually sent forward under Neuville's command. This irascible bully had been a
very genuine Republican from the beginning. He started
to the wars with enthusiasm, but got no farther than
Rheims, where he was hurt by a fall from his horse.
La Montansier rushed once more to his rescue and
brought him back safely to Paris and to his more peaceful and appropriate vocations as actor and joint director
of the little theatre in the Palais-Royal.

The breathless drama of the Revolution and the
Terror was in full tide. France, in the anguish of her
fear both of invasion and of betrayal, struck madly right
and left, killing her own and attacking the enemy. The
monarchy was abolished, the September massacres
flamed across the sky, the King and Queen were imprisoned and guillotined. Led by Dumouriez, the ragged
army of *sans-culottes* faced the enemy, and the Austrians
were driven out of France. Belgium was liberated, or
captured, and the Revolution triumphant. La Montansier watched all this with passionate interest and
excitement. When Dumouriez started toward Brussels,
she conceived the project of being made directress in the
suite of the conquering army as she had been directress
in the suite of the Court. Dumouriez laughingly ap-
proved her project when he talked to her in her salon
just before starting on his campaign. Her flattering
belief in his future success may have made him indulgent.
The Convention was equally enthusiastic and gave La
Montansier permission, and even money, to open a theatre
in Brussels and to teach the recalcitrant Belgians the
beauties and blessings of Liberty, Equality, and Frater-
nity, French brand, model of 1792.

We therefore find our intrepid directress in Brussels in
November of that year, ousting the unwilling manager
from the Théâtre de La Monnaie and installing there
her own company, combined with that of the resident

players, as La Troupe des Artistes Patriotes. She played for six weeks in a series of republican and anti-clerical dramas taken from her Paris repertory: Chenier's *Charles IX*, *Les Victimes cloitrées*, by Monvel; *La Fédération*, by Collot d'Herbois, and *Mélanie, ou La Religieuse malgré elle*, by La Harpe, all bitterly exaggerated attacks on the old régime and the clergy and prime favourites with the Paris mob. She also gave spectacular pieces built around the *Marseillaise* and other revolutionary songs, such as the *Départ des Volontaires* and *La Carmagnole à Chambéry* — a species of song, pantomime, and pageant very popular at the time. All this display of patriotism, however, failed to arouse the enthusiasm of the Belgian populace or to keep the Austrians and Prussians at bay. The French forces were defeated, Dumouriez went over to the enemy, and the comedians had to fly from Brussels, leaving all their possessions, scenes, costumes, and personal belongings in the hands of the enemy.

La Montansier was sixty-three years old when she came back to Paris and took up again the direction of her theatrical enterprises there. Time and troubles, the dangers of the day, and the ever-present menace of the guillotine, now swinging into its busiest year, might have dampened the ardour of the bravest, but Marguerite Brunet was of another stamp. In her hardy old age she launched the largest enterprise she had yet undertaken, and with a flourish of trumpets and much waving of flags she opened her own theatre in Paris, the Théâtre National, on August 15, 1793.

The project had, of course, been brewing for several years. Hampered by the smallness of her Palais-Royal stage, she had from the beginning nursed the hope of creating a really beautiful and adequate theatre which would be entirely her own. In 1791, she bought a plot of land opposite the Bibliothèque Nationale on the rue de Richelieu, sometimes called the rue de la Loi, on the very spot known to-day as the Place Louvois. She commis-

sioned the architect Louis to build for her the finest
theatre he could devise, and this he did in an astonish-
ingly short time. The theatre stood on an isolated plot,
a handsome building with grilled arcades and ample
exits and entrances on all four sides. The auditorium was
large and elaborately decorated, illuminated by a kind of
indirect lighting quite new in theatre architecture.

Another innovation was the elimination of stage-boxes:
'The Directors feel,' so the prospectus explains, 'that in
order to increase the pleasures of the spectacle and the
truth of theatrical representation, there should be a line
of demarcation between the spectator and the action
represented, and that in order to have the public enjoy
the performance to the full, the actor should, as it were,
be left alone with the character he is interpreting. This
consideration, so important to the progress as well as the
magic of art, has silenced all financial considerations, and
for the first time a theatre has been built without boxes
on the stage.' Behind the scenes the building was equally
well organised. The stage was seventy-five feet deep and
a hundred feet high. The scenery could be brought up
from below or lowered from above as required. The
building contained a studio for scene painting, as well as
the usual offices and greenrooms, a large foyer and an
assembly room for balls and receptions. It cost in all
some three million livres and was adjudged one of the
finest theatres of its day.

The first performance at the Théâtre National was
more notable for lavishness than for taste. Not content
with a curtain-raiser in praise of the architect, followed
by a sentimental drama in three acts and various songs
and ballets given by leading lights from the Opéra,
Mademoiselle Montansier seized the opportunity to stage
one of those mass scenes for which she had a very special
gift. The pageant was called the *Constitution à Constantinople* and put on the stage, besides a crowd of old
men and women, stalwart artisans, maidens in white,

children, beggars and Bedouins, a whole troupe of circus horses, the Chevaux Francini, which were at the moment extraordinarily popular in Paris. The scene showed the Tablets of the New Law carried in triumph on a chariot drawn by eight horses, while dashing riders on other noble steeds caracoled through the crowd. The effect was adjudged magnificent, and Mademoiselle Montansier's direction of the mob was particularly praised, but she was reminded that horses would not take the place of good actors and good plays even in the magnificent space of her admirable new theatre.

No one knew this better than Mademoiselle Montansier herself. It had always been her ambition to produce every variety of play, but a director's problem was nothing if not intricate in those dangerous days. It behooved her to step warily, for it was difficult to know what play, what scene, indeed, what line or phrase in an apparently harmless performance, would be judged unpatriotic and anti-revolutionary by some fire-eating denunciator or personal enemy in the *parterre*. The Revolution had brought legal freedom to the theatre by abolishing monopolies and civil incapacities in its decrees of 1791, but in actual practice the new rulers of the country were as tyrannous and capricious as any *ci-devant* king.

The citoyenne Montansier's summer repertory was chosen with extreme care. Voltaire was safe, and certain of Molière's plays had been declared harmless. Dubuisson's operettas, the comedies of Regnard and Destouches, were passed by the official censors. The more dangerous and noisy approval of the *tap-durs* in the audience was enlisted by new productions all of a violently propagandist nature; *La Fête civique*, reflecting in miniature the huge public festivals being held in and around Paris in which La Montansier's troupe had taken part; *La première Réquisition*, full of local allusions and flaming patriotism; two comedies by the erst-while court poet

Joseph Aude, now turned ardent Republican, an opera, *Séliko, ou les Nègres*, by Saint-Just, now one of the all-powerful and all-menacing Committee of Public Safety — what could be more *sans-culotide* than such a repertory and such playwrights! Her actors were equally above reproach. Her partner Neuville had been injured in the cause of freedom; Molé, whom she had just engaged, was the one important member of the Théâtre Français not arrested in September when that famous band was thrown into prison accompanied by the terrible threat that 'the head of the Comédie Française will be guillotined and the rest deported.'

La Montansier's plays, her company, her sentiments, and her actions seemed above suspicion, yet on November 13, 1793, Chaumette denounced her before the Revolutionary tribunal on the astounding charge that she had built her theatre in order to set fire to the Bibliothèque Nationale. Further, she was accused of having received money from England, from the Veuve Capet and the *émigrés* for the enterprise. Hébert added his word, and the unfortunate old lady was routed from her bed in the middle of the night and dragged off to the prison of the Petit-Force, there to await freedom or the guillotine as the whim of fate and accident decreed. The motive behind her arrest was simple enough. Her theatre was coveted by those interested in the opera, chief among them her old enemy Robespierre. After her imprisonment, her troupe continued to act for a few months, but in April, 1794, they were arbitrarily ejected from their theatre, and the opera took possession of it, under the name of Théâtre des Arts, the following August — a year after its inauguration.

In the mean while La Montansier was in prison and Neuville as well, the latter on the incriminating charge that a door led from his apartment into that of the suspect, Marguerite Brunet. As soon as she found herself in prison, La Montansier set vigorously to work in her own

defence. She at once drew up and had printed a Memorial
in which she pointed out all her services to the cause,
denied any royalist sentiments with a completeness which
did more credit to her good sense than to her heart,
made excellent sport of the grounds on which she had
been arrested, showing how absurd it was to suppose that
she could have induced any one to give her millions of
livres for so stupid an undertaking as the burning of the
Bibliothèque Nationale, and finally, having proved that
there was no evidence against her even after a careful
search had been made of all her papers, she demanded
her own and Neuville's release: 'Citizen,' she wrote in
her letter to Couthon, President of the Convention —
using not only the democratic 'tu' so popular at the
moment, but an orthography and grammar individual
to the writer and equally untranslatable, 'You are a true
republican — therefore just! I am assured that you love
to uphold the innocent. I send you a copy of my Memorial. You will there read the truth, nothing but the truth
— yet I languish in prison and have been there five
weeks!'

But these were the days of the great Terror. There
were few releases except by way of the scaffold, and
justice was a purely rhetorical term. Was La Montansier
saved from a meaningless death by Labussière, that
strange being, ex-actor, clown, and clerk of the Committee
of Public Safety, who, by destroying documents in the
dossiers of the condemned, managed to save some eleven
hundred people from the guillotine? He had a particular
liking for the theatrical profession and undoubtedly prevented the execution of the six actors and actresses of the
Comédie who were still in prison in the spring of 1794
and were in imminent danger of death. La Montansier's
name is on the long list of those he is supposed to have
saved, and it is quite likely that she owed her escape
from the tumbrils to the casual workings of this protective angel in an odd disguise. At any rate she managed

to keep alive until the 9th Thermidor, that joyful 27th of July, 1794, which saw the downfall of Robespierre and his satellites and the end of the acute phase of the Terror. News came to her in her prison of the deaths of her accusers Hébert and Chaumette. The Incorruptible himself mounted the scaffold, as well as her former friend and playwright, Saint-Just. She had escaped with her life, and hourly expected her liberty, but she had to wait two more months before she could obtain a hearing for her very just complaints. At last on September 16, she was released from prison, and arm in arm with Neuville returned to her home at number 82, Maison Égalité under the arcades of the *ci-devant* Palais-Royal.

Here she took account of stock once more, resumed control of the little theatre which on her imprisonment had promptly dropped her name, calling itself first the Théâtre du Péristyle de la Maison du Jardin-Égalité, and then for greater convenience — and protection — the Théâtre de la Montagne, a title so honourable at the moment that the grave legislators of the Convention hesitated long before permitting the players to adopt it. When the tide turned and the Mountain was swallowed by the rising flood of moderates who proclaimed themselves as much enemies of the Terror as of the monarchy, it was rechristened the Théâtre Montansier, with the indefatigable directress at its helm.

Once more, as in the early days of the Revolution, her salon and foyer became a centre of amusement and of politico-social activities. As the new-rich came into their money, as the *émigrés* floated back, and the city, weary of noble sentiments and great words, settled into its post-revolutionary disillusionment, the galleries of the Palais-Royal came to life again — a life which centred around the Théâtre Montansier, where the incomparable Volange delighted Republican France as he had diverted the Court, where Brunet created the type characters of the period — Cadet Rousselle and Jocrisse, and where the most beautiful courtesans of Paris held royal court in box and balcony. Freed at last from the fear of reprisals, the actors staged a series of satiric skits on the 'tyrants,' the 'butchers,' the 'boors,' and 'boobies' who had terrorised the country for so long. *Le Concert du jour* and *L'Intérieur des comités révolutionnaires* held up the former revolutionary leaders to derision, as in earlier plays the King and Court had been mocked and jeered at on the stage.

In and out of the theatre, under the arcades and in the gardens of the Palais-Royal, strolled a motley crowd of pleasure-seekers, *beaux* and *muscadins*, with their tight trousers, their flaring lapels, and flapping coat-tails, *incroyables* and *merveilleuses* in long straight dresses, high-waisted and transparent, on their heads deep poke bonnets denoting a modesty which had long ceased to be in fashion. In the foyer of La Montansier's theatre, two counters catered to her patrons' tastes, one where lemonade and sweets could be bought, the other devoted to the flood of scurrilous and indecent literature for which the arcades of the Palais-Royal were ever famous. Here in the evening came the rulers of the people, soldiers on leave, merchants making their fortune from their country's needs, foreigners bent on seeing the sights and snatching an evening's pleasure. Lovely ladies were there for the asking, of all kinds and at all prices, and over it all La Montansier presided benignly, seeing little difference in the methods by which mankind amuses itself whether the Government in power is King or Incorruptible, Director, Consul, or Dictator. She had entertained them all in her hospitable salon, and now the most spectacular of all these rulers of men came for a moment under her roof and sat at her table.

Only two years after the fall of Robespierre, La Montansier met, and, some would have us believe, nearly married, the man who was destined to 'confiscate the revolution' and restore autocratic rule to France. The

story comes to us from Barras himself, who at the time
was one of the five Directors and the friend and protector
of the young Napoleon Bonaparte. Barras had known
La Montansier in her Versailles days and had perhaps
been one of her casual lovers. He now lodged in a small
apartment under her roof, ate at her table, and was an
intimate in her house. One day he brought the hero of the
hour to see her. Napoleon Bonaparte, twenty-six years
old, had recently turned the tables in favour of Barras and
the Convention by stopping the threatening attack of
the Sections on that body with his famous whiff of
grapeshot. Bonaparte was looking for advancement and
a rich wife, and Barras, in his *Mémoires*, would have
us believe that he coquetted with the idea of marrying La Montansier, who was easily old enough to be his
grandmother, for the purpose of obtaining her reputed
wealth.

The story of the projected marriage is preposterous,
but it is not at all unlikely that the young man fresh from
Italy and Toulon found his way into La Montansier's
much-frequented drawing-room in Barras' wake, and
that he sat on the dilapidated old blue damask sofa beside Mademoiselle Montansier, as so many famous men
from the comte d'Artois to Danton and Robespierre had
done before him, and listened with interest to her racy
conversation. He may even have discussed with her the
possibility of finding an heiress to help him on his way —
he married Josephine de Beauharnais in March, '96 —
but anything else is absurd. Not only was La Montansier far too old, she had practically no money. Her fortune consisted of debts and lawsuits, particularly her
heavy claim against the Government for the confiscation
of her valuable property, the Théâtre National. Her last
years were one long legal argument with successive
governments, which was finally settled by Napoleon
himself in a decree from Moscow. In the mean while she
had been forced to sell her rights to the Théâtre Montan-

sier and several arcades of her Palais-Royal property in order to live at all.

Even in her old age, however, La Montansier was indefatigable. At sixty-nine she married Neuville, who died four years later, during the winter in which she was thrown into prison for the unsettled debts of the Théâtre National, now the Opéra, which was no longer hers. In 1810, when she was eighty years old, having through all these years retained interests in various theatrical enterprises, she once more took over the active direction of her little Palais-Royal theatre, now called the Jeux-Forains. There she gave fairy scenes, vaudeville, ballets, and pantomimes with the marionettes of the old Théâtre des Beaujolais, which she had kept stored away in the attic ever since she had evicted them in 1789.

Theatrical restrictions were once more the order of the day, and La Montansier had to content herself with marionettes, tight-rope walkers, and performing dogs in place of the actors, actresses, and opera singers who had formerly appeared on her stage. She was allowed one or two performers, but not enough to give real plays. She was further hampered, as in the old days of tyranny and revolution, with the vagaries of censorship, and she complained bitterly that her little fairy plays were kept indefinitely by the censor and that in consequence her theatre was failing. After a last spurt of energy in the winter of 1812, she closed her theatre for good, and nothing more is heard in the theatrical world of the little old woman whom Paul de Kock saw trotting across the Palais-Royal gardens — 'So old, so decrepit, so lined and shrunken, and in addition so grotesquely clothed, that I thought her the fairy Carabosse herself.'

A last word in her own handwriting closes the cycle of La Montansier's career. Louis XVIII, whom she had known as the comte de Provence, was on the throne, the duc de Duras once more in charge of theatre affairs. In April, 1819, she addressed a letter to the King pleading that she might be allowed to have a performance given for her benefit at the Opéra. 'I am the dean of theatre directors in France,' she wrote. 'I built the theatre in which the Opéra is housed. The leading actors of the French stage have been my pupils and members of my company. Fleury, Mademoiselle Mars, and many others have only words of praise for their old directress and are ready to prove their affection. Furthermore,' she adds, and here her canny business sense flashes out once again — 'this favour will cost no one anything, and will be advantageous all around, as these special gala performances are always good for trade.'

Her petition was never granted, for in February, 1820, the duc de Berry, nephew of the King, was assassinated as he left the Opéra and the building was incontinently condemned. La Montansier did not survive the destruction of her beloved theatre. She died on July 13, 1820, at the ripe age of ninety, after being cared for by no less a person than the King's own physician, Sue, father of Eugène Sue. At the time of her death she still owned her theatre in Versailles, her apartments in the Palais-Royal, and interests in various theatrical ventures. She left her estate to Francisque Alberico, former director of the Neapolitan Marionettes, and to her oldest friend and the companion of her last years, Mademoiselle Lillié, the 'sweet nightingale' of Versailles days.

The last glimpse we have of La Demoiselle de Montansier before her death is a description of her at a reception given by the actor Brunet. 'Her spicy reminiscences, her gay and witty conversation, held every one enthralled,' a fellow guest tells us. 'Old as she was she dominated the salon and made herself the focus of interest and attention.' And so we leave her, this *doyenne* of French directresses, surrounded by her friends and admirers and still holding centre stage in spite of time and tide. She was a woman of enormous energy and soaring imagination. Capable, conscienceless, and frankly self-indulgent, she had but one devotion — one loyalty — an undying passion for the theatre which she served to the best of her abilities through a long and dangerous life.

CHAPTER XII

MADAME VESTRIS

THE FIRST LESSEE LADY OF THE ENGLISH STAGE

JUST one hundred years ago, the date, to be exact was January 3, 1831, the first modern directress and the last of feminine theatrical pioneers walked out on the brightly lit stage of the Olympic Theatre in London, and, as she made her bow to an enthusiastically applauding crowd of elegants and 'fashionables' there assembled, she not only inaugurated the reign of the first lessee lady of the English stage, but also started a revolution in stage-craft and production which brought into being our theatre of to-day.

The scene at the Olympic, harmonising with its name, was appropriately mythological and Grecian. Eliza Vestris as Pandora, in an airy, classic costume almost as seductive as the breeches and hose for which she was famous, opened her box of surprises with verses written for the occasion: 'Nobles and Gentle matrons, patrons, friends,' she began in that winning and 'luscious' voice which seemed to speak directly to the heart of each listener present,

> Before you here a 'venturous woman bends —
> A warrior woman, who in strife embarks,
> The first of all dramatic Joan-of-Arcs!
> Cheer on the enterprize thus dared by me,
> The first that ever led a company;
> What though until this very hour and age,
> A Lessee lady never owned a stage,
> I'm that *Belle Sauvage* — only rather quieter —
> Like Mrs. Nelson, turn'd a stage proprietor.

The cheers asked for were granted on the spot and Vestris

could with difficulty finish her little poem for the noisy enthusiasm of her friends — noble and otherwise.

No one, on that festive occasion, had the heart to cavil over the purely technical point of the fair Lessee Lady's priority in stage-management. It would have been pedantic to draw attention to the fact that Lady D'Avenant had owned, and, to a certain extent, directed, her husband's Lincoln's Inn Field theatre when its worthy founder died in 1668. Since then two or three actresses had managed theatres both in London and in the provinces with passing success. Mrs. Waylett had tried her hand at the Tottenham Street Theatre in 1829, while Mrs. Nisbett, another star of the day, was about to reopen it as 'The Queen's' in the same month that Madame Vestris began her managerial career. But all these attempts were more or less abortive and short-lived.

Vestris could rightly claim for herself the title of pioneer in this particular field of theatrical endeavor, for she was the first woman in England to show a genuine capacity for effective and imaginative direction. More than that, she was one of the first English managers, man or woman, to sense the movement of the times toward perfection of detail and an effective realism. Working in her own particular medium of light comedy, extravaganza, and burlesque, she brought about, as Ernest Bradlee Watson has pointed out, a revolution in stage art more considerable and far-reaching than anything attempted by Kemble, Kean, or Macready. She is perhaps chiefly engaging as an outstanding example of the complete woman of the theatre. Débonair, light-hearted, and incurably extravagant, she is a true child of the drama's lighter moments. She could dance and sing, appear with equal effectiveness in 'male attire' or in the fluffs and furbelows of her own sex, and play with consummate skill every variety of light comedy and burlesque. The struggles, intrigues, dangers, and victories of the theatre were meat and drink to her, and her success as a directress was largely due to her intimate, her instinctive, knowledge of the stage.

The English theatre during the period in which Vestris flourished was a dull and uninspired affair. It gained what little glamour it possessed from such personalities as her own. The days of Garrick were long over; Mrs. Siddons, though still living, had retired majestically two years before Vestris made her début. Play-writing was at its lowest ebb, and the two great patent theatres, while crushing every 'upstart stage' that tried to compete with them, were bankrupting manager after manager and dying of their own unwieldy splendour. The two-headed theatrical monopoly, inaugurated by Charles II in his patent to D'Avenant and Killigrew, had continued to oppress the stage for a century and a half of changing fortunes. Legally there were only two theatres in London where so-called legitimate drama could be given; that is, where straight plays without music or other embellishment had the right to be produced. Only at Drury Lane and Covent Garden could the classics from Shakespeare to Sheridan be acted, only there could new plays see the light. The Haymarket had obtained a limited license permitting it to play legitimate drama during the summer months when the patent houses, the 'majors' as they were called, were closed. The twelve or fourteen 'minor' theatres, which were in lively existence in spite of rights and prohibitions, functioned under special licenses other than the original patents. They were limited to 'illegitimate' or 'irregular' plays in which music, ballet, pantomime, and show were supposed to predominate over any intellectual content.

The struggle between the majors and the minors was violent and bitter, leading to absurd ruses on the part of the minors to evade the law; while the majors resorted to interminable suits and prosecutions to enforce obedience to regulations that no one quite understood. The result was a state of chaos in the theatrical world which served to alienate the more intelligent public. Only the King's Theatre, the Opera House of the first quarter of the nineteenth century, still kept its social prestige and remained the resort of the aristocracy. Here, on gala nights, the dandies of the day could be seen displaying their elegant attire in Fop's Alley, the aisle which ran down the centre of the pit and was the resort of masculine fashion. The opera boxes were the most conspicuous spot in which to display the drooping line of a powdered shoulder, a new diamond necklace, or the latest coiffure from Paris. No one was allowed in this sanctuary of elegance except in full evening dress, and in consequence the audience presented a very different picture from that to be seen at the patent houses or the minor theatres.

In the hundred years that intervened between Mary Betterton's death and Vestris' appearance, a change had come over the complexion of London's playgoing public. The theatres were no longer the diversion of kings and the resort of a cultured court. German princes ruled at St. James's and Windsor where once the English Stuarts had patronised the arts. Following the French post-revolutionary styles, the dandies and beaux of London society were more interested in the cut of a coat or the set of a neckerchief than in the niceties of composition or the witty polish of a line.

The theatre buildings themselves had changed. At each reconstruction following on the inevitable fires, Drury Lane and Covent Garden had grown larger and larger to accommodate the new rulers of taste, the people. The tyranny of the pit had replaced the tyranny of the royal box, as was amply proved by the famous O. P. riots of 1809. This extraordinary exhibition of mob violence, reminiscent of the heated scenes in the French theatres at the outbreak of the Revolution, took place when John Philip Kemble, Mrs. Siddons' brother and an actor and manager of repute, dared to raise the prices of admission to Covent Garden. He was lessee of that theatre which had been burned to the ground nine months before and rebuilt at enormous expense.

To meet the current costs of his enterprise, Kemble added sixpence to the price of entrance to the pit. When the curtain rose on his first performance, bedlam broke loose, and this in spite of the fact that the play was *Macbeth*, with Siddons in what was perhaps her greatest rôle. The audience rose in its wrath and drowned out all proceedings on the stage, vociferously demanding a return to 'old prices.' The rioting continued for sixty-one nights, during which the actors performed in dumb show amid a rain of missiles, while the auditorium reverberated to the din of whistles, cat-calls, shrieks, and shouting, interspersed with free fights between Kemble's hired bruisers and the more bellicose among the rioters. The battle ended in Kemble's defeat. The management returned to the old prices and the pitites once again permitted Mrs. Siddons' vibrant periods, Cooke's force, and Munden's incomparable clownery, to dominate the scene.

It would be amusing to know whether the future lady lessee of Covent Garden had seen this bear-baiting of her predecessor. She was only twelve years old at the time, but Eliza was a precocious child, and, as her first biographers take pains to tell us, 'her parents denied her none of the amusements of the metropolis and her interesting and brilliant features might have been seen at opera, concerts, balls, etc., at a very early age.' In other words, this piquant little person, with her snapping black eyes and bobbing corkscrew curls, her graceful figure and eager, intelligent face, was soon initiated into the fascination and dangers of theatrical life. She came of a family of artists; her grandfather was Francesco Bartolozzi, the famous Italian engraver who settled in London toward the close of the eighteenth century. Her father, Gaetano

Bartolozzi, after learning his father's trade, preferred to devote himself to music and the dance. He married Theresa Janssen, daughter of a dancing-master and herself a musician of some distinction who eventually was called upon to support her two daughters, Eliza and Josephine, while Gaetano betook himself to Paris and a life unencumbered by domestic responsibilities.

Lucia Elizabetta Bartolozzi was born in London in 1797 in the same decade as Keats and Shelley, and at the very moment when 'Bony,' that future ogre of English nurseries, was dawdling on Mademoiselle Montansier's blue brocade sofa and looking about him for a wife and a career. She grew up during the troubled period of the French wars and witnessed England's struggle to adjust herself to the new currents of democracy without losing her constitutional monarchy represented at the moment by the deliquescent German Georges. In 1811, the third of the name, who had attempted to run England single-handed and had lost the American colonies in the process, went definitely mad and his place was taken by the Prince Regent, the oldest of his seven eccentric and more or less incompetent sons, who later became George IV. With the army fighting abroad, the forces of reaction at home were sufficiently strengthened to prevent the political upheaval which constantly threatened this unpopular Regent and King; but a revolution far more profound than any change of government was taking place in the very fabric of that society which it was to be Elizabetta's destiny to serve. A year before Waterloo, Stephenson perfected the first locomotive engine. Five years later, in 1819, the first steam-driven vessel crossed the Atlantic. With the railroad act of 1823 and the widespread intro-duction of the new power into industry, that ugly baby, the machine age, was fairly launched on its devastating career.

Elizabetta's youth was passed in the dashing days of the Regency when the young bloods and bullies of the

Prince's circle dominated society and the pace, financially and morally, was fast and furious. Beau Brummel led the way with his faultless elegance, his barbed wit, his incredible luck at Macao, and his equally incredible debts. With Alvaney, Yarmouth, Greville, and the rest he throned it at White's and Watier's, led the fashion at Almack's, and dictated good taste from the exclusive drawing-rooms where Lady Melbourne, Lady Jersey, and the other *grandes dames* and beauties of the day held undisputed sway. While Elisabetta was still a child, learning French, German, and Italian in her polyglot home, acquiring from her mother the rudiments of music, and from her father, when he deigned to honour his family with his presence, the first steps in the dance, London society was electrified by the meteoric appearance of Lord Byron. 'Mad, bad, and dangerous to know,' Lady Caroline Lamb's phrase, caught the essence of his fascination. Every one was at his feet. The ladies of Mayfair adored him; the Regent talked to him of poetry and pleasure. When the Drury Lane Theatre rose once more from the ashes of its latest fire, it was put under the control of a committee of lords and gentlemen in which he was included.

Elizabetta Bartolozzi may have been present when the new house was inaugurated with Byron's verse in October, 1812. She was just fifteen and her interest in things theatrical was growing apace. During that winter she was often to be seen in the boxes at the King's Theatre, where all fashionable London congregated to hear Italian opera and to admire the dancing of Armand Vestris, grandson of the famous French dancer who had been known in his day as *le dieu de la danse*. Young Vestris was immensely popular in London and was in charge of the ballet at the opera. Off-stage he was a round-faced, clumsy youth of twenty-two whose dissipations had already made their imprint on an unprepossessing countenance, but once on the stage he was the very incarnation of grace and masculine beauty. He created a sensation in London, and Elizabetta fell victim to his choreographic charms. She studied dancing with him, fell in love with him, and married him in January, 1813, a youthful indiscretion the sixteen-year-old bride was soon to regret.

Her early and disastrous marriage had a profound effect on Elizabetta's career. On the one hand it introduced her to a back-stage and greenroom world which was notorious for its immorality. On the other, it started her in a profession eminently suited to her gifts and where she was to win an unprecedented position. Her disillusionment was complete and permanent, but her husband's ambition, and more especially his financial needs, set her feet on the path of success and made possible her extraordinary theatric triumphs. Two years after they were married, Armand conceived the excellent idea of exploiting Elizabetta's talents on the stage. After due coaching from various singing teachers and much encouragement from the beaux and dandies of the greenroom circle, who had already discovered the budding charms of the ballet-master's young wife, Madame Vestris made her début. The advertisement proclaimed that this was her 'first appearance on any stage,' and that she would play the part of Proserpina in von Winter's opera, *Il Ratto di Proserpina*, at her husband's benefit performance at the King's Theatre on July 20, 1815.

The event was a success, the audience enthusiastic, the newspapers full of praise. 'Her voice is a perfect contralto,' says the *Theatrical Inquisitor*, 'possessing a peculiar sweetness accompanied by a correct, harmonious articulation which imparts to each note a mellowness creating delight rather than astonishment. She appears about eighteen, is elegant in her person and has a countenance expressive rather of modest loveliness than of any marked passion. There is a chasteness in her acting which seldom fails to please. We scarcely ever remember to have seen so much ease and simplicity evinced on a first appearance.' Through the stilted phrases of this, Vestris' first notice, certain important characteristics of her later style can be discerned. She had already sensed the value of a restrained and apparently natural acting as against the artificial theatricality of her period. Her first performance, as her later direction, was marked by those essentials of genuine realism, simplicity, and good taste. Even on her initial trial these virtues were apparent. The pit was enthusiastic, Fop's Alley marked its approval, and the management promptly engaged her for the rest of the season and for the following year.

The second performance of *Proserpina* was a gala occasion. On the stage Eliza Vestris, glowing with youth and the excitement of her first public triumph, divided the attention of a brilliant audience with Princess Charlotte who graced the royal box. Charlotte, the Prince Regent's only daughter, was the one member of the huge royal family to enjoy a genuine popularity. Among the guzzling, gambling, quarrelling royal dukes with their debts, their mistresses, their illegitimate children, their ceaseless demands for money and sinecures, the young princess stood alone. Her unhappy life, torn between devotion to a discredited mother and enforced obedience to a tyrannical father, was in striking contrast to her exalted position as heir apparent to the throne. The people loved her for her troubles and her youth. When she appeared in the box at the King's Theatre on that festive night, she was greeted with affectionate enthusiasm by the entire audience. The cast, led by the young débutante, sang the customary 'God Save the King' with unusual fervour. Patriotism ran high in these weeks following Waterloo, and so happy an occasion as the public appearance of Charlotte combined with the launching of a new operatic star was made the excuse for a lively demonstration of loyalty and enthusiasm.

A second season at the King's Theatre saw Vestris well established as a singer of light opera, but becoming increasingly involved in matrimonial and financial difficulties. Both young people were incurably extravagant, and in addition Armand had a roving eye. Eliza very probably retaliated with flirtations on her own account, though much that is told of her in this respect is palpably untrue. One of the liveliest and least credible of these imaginary adventures, constructed in the style of Aphra Behn's comedies of intrigue, shows Eliza and another young actress indulging in a chance encounter with a pair of handsome and gallant gentlemen whom they met in the park, only to discover later that one of these dashing beaux was the Prince Regent himself. Amorous adventures aside, however, London was becoming too difficult for the young couple. Bankruptcy threatened Armand, and the two departed for France, there to accumulate more debts and scandals and finally to separate for ever.

In Paris, Eliza Vestris found herself in her element. The new school of acting introduced by Talma appealed to her taste for a nearer approach to realism than the English theatre afforded. She played *Proserpina* at the Italian Opera, and, more important still, Camille — in French, of course — to Talma's Horace at the Comédie Française. Talma as Horace wore a Roman toga, quite literally 'sans-culotte,' an innovation which struck Vestris with such surprise that for a moment she thought the actor had gone crazy. 'Talma, are you mad!' she whispered in consternation; 'you have forgotten to put on your breeches.' To which Talma retorted that Romans never wore them, and thereupon gave Eliza her first lesson in appropriate costuming.

Outside the theatre and her very occasional appearance at the opera, Eliza led a gay life, surrounded by a group of pleasure-seeking Englishmen who found Paris under the recently restored Bourbon rule a city after their own hearts. At this point Armand eloped with one of his

numerous flames and Eliza saw him no more. She herself promptly acquired a protector, and for the next few
years divided her time between Paris and London. In
1820, she obtained an introduction to Elliston, autocrat
and lessee of the Drury Lane Theatre, and resumed once
more her professional career in England.

Robert William Elliston, that 'pleasant creature' of
Lamb's affectionate memories, was one of the strangest
beings who ever graced the English stage. Showman and
charlatan at once, he was a brilliant comedian as well as
the most eccentric of men. When he had been manager
of the little Olympic, he had championed the cause of the
minor theatres and cast reflections on the tendency of the
majors to resort to horses and aquatics in order to fill
their houses. Once he himself became a major at Drury
Lane, he outdid all his predecessors in inane display. His
Coronation, staged in honour of George IV's crowning, in
which he himself took the part of the king and solemnly
blessed his 'people,' the pitites, as though he were a real
monarch, was more elaborate and spectacular than anything yet produced, while the *Cataract of the Ganges*, as
the name suggests, employed more cubic feet of water
than any drama ever launched at Drury Lane.

Yet, in spite of his love of circus display, in spite of his
conceit and inordinate self-puffing, he appreciated and
fostered good acting. The company playing at Drury
Lane when Eliza Vestris joined it, in 1820, included such
brilliant dramatic stars as Edmund Kean and Charles
Munden. Kean had made his spectacular début in 1814,
and was still undisputed master of the stage. His tor-
rential power, his magnificent, if uneven, performance,
his force and his passion were the wonder of his day. It
was of Kean that Coleridge said that to see him act was
like reading Shakespeare by flashes of lightning. Keats
haunted the theatre for the joy of hearing him. 'There is
an indescribable gusto in his voice,' he wrote in one of his
rare essays in dramatic criticism. 'The sensual life of

verse springs warm from his lips. His tongue seems to have robbed the Hybla bees and left them honeyless.'

Charles Munden was almost equally unrivalled in the field of comedy. 'In the grand grotesque of farce,' Elia tells us, 'Munden stands out as single and unaccompanied as Hogarth. He is not one but legion. Not so much a comedian as a company. Who can wonder like him, who, like him, can throw, or even attempt to throw, interest over the commonest daily-life object? He understands a leg of mutton in its quiddity.' The lesser lights of Elliston's company included such popular actresses as Mrs. Glover, Miss Kelly, and Mrs. Orger. Elliston himself was a tower of comic strength. In 1820 he dominated the London theatrical world, out-showing and out-rivalling Covent Garden, which was suffering an interregnum between Kemble managements, and quite eclipsing all the minor theatres.

The Great Lessee, as he was called, was quick to appreciate Eliza's latent powers. He tried her out in a small part in the *Siege of Belgrade*, a poor play hardly enlivened by its incidental songs, and then in Arne's opera *Artaxerxes*, in which she took the rôle of the hero, her first appearance in a boy's part. The newspaper notices on her reappearance sound the same note as at her début. Her grace, her pathos, and her just intonation are praised as well as 'the chaste and touching way' in which she rendered a certain song. Her method, so the *Times* critic tells us, 'might almost be adduced as a specimen of the true style of simple singing.'

The hit of the Drury Lane season, however, was her appearance as Don Giovanni in Moncrieff's *Don Giovanni in London*, an insipid burlesque of Mozart's opera to which Vestris lent such vivacity, brilliance, and charm that it became overnight the rage of London's fashionable society. Among the many curious phenomena by which the history of the theatre is enlivened, none is more surprising than the unbounded enthusiasm with

which English audiences acclaimed the long series of its
'principal boys.' Beginning at the Restoration with such
actresses as Mrs. Long and Nell Gwyn, and continuing
through those all-female performances of Dryden's and
Killigrew's plays which shocked even the tolerant Pepys,
the idea of women in men's parts has appealed to British
taste. Peg Woffington was a devastating Sir Harry
Wildair; Anne Cateley was the first woman to play
Captain Macheath in *The Beggar's Opera*; Mrs. Abington
not only acted the dashing beaux usually favoured by the
ladies, but men's character parts as well, to the disgust of
certain critics; Dora Jordan, who was for so many years
the companion of the Duke of Clarence, later William
IV, and bore him no less than ten little Fitz-Clarences,
was famous for her Sir Harry Wildair and other men's
rôles, while even the incomparable Siddons deigned to
try Hamlet duly arrayed in a 'shawl-like garment' to
protect her modesty.

It was not modesty but audacity that lay at the root
of Vestris' fascination as Don Giovanni, and later as
Macheath in a revival of *The Beggar's Opera* staged for
her at the Haymarket during the summer of 1820. Her
easy display of a perfect leg, clad in the tightest of tight
hose and set off by flaring top boots and an elegant tunic-
like coat falling almost to her knees, represented a more
enlivening departure from ordinary feminine apparel
than we, who have long been immunised to short skirts
and scanty garments, can well imagine. Vestris' originality as a 'principal boy' lay in the fact that, while
swaggering about the stage and giving an excellent impersonation of a jaunty, roistering amorous gallant, she
was never coarse or vulgar. Her native good taste, the
restraint for which she was so much praised, and her
manner of conveying to the audience that it was all a
lark and should be taken as such, made her performance
irresistible. She was rollicking and high-spirited in the
true tradition of Nell Gwyn, but she had in addition a

MADAME VESTRIS as DON GIOVANNI.

London Published by Orlando Hodgson 10 Maiden Lane Wood Street, &c.

VESTRIS AS DON GIOVANNI

MADAME VESTRIS (IN THE CENTRE) WITH MISS GLOVER AND
MR. LISTON IN 'PAUL PRY'

polish and refinement all her own. Her 'dapper' Don
created an unprecedented excitement in London. Like
the furor which first greeted Lavinia Fenton on the
first production of *The Beggar's Opera*, like the rage over
Master Betty or the hysterical excitement which, on the
publication of *Childe Harold* eight years before, had
made Byron famous overnight, Vestris' popularity was
instantaneous and devastating. Every one rushed to see
her, her picture appeared in every bookstore, casts of
la jambe Vestris were sold to credulous admirers. She
became, in fact, the latest nine days' wonder, but unlike
most phenomena of the kind, she was sufficiently wise
and sufficiently talented to consolidate her popularity
and to build for herself a permanent niche in the hearts
of her volatile countrymen.

For ten years Vestris was London's most popular
ballad-singing comedienne, alternating her breeches parts
of Macheath and Don Giovanni with light opera at the
King's Theatre and sundry excursions into the legitimate at Drury Lane, Covent Garden, and the Haymarket. She played Lydia Languish in *The Rivals*, Paul
in a Drury Lane dramatisation of *Paul and Virginia*,
and Rosalind, Ariel, and Mrs. Ford in various Shakespearean revivals. One of her most successful parts was
that of Phœbe in *Paul Pry*, Poole's amusing farce in
which Liston made an amazing hit. The play ran one
hundred and fourteen nights in succession, an unheard-of
proceeding in those days, and not a little of its success
was due to Vestris' singing of *Cherry Ripe*, a ballad so
popular that every one in London from Prince to pauper
was whistling, humming, or singing it before the week
was old. Wherever Vestris appeared,

The fiddles, though quietly placed on their shelves,
Would from habit squeak out *Cherry Ripe* of themselves.

Vestris started the vogue for a number of tuneful ballads which remained in favour till the end of the century.

'I've been roaming,' and the even more familiar 'Buy a Broom,' with its 'Ach, du lieber Augustine' refrain, were sung in drawing-rooms and music-halls for many years after she had launched them in her inimitably piquant and engaging manner.

Popular and thoroughly occupied as she was, Vestris was not content. She could command an excellent salary, she could secure a variety of engagements both in London and the provinces, and her ascendancy over recalcitrant and ill-bred audiences was remarkable, but she was essentially a leader and not a follower. The capricious rule of lessees and managers irked her. She quarrelled with them all and would not submit to their terms. She was mortally weary of Don Giovanni and *Cherry Ripe*, and she disapproved of the shoddy way in which plays were produced, whether at the minor or the major theatres. Little by little her ideas on management, staging, and direction were becoming more clearly defined. A brief experience as assistant stage manager at the Haymarket confirmed her in the opinion that she could handle a theatre of her own, and taking her courage, and all the cash she could earn, beg, or borrow, in hand, she leased the little Olympic Theatre in Wych Street, Drury Lane, and started, as we have already seen, on her managerial career.

The first difficulty that confronted the spirited directress was the perennial one of the monopoly. Like all minors she was not allowed to produce legitimate drama and was confined to the use of burlettas, farces with music, extravaganzas, and the other methods which had slowly evolved for dodging the law. It was particularly difficult for Vestris to secure a license, as her personal popularity and success made the patentees of the two regular theatres more than usually anxious to suppress her. She finally obtained one, however, as well as the lease of the Olympic, and started, quite unconsciously on her part, toward a much-needed reformation of the English stage.

Her first act was that of any good housekeeper, and, incidentally, of a very clever business woman. She entirely refurbished the interior of her theatre, making it as attractive and comfortable as the space permitted. She decorated it with painted panels, the subjects of which were taken from her grandfather's work. She stretched silk across the ceiling, and arranged the lights so that the ladies in the boxes would look their best. The effect of the whole was gay, light, and attractive, in striking contrast to the dinginess and gloom of the patent houses. She had taken a neglected and discredited theatre and turned it into what seemed to her contemporaries a fairy palace, transforming not only the auditorium, but the scene itself, into a thing of beauty and delight.

Her opening bill contained one of those charming extravaganzas by J. R. Planché for which her management was to become famous. Planché had written and produced plays for the patentees, but it was not until he joined forces with Madame Vestris that he found a sympathetic leader with whom he could work. Vestris grasped at once the force of his suggestions and put them into effect. He wanted his burlesque clothed with a certain degree of verisimilitude so that the absurdity of the lines would be all the more striking contrasted with an appropriate and picturesque background. Vestris carried his idea still further and insisted that the acting should be natural and unaffected. The whole conception was so at variance with the tradition of burlesque in which meaningless and grotesque costume were supplemented by equally exaggerated mannerisms in acting, that some of the older performers never fully accepted the Vestris innovation. Liston had joined her company, but he was never entirely sympathetic with the new way. 'He thought to the last,' so Planché tells us, 'that Prometheus, instead of wearing a Phrygian cap, tunic, and trousers, should have been dressed like a great

lubberly boy, in a red jacket and nankeens, with a pina-
fore besmeared with lollipops.'

This was not Vestris' style, and the effect of her new
method, as shown to her first night audience, was so
startling that it seemed like a miracle. Her little theatre
sprang into instant popularity. It had been her aim to
attract the patronage of the 'fashionables,' to make the
theatre as much a rendezvous of elegance as the opera, to
restore to it something of its past social prestige. This
she did most admirably, as eight years of continued success and patronage amply proved. Every night her
doors were besieged by a distinguished crowd of pleasure-
seekers. Private carriages and hackney coaches filled
Wych Street and extended up Drury Lane as far as
old Drury itself, whose lessee raged at this noisy witness of an upstart's success. The worst fears of the
patentees were confirmed. Vestris, at her absurd little
dump of a theatre, had attracted a *beau monde* which
Drury Lane and Covent Garden still yearned for in
vain.

Not only was Vestris herself, as an actress, a strong
drawing card, but she had also gathered about her an
excellent company. Maria Foote, for a while her partner
in the venture, was a beautiful young woman with a large
following among the bucks and dandies of Fop's Alley.
Her breach-of-promise suit against 'Pea Green' Hayne,
from which she had emerged with three thousand pounds'
damages and an enormously increased popularity, had
made her the talk of the Town a few years before. Mrs.
Glover was an able and experienced comedienne, and since
Munden's retirement Liston was undoubtedly the leading
low comedian of his day. Hazlitt said that he had 'more
comic humor, more power of face, and a more genial,
happy vein of folly than any other actor we remember.
His voice is a pitch-pipe of laughter.' In 1835, Charles
Mathews made his début under her management, and in
him she gained a light comedian of great talent and one

who carried to perfection her own ideals of moderation and naturalism in acting.

During her eight years at the Olympic, Vestris, though always limited to burletta by the ever-watchful and inimical patentees, continued to carry into effect her theatrical reforms, clothing what was the first important movement toward modern staging in the engaging lightness of her extravaganzas and burlesques. Her extraordinary energy and devotion to the theatre accounted in no small measure for her success. She rehearsed her company carefully, a custom so unusual at that date, that when Macready as a young actor had tried a few years before to do it for himself, he was almost thrown out of the company. No manager had as yet attempted anything as revolutionary as Vestris did in inaugurating the custom of rehearsals. She was careful of every detail of her productions, and when she was not on the stage herself, she would watch the play from a box, checking up on any slovenly performance and assuring herself that the stage effects were as fresh and successful on the last as on the first night. Planché tells us with admiration and surprise that she would re-costume a whole burletta if, in the course of a 'run,' it began to look shabby.

Her desire for realism, accuracy, and perfection was so great that it led her into enormous expenditures. When she staged *The Court Beauties*, she went to the trouble of obtaining permission for her artists to study the portraits of Charles II's mistresses in the Gallery at Hampton Court. For this same play she bought a certain historic tapestry which had been made by the ladies of Charles' Court, as well as the actual curtain, green with gold embroidery, which had for years covered the Lely portraits at the Palace. Now it was used to hide her actress-beauties before they were revealed, living pictures of the Restoration belles on the stage of the Olympic. King Charles spaniels, real silks and laces, and furniture of the period picked up in London's old curiosity shops, completed an effective and historically accurate picture of the Court of the Merrie Monarch. This accomplishment is all the more surprising when we realise that it occurred as early as 1831, nineteen years before Charles Kean, who is supposed to have started the movement toward realistic staging, inaugurated the Princess Theatre with the series of elaborate, not to say pedantically correct productions of Shakespeare for which he is famous.

'With full recollection of all that has been accomplished since by Macready, Madame herself, and Mr. Charles Kean,' writes an 'old Stager' quoted by John Coleman, 'I believe that no more perfect sets were ever seen on any stage.' The 'old Stager' had worked under Vestris, and gives us some interesting details of the equipment of her theatre. 'The stage itself,' he says, 'was formed upon a principle then quite novel, being elaborately yet simply built of component parts, each of which was four feet in depth from the footlights, and divided into six sections, upon which were set all the properties for each scene, thus avoiding any awkward changes in sight of the audience.' Vestris also had her curtain divided in the middle and parting sideways in the graceful way of the old theatres, avoiding the ugly green baize rolled curtain then in use.

One of her most important innovations was the introduction of boxed-in sets for her interiors. For the first time in England, a stage room was given walls and a ceiling, and furnished according to the standards of reality. Her outdoor scenes were equally effective. In order to reproduce Birdcage Walk in *The Court Beauties*, she arranged to open the back part of her stage on to a long corridor which led to the adjacent Craven Buildings, a passage one hundred feet long, which she lined with trees and decorated with hanging lanterns and real birds in their cages, birds who were incited to sing by their masters hidden behind the shrubbery for the purpose. When the ingenious manageress came walking down this

miniature mall, clad as a page of Charlie's household and
leading a brace of magnificent buckhounds which her
royal friends at Windsor had lent her, the effect was so
lovely that the pit stormed its applause, and Vestris
forgot all too quickly the sums spent in producing so
thrilling a result.

During her years of Olympic management she produced an astonishing number of new pieces. Now that
she could plan matters herself, she abjured the thread-
bare plays she had been forced to perform endlessly in
other theatres. New burletta followed burletta on her
bills, as well as farces, comedies, and extravaganzas.
After seven years of classic festivities, such as *The Olympic Revels*, *The Olympic Devils*, *The Paphian Bower*,
Perseus and Andromeda, and the rest, Planché devised his
fairy-tale extravaganza, adapted from the French and
put on the stage with such admirable spirit and beauty of
costume and setting that they delighted the Olympic's
patrons.

In addition to her unceasing efforts as manager, stage
director, and responsible head of a busy and tempera-
mental organisation, Vestris took the leading part in
most of her more important productions. Hers was the
guiding hand, the inspiration and the force that made
of the little Olympic the theatre of the moment. Her
superhuman energy never seemed to flag; she was always
hunting for new ideas, new music, new stage effects, and
new production methods. As an actress she had frequently quarrelled with her managers, but now that she
was in power a different picture presents itself. The
'Beautiful Rebel' had become the 'Liberal Lessee.' Her
generosity was proverbial, and though she made her
actors work as they had never done before, she also paid
them well. She gave them a whole week's salary as
a bonus on the Saturday before the Olympic opened,
a most unusual procedure at the time and probably the
first occasion on which actors were paid for rehearsal.

Her authors also spoke highly of her liberality. Not only did she pay them well for their scripts, but she spent time and money on the production of their plays, giving as much attention to the work of a living writer as was usually lavished on Shakespeare and Shakespeare alone.

Vestris was only thirty-four when she began her career as a manager. Though she had sixteen years of acting experience to her credit she was at the height of her powers, full of vitality and energy and the charm of a ripe and seductive beauty. Her black eyes sparkling with mischievous coquetry, her ink-black, bobbing curls, her red lips, curving, pouting, merry, and provocative, were accounted irresistible. Her contemporaries are lyric in their praises. They tell us that her proportions were perfect, 'she had the figure of the Medicean Venus, she was a veritable Phœbus Apollo, indeed the most perfectly symmetrical girl that ever donned the dress of a boy; she sang like an angel and danced like a sylphid; when she played high comedy she was the beau ideal of a woman of fashion' — these are a few of the less frenzied and less intimate comments on her physical perfections. To counterbalance this praise, we are regaled with absurd descriptions of her methods of preserving her beauty and with lurid tales of her high living and free spending. The scandal-mongers were ever at her heels pouring out stories of intrigues and amours adorned with details that only an imagination unchecked by facts could devise. A little dialogue supposed to have taken place between three of her friends, all at one time or another actresses in her company, is typical of the stories current during her lifetime and after. The conversation turned on the rumour that Madame Vestris, who, since the death of Armand in 1825, had been a widow, was about to remarry. 'They say,' said Mrs. Humby, with assumed simplicity, 'that before accepting him, Vestris made a full confession to her future husband of all her lovers.'

'What touching confidence!' she added archly.

'What needless trouble!' remarked Mrs. Orger.

'What a wonderful memory!' wound up Mrs. Glover — capping a story which has become a classic, and very probably originated among the gossips of ancient Egypt.

Vestris herself showed more good taste than her traducers by never paying any attention to the scandals circulated concerning her private life. That it was agitated and somewhat varied there can be no doubt. Armand Vestris had taught her the way of the world, and she was an apt, though always a charming, pupil. She succeeded in keeping out of love for many years, until a certain 'young nobleman' appeared on the scene who unfortunately touched her heart and at the same time emptied her purse. The episode occurred during her management of the Olympic and did nothing to improve her financial situation. A spendthrift by nature, she was also, in the theatre, a spendthrift by design, but when a spendthrift lover was added to the situation, disaster was inevitable. While still in control of the Olympic, she went through the bankruptcy court, losing in the process both her debts and her young nobleman, greatly to her advantage. With the advent of Charles James Mathews, who became the leading young comedian of her company, a new era opened in Vestris' affairs.

Mathews was the son of the famous actor of that name whose 'At Homes' had been a feature of the early nineteenth-century theatre. He began his career as an architect, but finding that pursuit unexciting as well as unremunerative, he reverted to his father's profession and made his bow at the Olympic on November 6, 1835. Liston had delayed his retirement from the stage in order to take part in the début of the son of his old friend, and they appeared together in *The Old and the Young Stager*, a skit written for the occasion and received with one of those bursts of sentimental approval to which English audiences were as subject as they were to more hostile demonstrations. Charles Mathews had been attracted to the Olympic by Vestris' acting and direction. He was in sympathy with her ideas and methods and his success was immediate. He became, in the course of a phenomenally long career, England's leading light comedian, developing a new form of realistic acting, restrained and gentlemanly in contrast to the old grotesque exaggeration. Handsome, suave, and faultlessly turned out, he was the embodiment of lively good nature, of gaiety, high spirits, and mirth. On July 18, 1838, three years after he had joined her company, the young comedian and the ever-fascinating directress were married in Kensington Church.

The ceremony, so gossip tells us, was performed in deference to the puritanical tastes of the American public whose good will Vestris and her companion were about to test. Mr. Price, of the Park Theatre in New York, had made Madame Vestris a glowing offer for an American tour. She hoped to earn enough money to pay off her debts, and with this prospect in mind she accepted the contract, only specifying that her leading man should accompany her. Price thought it wise for Mathews to go as her husband, and this being duly and satisfactorily arranged, the couple started on their journey of adventure.

The American episode was the only personal failure in Vestris' long theatrical career. Her managerial enterprises may have ended in financial difficulties, but artistically speaking they were entirely successful, and she never for a moment lost her popularity. New York, however, would have none of her. She was the scarlet woman incarnate, foreign, wicked, and, worst of all, proud. Absurd stories of her alleged haughtiness were circulated. She was said to have refused to go to a ball at a country hotel, for the excellent reason that she was tired after a long, hot journey. Scandal-mongers rehashed the tale of her past love affairs. Details of her extravagance, her airs, her indifference to the fascinations of

America were circulated to her great disadvantage. When she finally appeared in the theatre, she was hooted and hissed off the stage. Outraged virtue won the day, and sin in the person of England's most bewitching comedienne was forced to retire in debt and discomfort.

It is no defence of New York audiences to say that those of London were often no better, but it is as well to realise that the absurd moral indignation expressed by this episode was not confined to America. When the great Edmund Kean himself appeared on the boards of Old Drury while he was being sued by the irate husband of one of his *innamorate*, he was hissed, hooted, and pelted with rotten fruit. He played what was probably the most thrilling and electric performance of the age, his Richard III, to a howling mob. The pitites of London, hot from championing Queen Caroline, Charlotte's mother, whom George IV had tried to divorce for misconduct in one of the most astonishing and sordid performances ever staged in Westminster Hall, decided Kean's case without evidence and damned the greatest actor of the day. Behind the Vestris episode there was a tangle of bad management, theatre feuds, and anti-British feeling, which was to explode ten years later in the famous Macready-Forrest quarrel with its bloody closing in the riot at Astor Place. For the moment the Mathewses were merely discomfited and retired poorer, if not wiser, from a disastrous venture.

Vestris' reappearance at the Olympic must have been comforting to the feelings of the harassed traveller. Her personal popularity was unaffected by her American reverses, but the Olympic had suffered financially during her absence. The American tour planned as a means of strengthening her position only served to increase her troubles. Mathews, though devoted as a husband and brilliant as an actor, was, if possible, even more extravagant, heedless, and unbusiness-like than his lady. He went into bankruptcy no less than four times in the course of his managerial venture, and did not learn to live within his income till long after Vestris' death. In the mean while he and Vestris continued their struggle with debt, and were driven into a new and larger enterprise in their efforts to redeem their situation. The little Olympic, even running to capacity, as it did when Vestris and Mathews played, could not bring in enough revenue to supply their pressing needs. With an enthusiasm and a hope hardly warranted by their predecessors' experiences, they took over the lease of Covent Garden Theatre just after Macready's first trial at managership.

Macready in his scholarly, determined, serious way had tried to bring order and beauty into his production of Shakespeare, but his mind was so rooted in the past, his prejudices so violent, that his work was rather the perfection of a dying period than the opening of a new one. To him the drama could only be saved — and it was evidently in desperate need of saving — by poetry of a neo-Shakespearean type. *Richelieu* and *The Lady of Lyons* were his great finds, Sheridan Knowles and Bulwer-Lytton his hope. But unfortunately for his later fame, the future of the theatre did not lie in the direction he pursued. Madame Vestris, whom it is to be feared he did not like at all, whose light-hearted ways he distrusted and whose success he deplored, had a keener sense than he of the way by which theatrical salvation would arrive.

Vestris inaugurated her rule at Covent Garden by a revival of *Love's Labour's Lost*, her first essay in Shakespearean production. The comedy had not been played since the closing of the theatres in 1642, and Vestris staged it with a care for detail and a respect for the text that might have won for it some measure of the success it deserved had she not, on the opening night, suppressed the shilling gallery and thereby brought down upon herself one of those delightful little riots that added to the dangers and uncertainties of nineteenth-century management. The gallery had to be restored, but in the mean while the play failed. Vestris, however, was not done with

Shakespeare. In the course of the winter she produced *The Merry Wives of Windsor* with Mrs. Nisbett as Mistress Ford and herself as Mistress Page. Mathews as Slender and Bartley as Falstaff rounded out an excellent cast, and the play, given with Bishop's music and with much of its real text, was warmly received. Her most important venture in Shakespearean production was in her second season. Taking full advantage of her experience on the little Olympic stage, she brought out *A Midsummer Night's Dream* with a beauty of spectacle and a charm of detail that had never before been achieved. For the first time since D'Avenant had begun his tinkerings, Shakespeare's play was allowed to follow its own course. There were a few omissions, a few slight rearrangements, but not a line was added to the original text. The scenery, costumes, and lighting effects were epochmaking and the whole production extraordinarily effective.

Another interesting Shakespearean revival launched by the intrepid manageress in her second season was *Romeo and Juliet* in its original form. For the first time since Mary Betterton played the part alternately in Shakespeare's and Howard's manner, Juliet was allowed to die as her creator had intended. The Juliet of the occasion was Jane Mordaunt, a young sister of Mrs. Nisbett; Mercutio, Betterton's part, was played once or twice by Charles Kemble, long retired from the stage, who at the age of seventy returned for a few performances at the command of the Queen. The public, however, were not interested in Vestris' excellent idea of giving the plays 'as wrote by Mr. Shakespeare,' and this, as well as a series of productions put on to star a promising but unsuccessful actor named Moore, were only moderately successful.

As an antidote against Shakespeare, Madame Vestris turned her expert hand to *The Beggar's Opera*. That battle-scarred veteran of the stage was an old friend of the manageress, who had suffered, probably not in silence, from the many inept and ugly productions in which she had appeared in her 'principal boy' days. Now, for the first time since its original performance, Vestris revived it in costumes of its own day. The conception was fantastic, for until now Shakespeare alone, and he only within Vestris' time, had been considered worthy of historically accurate productions. To put on *The Beggar* in eighteenth-century clothes was an absurdity, but Vestris did it, and with such success that even the Covent Garden money-boxes, those bottomless pits of need, showed signs of filling up. Vestris played Lucy, as more fitting for her managerial state than her old breeches part, and Macheath was performed by Harrison, an opera singer and later opera manager of repute. *The Beggar* saved the day for the Mathews firm, and for a while all went well with them.

The most important theatrical event of Vestris' Covent Garden management was her production of Boucicault's *London Assurance*. In the history of English drama this play, artificial and theatre-made as it seems to us to-day, stands as the first landmark in a new dispensation. Its claim to novelty did not lie in the play itself, but rather in the manner of its presentation. For the first time in a London theatre a modern scene was shown on the stage with all the realistic detail with which we are to-day so wearisomely familiar. At that time, however, the care, taste, and refinement displayed in the production were phenomenal. The boxed-in set, real carpets, furniture such as would ordinarily grace an English home, appropriate clothes, a style of acting in keeping with the settings, flashed on the Covent Garden audience on that 4th of March, 1841, as novel and delightful surprises.

The innovations were enthusiastically received. The play ran fifty-two nights in succession, and it seemed as though Vestris had really inaugurated a new comedy of modern manners. She herself, at any rate, was ready for the new style, but neither playwrights nor perhaps the larger public were as yet ripe for change. The text of *London Assurance* shows up in print as a shabby enough patchwork of old stage tricks, and though the polish of its performance was enough to give it the appearance of novelty, it was not enough to stimulate a new school of play-writing. Not until 1867, with Robertson's appearance and the Bancroft management, did the new theatre foreshadowed by Eliza Vestris, the theatre of Pinero, Jones, Ibsen, and Galsworthy, come into permanent being.

Vestris' direction at Covent Garden was marked by other reforms than those on the stage. She made the auditorium more comfortable, abolished the ugly gas-lighting and restored the soft splendour of wax candles. She instituted a greenroom which became under her guidance a pleasant salon, a gathering-place for agreeable and distinguished people and a welcome retreat for her actors and actresses. Her staff always spoke of her with affection and respect. For all her quick temper and imperious ways, Vestris was a considerate director. Invariably courteous to her company and thoughtful of its comfort, she created a pleasant atmosphere in her theatre which was warmly appreciated by every one who worked with her.

A change had come over the complexion of English society since Vestris had made her début in the gay days of the Regency, a change which affected the whole country and was reflected in her 'drawing-room management.' The seven German princes had disappeared from the scene. In their place a slim, upright girl with smooth, dark hair and a round, obstinate face dominated the scene. The unfortunate Princess Charlotte, who had seen Vestris make her bow, had died after a brief year of happy married life. Born a year after Charlotte's death and brought up in strict seclusion in Kensington Palace under the firm and godly rule of a German governess, the new Queen of England had inaugurated her era with a sincere little-girl promise. 'I will be good!' she said when her guardians broke to her the awful news of her probable destiny. And now, snatched from the dangerous influence of Lord Melbourne, husband of Byron's Caroline Lamb, the last of a great race of worldly, subtle, cynical gentlemen, and safely married to the *best*, the *handsomest*, the *most perfect* of men, Prince Albert of Saxe-Coburg, Queen Victoria had come into her own. The epoch known by her name found its source in the bourgeois happiness of the nursery at Windsor, and 'goodness' became the order of the day.

Victoria and Albert, however, for all their seriousness of purpose, were not indifferent to the theatre. They came to Covent Garden often, and were particularly delighted with Vestris' spectacle, *The Fortunate Isles*, staged in honour of their marriage on February 10, 1840. They attended a performance two days after that great event, as Thackeray's sketch has delightfully recorded. When the Queen came to the play, Vestris' greenroom put on a gala appearance; tea was served to the assembled company and the Gentlemen of the Court were courteously received, the occasion leading, so we are told, 'to agreeable and sometimes advantageous acquaintances.' It would be amusing to know whether Vestris, following the ancient ceremony long in vogue, met the young Queen at the entrance of the theatre and escorted her, walking backward and carrying two lighted candelabra, to the door of the royal box. Probably this duty was left to Charles Mathews, who would have looked very smart in the prescribed court costume. With his grace and assurance, he could have executed his part to perfection, avoiding the accidents which overtook Buckstone in his discharge of the same function. That worthy comedian first had his candles blown out by a draft from the open door and then fell flat in the process of walking backward, though he carried off both misadventures with such comic

effect that his royal patroness was reduced to helpless
laughter before she reached her seat.

Not content with Shakespeare, with comedy, farce,
and extravaganza, Vestris, following the tradition of the
patent theatres whose days were drawing rapidly to
a close, produced opera as well. It was her good, or perhaps bad, fortune to launch Adelaide Kemble, first in
Norma and later in an excellent production of *The Marriage of Figaro*, Miss Kemble as Susanna, and she herself as Cherubino, a part she had sung before and one
excellently suited to her style. Miss Kemble's enormous
success brought money to the house and the hope of
ultimate solvency, but it also stimulated Charles Kemble's ambition. The owners of the theatre refused to
wait for a small part of their rent which was overdue,
the Mathewses were turned out and Kemble took their
place.

Once again bankruptcy proceedings and a brief sojourn
in the Queen's Bench Prison freed Mathews from the
swarm of creditors and process-servers who were ever at
his heels, and he was ready to resume his professional
engagements. Macready, who was at the time manager
of Drury Lane, had followed Vestris' career with distaste
and foreboding. Though he spoke of her contemptu-
ously, he had found it expedient to filch some of her
ideas, and now he thought it wise to try to prevent her
rivalry altogether by engaging her in his own company.
He paid her, so he notes in his journal, 'a very great
salary, but it is paid in consideration of enfeebling a position as well as adding to my own strength.' Such an attitude was of course fatal to harmony. Macready gave
both Vestris and Mathews small parts and no proper
billing, and after a few weeks of quarrels and scenes, they
left his theatre for good. A tour in the provinces followed,
engagements at the Haymarket and other small theatres,
but the urge for management was in Vestris' blood and
she could not exist happily without a theatre of her own.

In 1847, they leased the Lyceum and opened there on the 18th of October.

The theatre monopoly had been finally abolished in 1843, so that now Vestris was not hampered by the restrictions which had tied her hands in her first small theatre. The Lyceum, like the Olympic of old, was refurnished and redecorated. The evil practice of 'orders' giving free admission to indiscriminate masses of people was abolished, elegance and refinement were once more the rule before and behind the curtain. But though she was eager to produce legitimate plays, Vestris' name was by now so closely associated with burletta and light comedy that she could not entirely discard the type of production she had made so popular at the Olympic. New fairy dramas by Planché and Dance were brought out with unsurpassed splendour, and once more her touch was seen in the perfection of detail, wealth of material appointments, and the smooth working of a well-organised company.

A series of light, farcical plays were staged, all of which, except that old standby of amateur theatricals, *Box and Cox*, have long been forgotten. English playwrights were still grappling feebly with old formulas and failed to give Vestris material fitted to her skill and her ambition. In default of home talent, she turned to the French stage, with which she was thoroughly familiar, and there found plays better suited to her needs. Perhaps the most important contribution of Vestris' Lyceum management was her introduction of French plays to British audiences. Through her efforts the way was prepared for the acceptance of a new type of drama, which at that very moment was taking shape in the mind of the young man who acted as prompter to her company. Fifteen years later, T. W. Robertson was to bring into actual being the ideals toward which he saw Vestris working during his association with her at the Lyceum.

Though she was no longer in her first youth, Vestris

was as enterprising as ever, and her new management saw her embark on another experiment in production. In 1852, she staged a huge melodramatic tale in eight acts called *A Chain of Events*, a drama translated for her from the French by G. H. Lewes. The plot was sensational in the extreme, including in its many scenes a complete shipwreck on the stage, but Vestris was chiefly interested in the realism with which she could invest it. Here, as in her second effort of the kind, *A Strange History* in nine scenes, she carried into melodrama the experiments she had begun in burlesque.

The Lyceum management marked the beginning of the end of Vestris' career. She was fifty years old when she took up this new burden, but she had somehow captured the secret of an enduring youthfulness. She played old parts and new with characteristic verve, her voice was still delightful, her figure exquisite, her energy and vivacity unflagging. On the opening night of the new venture, her devoted followers applauded and shouted their appreciation until the 'fair manageress' was almost reduced to tears. She had been acting for nearly thirty years, yet her freshness was undimmed. 'When I saw her as Lady Bell,' John Coleman writes, describing her at about this time, 'she might have been any age twixt five and twenty and thirty. Her high powdered head-dress made her appear tall; the rich brocaded sacque of exquisite cut, colour and texture and her grace of motion imparted a remarkable air of distinction rendered piquant by a certain *espièglerie* which was all her own and was perfectly irresistible.' As for her acting, it showed, according to Westland Marston, 'a union of elegance and mirth in which she never failed to excel. She was probably more fascinating than any of her time.'

The most surprising development of these last years, however, was expressed by no less a critic than George Henry Lewes, who, writing of her appearance in one of the few tragic rôles she ever attempted, says: 'The lasting astonishment is that Vestris should have performed [the part] as no actress of our stage could do it. That is something to marvel at. Vestris, the greatest pet of the public, will startle even her greatest admirers in this part, for assuredly no one ever believed her powers lay at all in that direction. Yet I assure you that her acting is quite a study.... Vestris and Mathews were *natural* — nothing more nor less. They were a lady and a gentleman such as we meet in a drawing-room, graceful, quiet, well-bred, perfectly dressed, perfectly oblivious of the footlights. ... I carry away from the theatre an exquisite picture on which it is delightful to dwell, which reflection tells me was perfect art.' His criticism is an indication of the lines along which Vestris' talent might have developed had she not been hampered during her formative period by the exigencies of managers and, when she was her own manager, by the restrictions of the monopoly. Her liberation came too late. Her career in the theatre, as in the world, was drawing to a close.

On the 26th of July, 1854, after a winter of illness, worries, and losses, Vestris appeared at her husband's benefit in a little play optimistically entitled *Sunshine Through Clouds*. She seemed as gay, as young, as spirited as ever, and her public bade her an affectionate farewell for the summer, little realising that it would never see her again. The following year she was too ill to act at all, and Mathews, unable to face the financial difficulties of the enterprise without her assistance and coöperation, gave up the struggle and with it the management of the Lyceum. In July, 1856, while he was acting in the provinces, he was thrown into prison for debt.

Vestris made one last futile effort to go to him in his trouble, but she was unable to leave her bed. Through the intervention of some of his many devoted friends, he was released just in time to reach his wife before the end. She died on the 8th of August, 1856, on the eve of the rebirth of the English theatre. Robertson was already

writing his plays, Henry Arthur Jones was five years old,
Pinero a baby in arms. In Norway, the 'theatre poet' of
Bergen, Henrik Ibsen, was about to become director of
the Norwegian National Theatre. Paris, revelling in
Scribe, Augier, and Dumas *fils*, did not even know that
André Antoine, who would eventually found a true
Théâtre Libre, had just been born to supplant them.
Vestris died before her ideas found their full expression,
but she had shown the way and others followed in her
footsteps. With her the tale of pioneer women in the
theatre comes to an end. In acting and play-writing,
in management and direction, women had won an undisputed place upon the stages of the world. The day of
innovation was over. The day of achievement was, and
still is, at hand.

THE END

INDEX

Abington, Mrs., 270
Academicians, attack *Le Cid*, 93
Académie de Musique, 241, 243
Acrobats, women, 9; in France, 82–83; in England, 135; in Germany, 206
Acte, Roman *mima*, 14
Actors, GREEK, 4–6; ROMAN, 13–15; ITALIAN, 52, 56; in FRANCE, 62–63, 86–88; 71; 76; 78; FRENCH, 63, 82; better than Italians, 88; 92; 95; 114; 117; ENGLISH, 132, 137–40; GERMAN, 204–06, 209, 214–15; 219; 225–26. *See also* Men as women
Actor's Remonstrance, The, 137
Actresses, women achieve greatness as, xv; pioneers, xvi; priestess in primitive cults, 1–2, 9–10; ROMAN, *mimæ*, 13–15; legal and moral standing of, 13, 16–17; protected by early Church, 17–18; nuns, 31; ITALIAN, position prepared by Renaissance, 47–48; earliest, 51–54; initial appearance of, 55–56; early *commedia* troupes, 56–57; travel in France, 56, 62–63, 86–88, 91; in England, 60, 136, 145; in Spain, 60–61; fully accepted, 64–66; first important, 66–67; banned by Church, 53, 64–65; superiority to boys, 66; abilities of early, 71–72; types of acting, 76–78; 82; moral standing, 66, 81, 97–98; FRENCH, *farceurs*, 82; allowed in mystery plays, 83–85; first professional, 86–88; excluded from farces, 89; morals and standing of, 89, 96–98; in strolling companies, 90; introduced in Paris, 90–91; early groups, 91–99; share in creation of great French drama, 92–94, 99–100; fully established, 96; types of, 101, 131; trained by Molière, 114; go to England, 136;

145; 229; 232; ENGLISH, first, 132–36; Ianthe, 134–35; established after the Restoration, 141–43; regulations for, 147–49; difficulties confronting, 150, 157; all women casts, 169–70; defence of, 171; recognition of, 162–72; GERMAN, introduced, 138; early, 204, 205–06, 209, 214–15, 225; blamed for corruption of stage in Rome, 16; in Spain, 60; in Italy, 66; in France, 89; in England, 170–71. *See also* Women *and* Women as men
Actress-Managers. *See* Managers
Æschylus, 5, 6, 100
Æsop, translated by Aphra Behn, 193
Age of Gold, 123
Ajax, dance of, 10
Ajax and Agamemnon, pantomime of, 15
Alançon, Duke of, 62
Alberico, Francisque, 256
Albert, Prince, 286
Aldobrandini, Cardinal, 79
Alexander the Great, 10
Alizon, actor of women's parts, 89
Alvaney, Lord, 264
America, 230, 280, 282
Amis, Ayfara. *See* Behn, Aphra
Amis, John and Amy, 177
Ancona, d', 56
Andreini, Francesco, 69–70; as Capitano Spavento, 71; 73; 75; 81
Andreini, Giovanni Battista, 69–70; 81
Andreini, Isabella, xvi, xviii, 66; importance of, 67, 79–81; portraits of, 68, 78; birth, 68; joins *Gelosi*, 68–69; marriage and children, 69; contribution to *commedia* types, 71, 72; *concetti*, 72–74, 78; poetry, 74; tributes to, 79–80; death, 80–

THE AUTHOR

ROSAMOND GILDER was born in Marion, Massachusetts, and brought up in New York in the literary circle of her father, Richard Watson Gilder, the celebrated poet and editor of *The Century*. As a child she thus knew such theatre persons as Eleanora Duse, Julia Marlowe, and Modjeska. Her first published work was a life of her father, built largely around his own letters and called LETTERS OF RICHARD WATSON GILDER. She translated and assisted in writing the memoirs of Emma Calvé, world-famous Carmen. In 1924 she joined the staff of *Theatre Arts Monthly* as assistant editor and feature writer, became its Broadway drama critic in 1938 and its editor-in-chief in 1945, remaining in that position until February, 1948, when the magazine changed hands. Author of a unique study of *Hamlet* in production, JOHN GIELGUD'S HAMLET (Oxford University Press) and a number of bibliographies and special studies on the theatre, she has been active in most of the movements toward better theatre in the United States: the National Theatre Conference, the Federal Theatre, the American National Theatre and Academy (ANTA)—all organizations of which she has been Secretary at one time or another. In 1947 at the invitation of UNESCO she took part in founding the International Theatre Institute, of which she is now vice-president. As Director of the U. S. Center of that organization (which is part of ANTA), she is in constant touch with the theatres of the world, and is at work on two books concerned with the international theatre scene. She has also been chairman of the U. S. Delegations to the bi-annual International Theatre Congresses, and has been invited to India for three months of lectures and seminars on theatre by the Indian Theatre Center and the U. S. State Department. Miss Gilder is an honorary member of the New York Drama Critics Circle and a member of the International Drama Critics Association, and she writes regularly for various international publications. ENTER THE ACTRESS was first published in 1931 by Houghton Mifflin.

SOME OTHER THEATRE ARTS PAPERBOOKS

THEATRE ARTS ANTHOLOGY (1916-1948), edited by Rosamond Gilder, Hermine Rich Isaacs, Robert M. MacGregor and Edward Reed. A massive collection from the great days of a great theatre magazine, *Theatre Arts Monthly,* and a handbook of theatre in all its multitude of component parts. 132 articles by 78 authors, all of them leaders in the theatre and allied fields—from La Argentina and Mary Austin to Thornton Wilder and Stark Young, and including such well known writers as John Mason Brown, Edith Hamilton, John K. Hutchens, William Saroyan, Robert E. Sherwood and Cornelia Otis Skinner. The pieces are divided into the following sections: 'The Dwelling Place of Wonder,' History, Playwrights and Playwriting, Music and the Dance, Actors and Acting, The Film, Scene and Costume Design, Architecture, Radio and Television, Tributary Theatre, Directing and Producing, The Films in Review and Broadway in Review. 703 pages, 5 by 8 inches.

SHAW'S LETTERS TO GRANVILLE BARKER, edited by C. B. Purdom. One of the most productive friendships of the 20th century resulted in this correspondence, rich in theatre wisdom and wit. Granville Barker produced many of Shaw's plays for the first time and Shaw's letters to him distill his knowledge of playwriting and production. "Shaw's ideas on the functions of censorship, society, and the dramatist . . . colored by his wit, his spirit, and his wholehearted generosity."—*The New Yorker.* 5 by 8 inches.

MUSICAL COMEDY IN AMERICA, From *The Black Crook* to *South Pacific,* by Cecil Smith. The whole panorama of the American musical stage, written with authority and wit by a noted music critic. 374 pages plus 64 pages of pictures. "It is the honesty and individuality of his views which distinguish this book, for although it is a history with dates, places, names and other factual data relating to a long succession of theatrical productions, it is held together and illuminated by the critical comment of the author. . . . I find it fascinating to read and invaluable as a book to keep in my study for future reference."—Oscar Hammerstein, 2nd, in the *New York Herald Tribune.*

write for a complete catalog of

THEATRE ARTS BOOKS

333 Sixth Avenue   New York 14